DISASTER DATES & LUCKY ESCAPES

FINDING THE ONE IN THE AGE OF ONLINE DATING

AN HACHETTE UK COMPANY
WWW.HACHETTE.CO.UK

FIRST PUBLISHED IN GREAT BRITAIN IN 2023 BY
KYLE BOOKS, AN IMPRINT OF OCTOPUS PUBLISHING GROUP LIMITED

CARMELITE HOUSE, 50 VICTORIA EMBANKMENT
LONDON, EC4Y 0DZ
WWW.KYLEBOOKS.CO.UK

ISBN: 9781804190937

TEXT COPYRIGHT @TESS SMITH-ROBERTS 2023
DESIGN AND LAYOUT COPYRIGHT 2018 @OCTOPUS PUBLISHING
GROUP LIMITED

DISTRIBUTED IN THE US BY HACHETTE BOOK GROUP, 1290 AVENUE
OF THE AMERICAS, 4TH AND 5TH FLOORS, NEW YORK, NY 10104

DISTRIBUTED IN CANADA BY CANADIAN MANDA GROUP,
664 ANNETTE ST., TORONTO, ONTARIO, CANADA M6S 2C8

TESS SMITH-ROBERTS IS HEREBY IDENTIFIED AS THE AUTHOR OF
THIS WORK IN ACCORDANCE WITH SECTION 77 OF THE COPYRIGHT,
DESIGNS AND PATENTS ACT 1988.

Publisher: Joanna Copestick
Junior Commissioning Editor: Samhita Foria
Design: Lydia Fisher
Cover Design: Rachael Shone
Production: Allison Gonsalves

Printed and bound in China

10 9 8 7 6 5 4 3 2 1

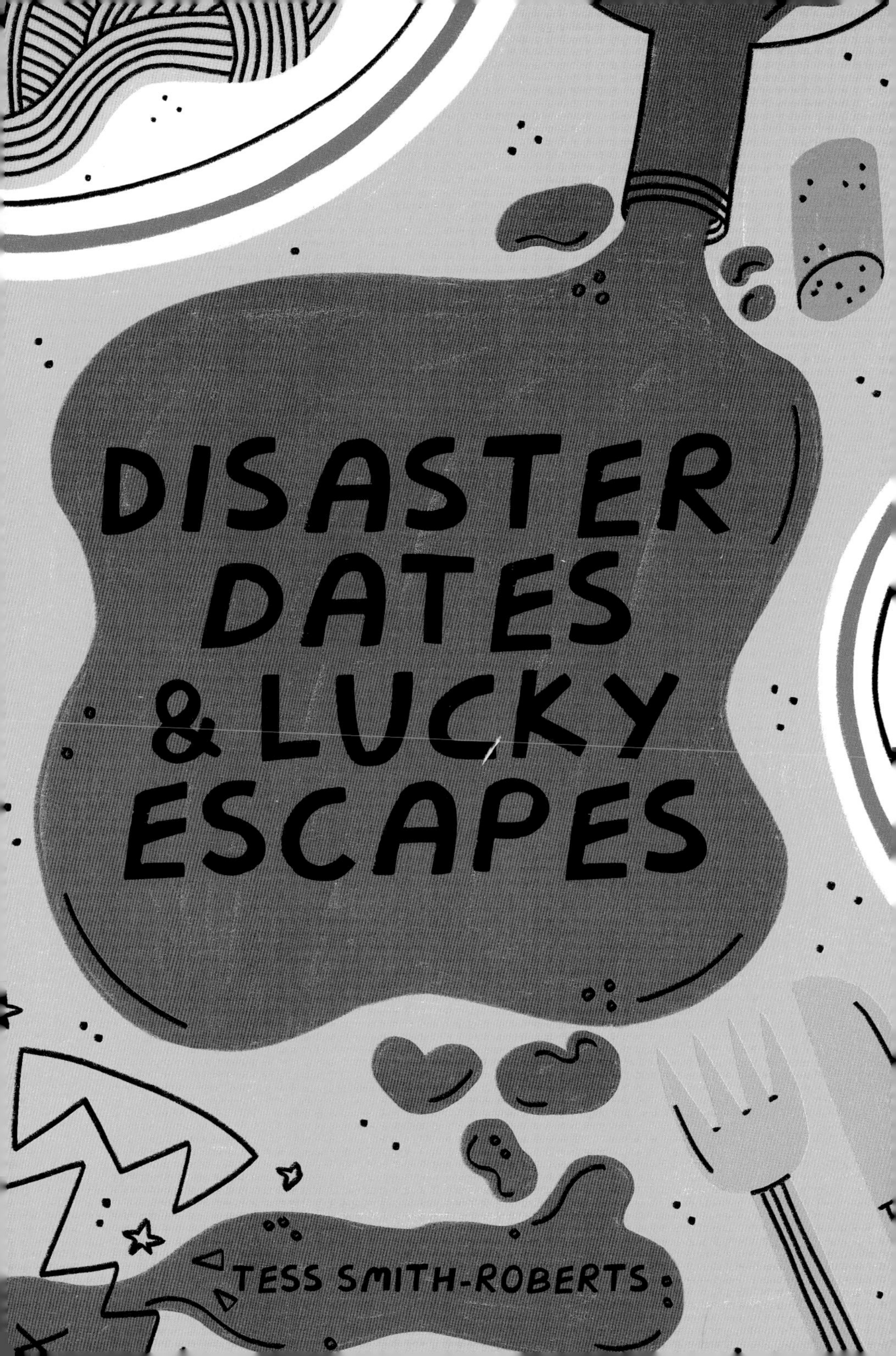
DISASTER DATES & LUCKY ESCAPES
TESS SMITH-ROBERTS

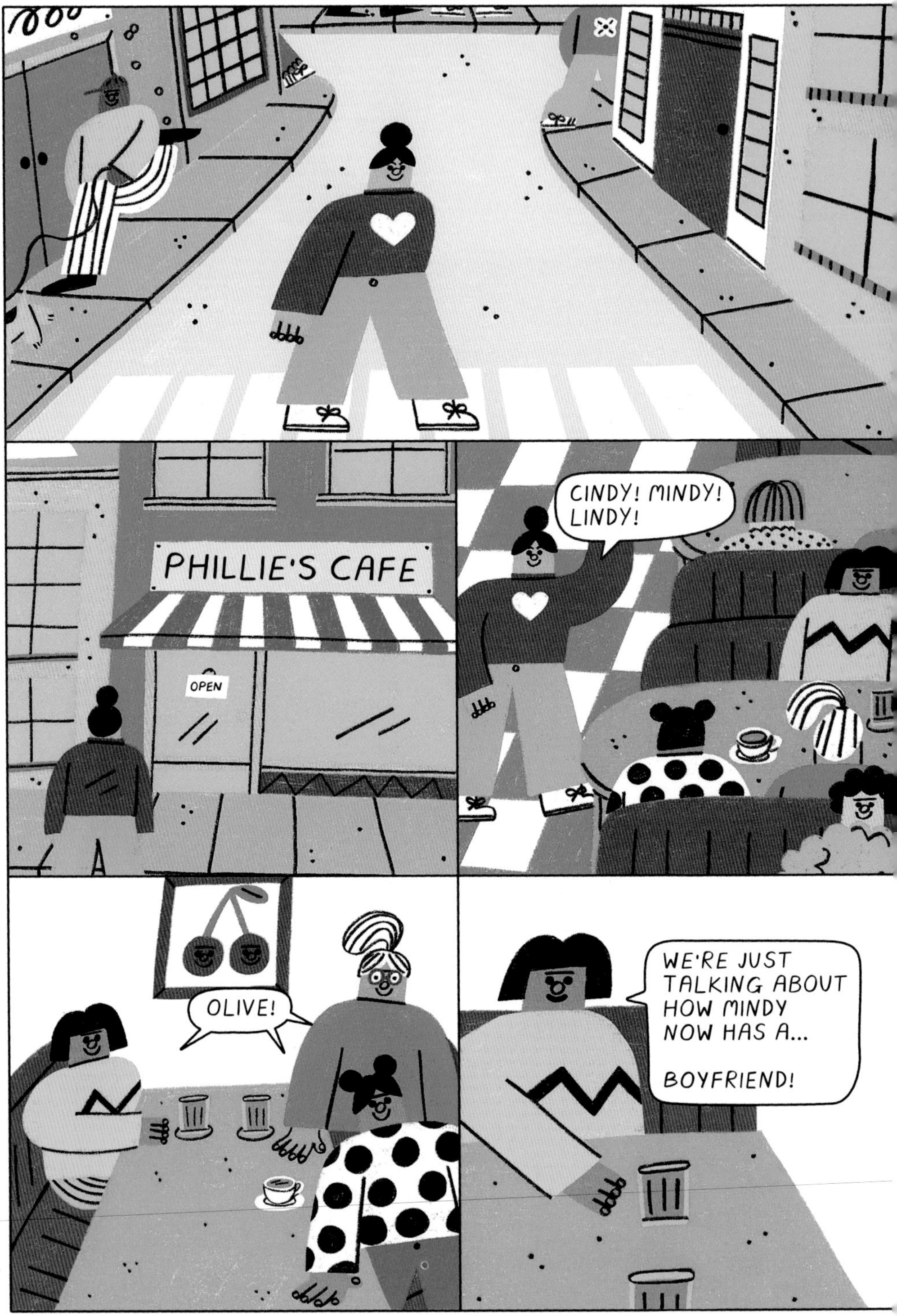
PHILLIE'S CAFE
OPEN
CINDY! MINDY! LINDY!
OLIVE!
WE'RE JUST TALKING ABOUT HOW MINDY NOW HAS A...
BOYFRIEND!

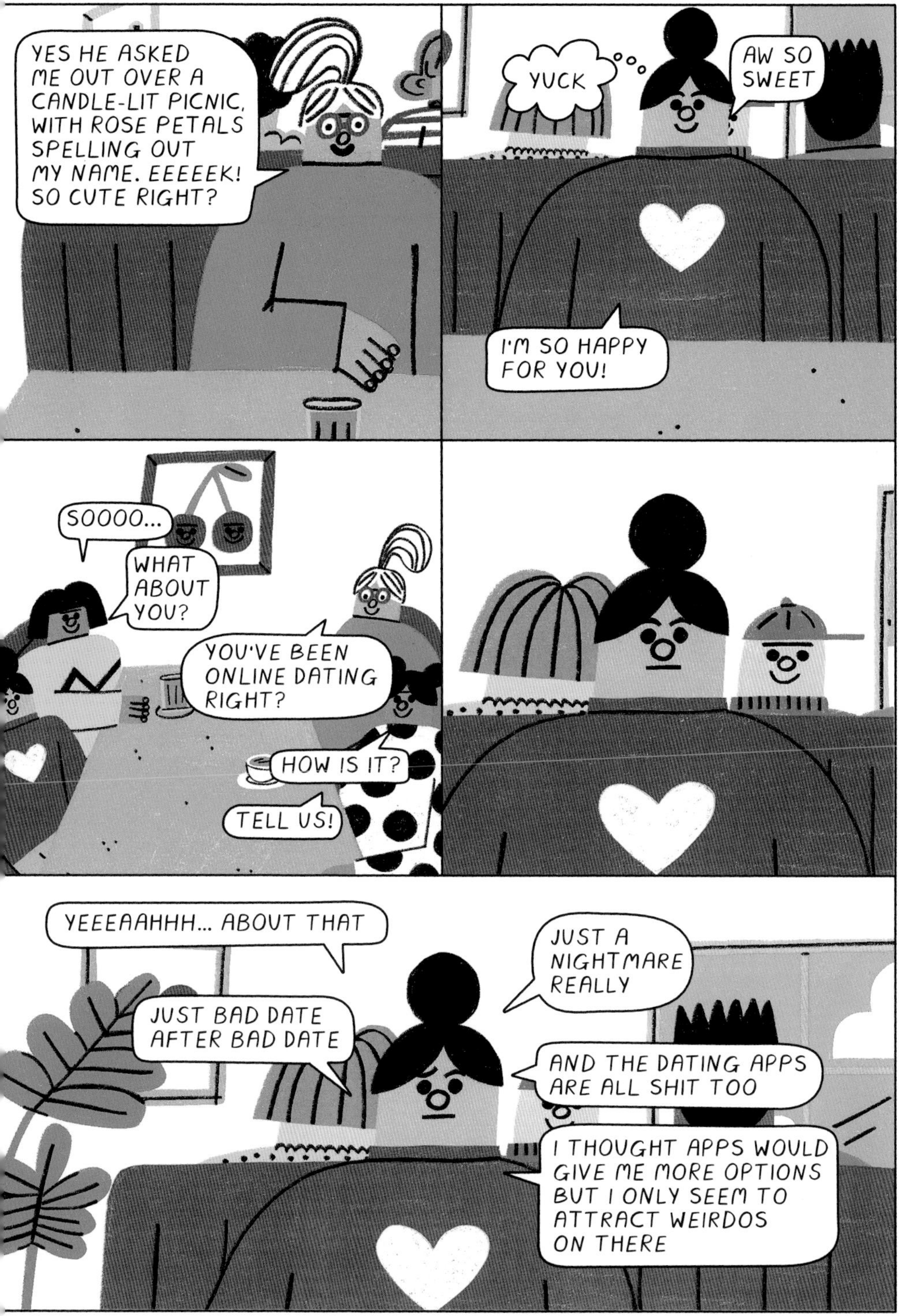
YES HE ASKED ME OUT OVER A CANDLE-LIT PICNIC, WITH ROSE PETALS SPELLING OUT MY NAME. EEEEEK! SO CUTE RIGHT?
YUCK
AW SO SWEET
I'M SO HAPPY FOR YOU!
SOOOO...
WHAT ABOUT YOU?
YOU'VE BEEN ONLINE DATING RIGHT?
HOW IS IT?
TELL US!
YEEEAAHHH... ABOUT THAT
JUST BAD DATE AFTER BAD DATE
JUST A NIGHTMARE REALLY
AND THE DATING APPS ARE ALL SHIT TOO
I THOUGHT APPS WOULD GIVE ME MORE OPTIONS BUT I ONLY SEEM TO ATTRACT WEIRDOS ON THERE

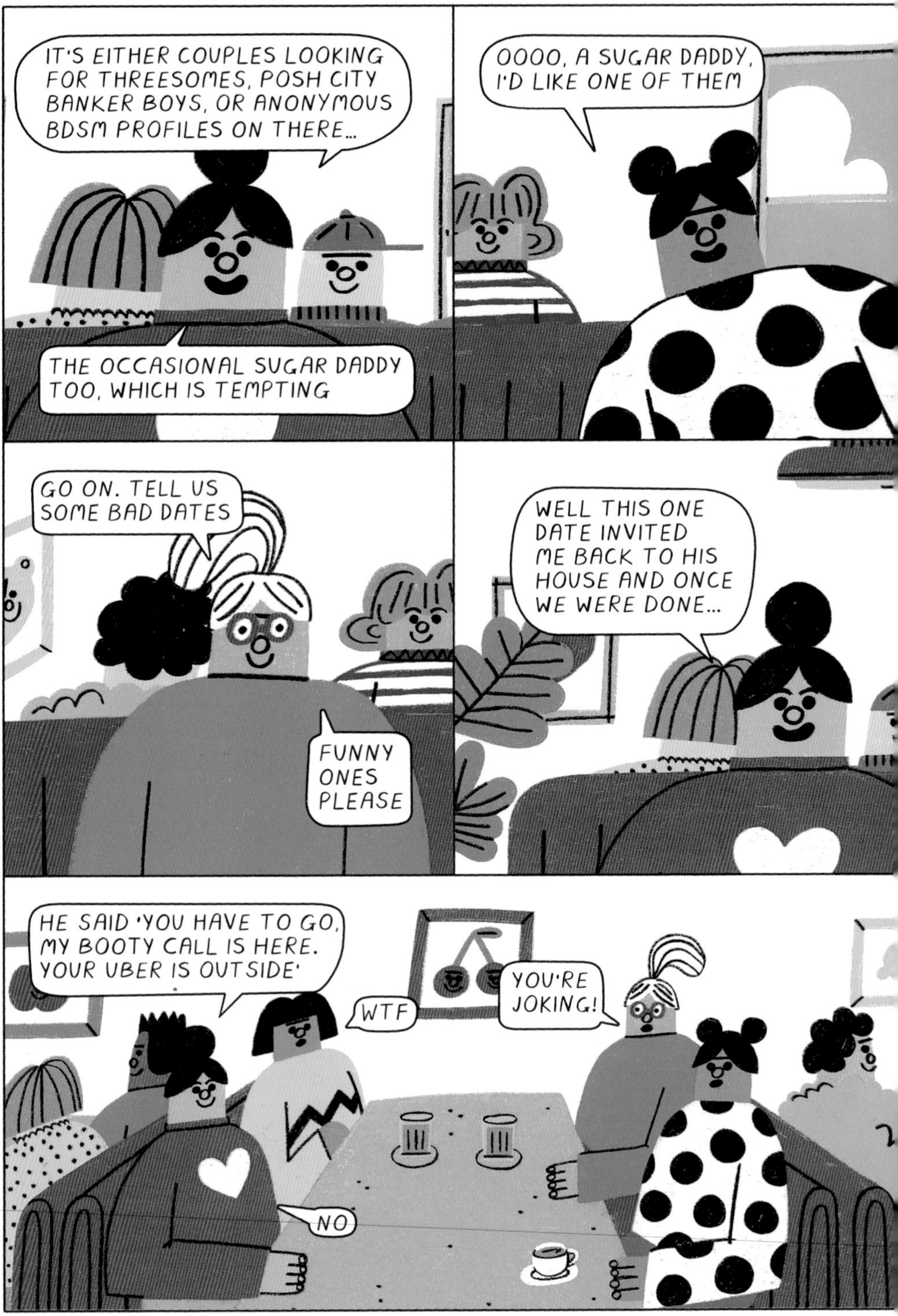
IT'S EITHER COUPLES LOOKING FOR THREESOMES, POSH CITY BANKER BOYS, OR ANONYMOUS BDSM PROFILES ON THERE...
THE OCCASIONAL SUGAR DADDY TOO, WHICH IS TEMPTING
OOOO, A SUGAR DADDY, I'D LIKE ONE OF THEM
GO ON. TELL US SOME BAD DATES
FUNNY ONES PLEASE
WELL THIS ONE DATE INVITED ME BACK TO HIS HOUSE AND ONCE WE WERE DONE...
HE SAID 'YOU HAVE TO GO, MY BOOTY CALL IS HERE. YOUR UBER IS OUTSIDE'
WTF
YOU'RE JOKING!
NO

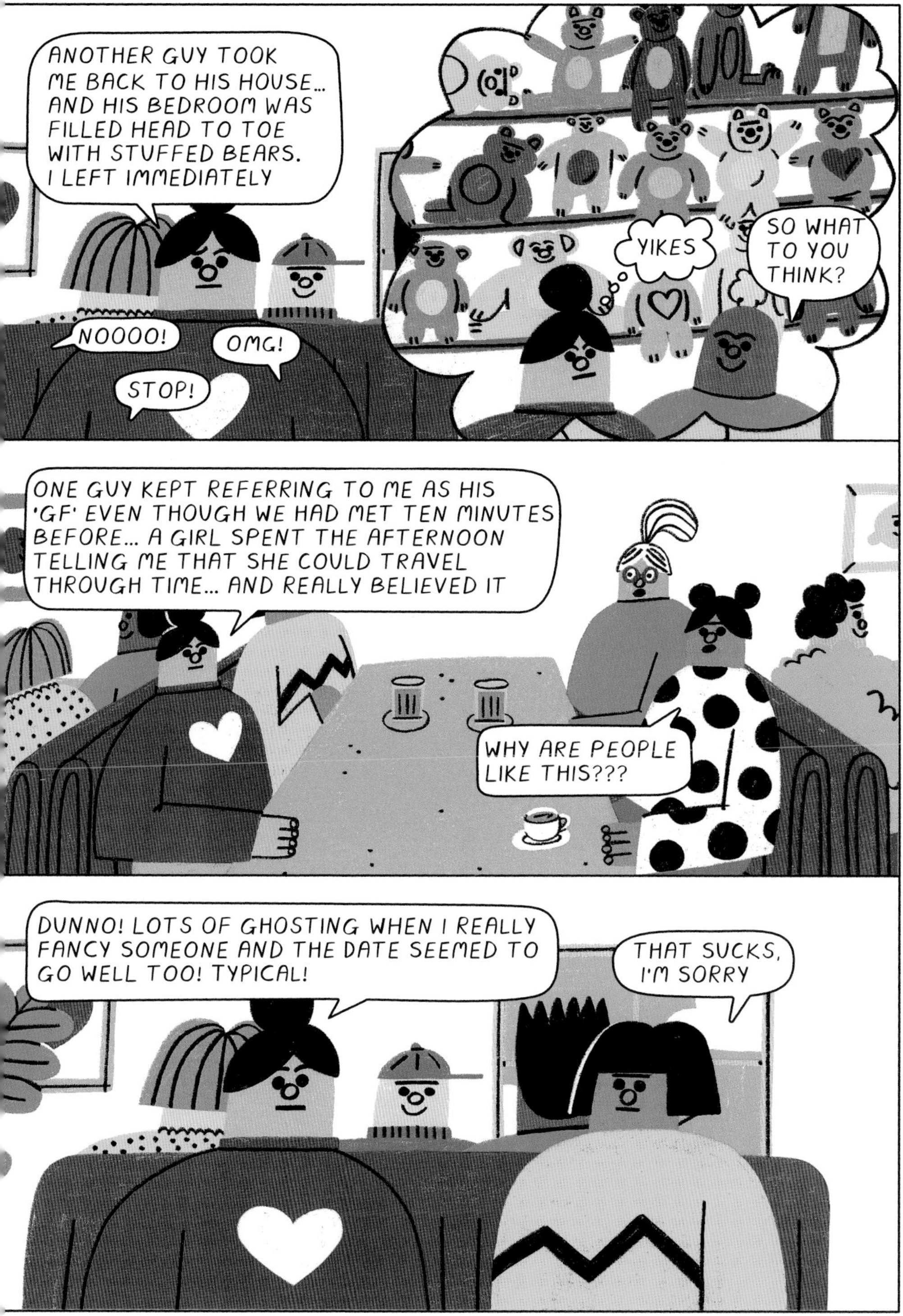
ANOTHER GUY TOOK ME BACK TO HIS HOUSE... AND HIS BEDROOM WAS FILLED HEAD TO TOE WITH STUFFED BEARS. I LEFT IMMEDIATELY
YIKES
SO WHAT TO YOU THINK?
NOOOO!
OMG!
STOP!
ONE GUY KEPT REFERRING TO ME AS HIS 'GF' EVEN THOUGH WE HAD MET TEN MINUTES BEFORE... A GIRL SPENT THE AFTERNOON TELLING ME THAT SHE COULD TRAVEL THROUGH TIME... AND REALLY BELIEVED IT
WHY ARE PEOPLE LIKE THIS???
DUNNO! LOTS OF GHOSTING WHEN I REALLY FANCY SOMEONE AND THE DATE SEEMED TO GO WELL TOO! TYPICAL!
THAT SUCKS, I'M SORRY

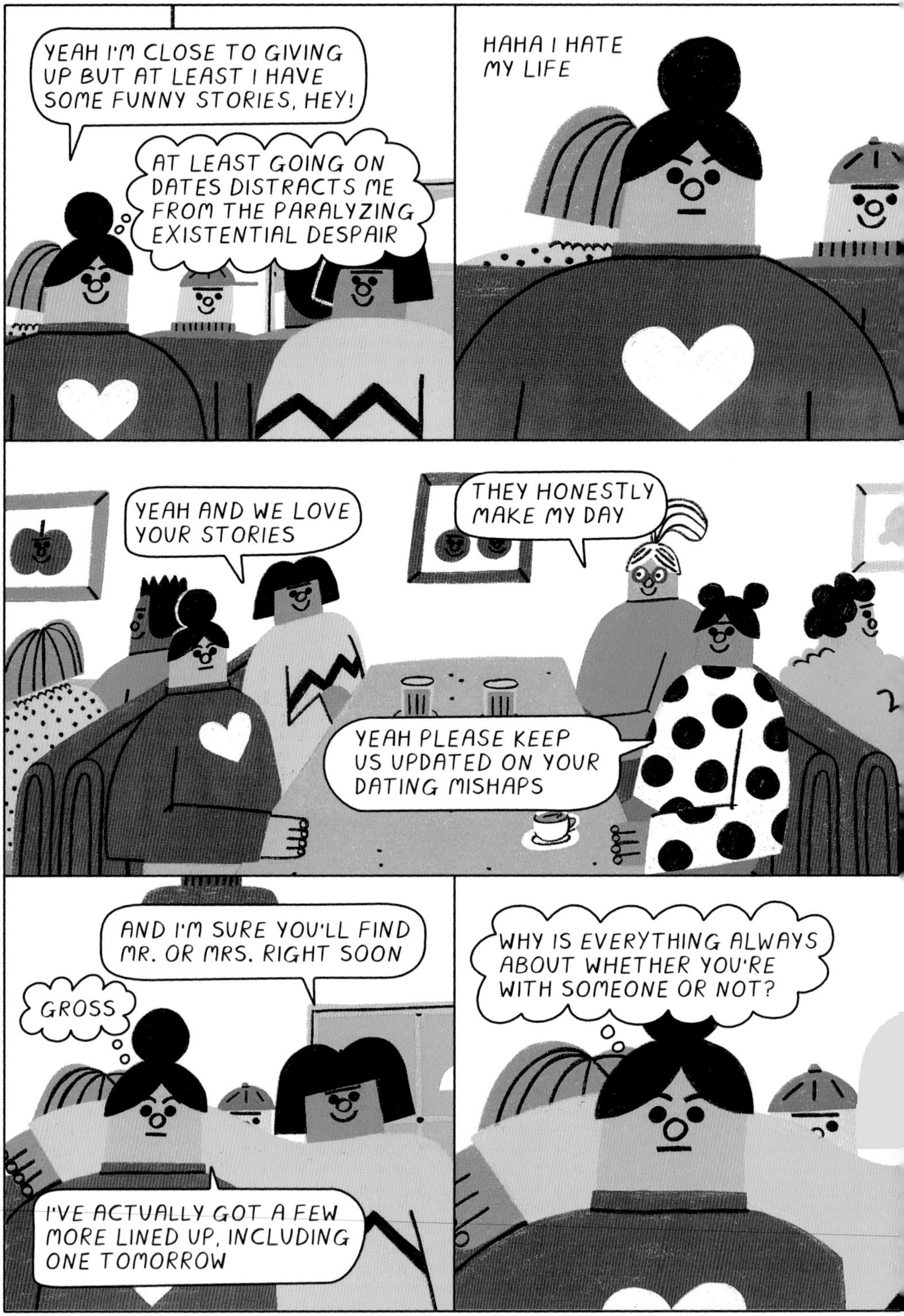
YEAH I'M CLOSE TO GIVING UP BUT AT LEAST I HAVE SOME FUNNY STORIES, HEY!
AT LEAST GOING ON DATES DISTRACTS ME FROM THE PARALYZING EXISTENTIAL DESPAIR
HAHA I HATE MY LIFE
YEAH AND WE LOVE YOUR STORIES
THEY HONESTLY MAKE MY DAY
YEAH PLEASE KEEP US UPDATED ON YOUR DATING MISHAPS
AND I'M SURE YOU'LL FIND MR. OR MRS. RIGHT SOON
GROSS
I'VE ACTUALLY GOT A FEW MORE LINED UP, INCLUDING ONE TOMORROW
WHY IS EVERYTHING ALWAYS ABOUT WHETHER YOU'RE WITH SOMEONE OR NOT?

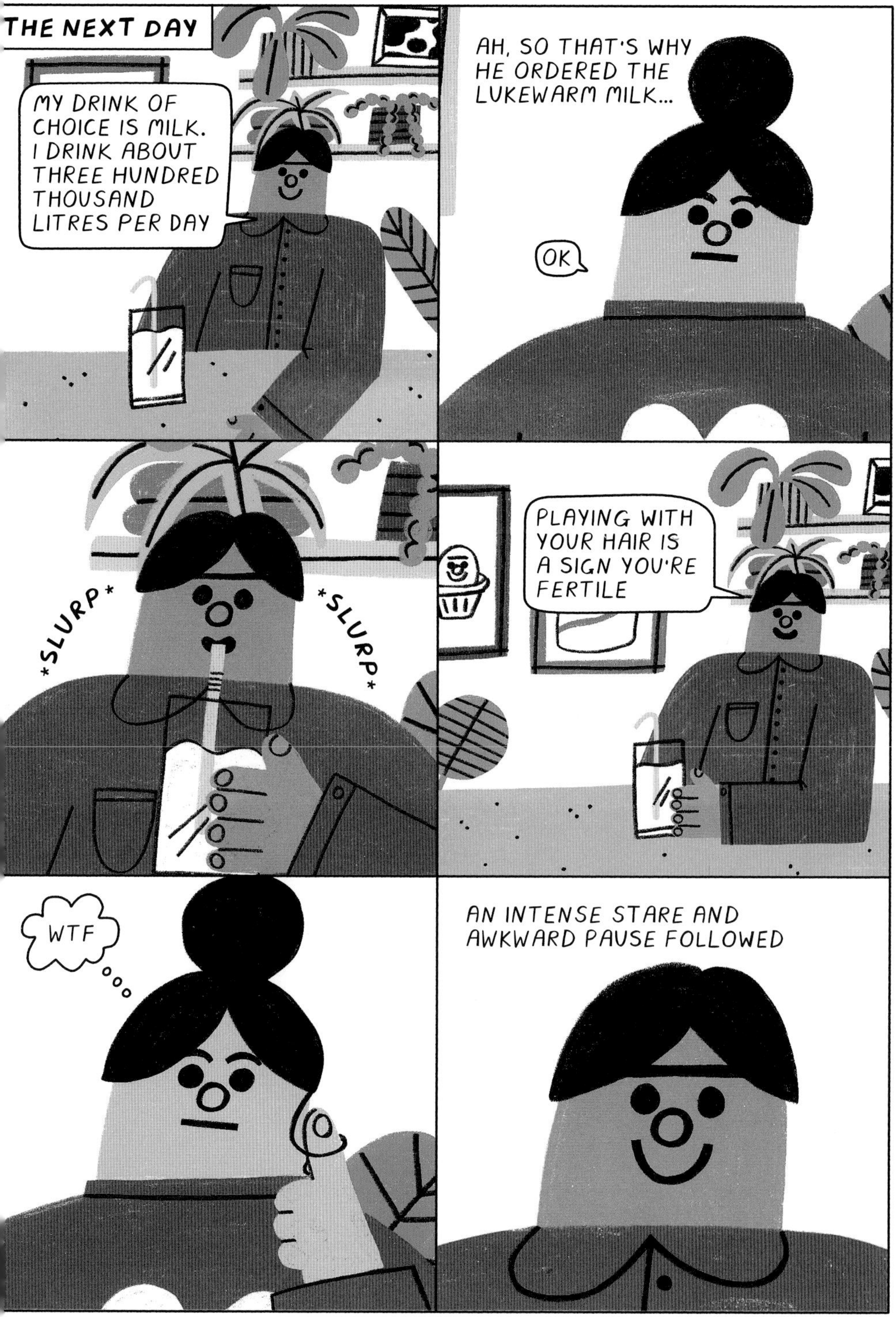
THE NEXT DAY
MY DRINK OF CHOICE IS MILK. I DRINK ABOUT THREE HUNDRED THOUSAND LITRES PER DAY
AH, SO THAT'S WHY HE ORDERED THE LUKEWARM MILK...
OK
SLURP
SLURP
PLAYING WITH YOUR HAIR IS A SIGN YOU'RE FERTILE
WTF
AN INTENSE STARE AND AWKWARD PAUSE FOLLOWED

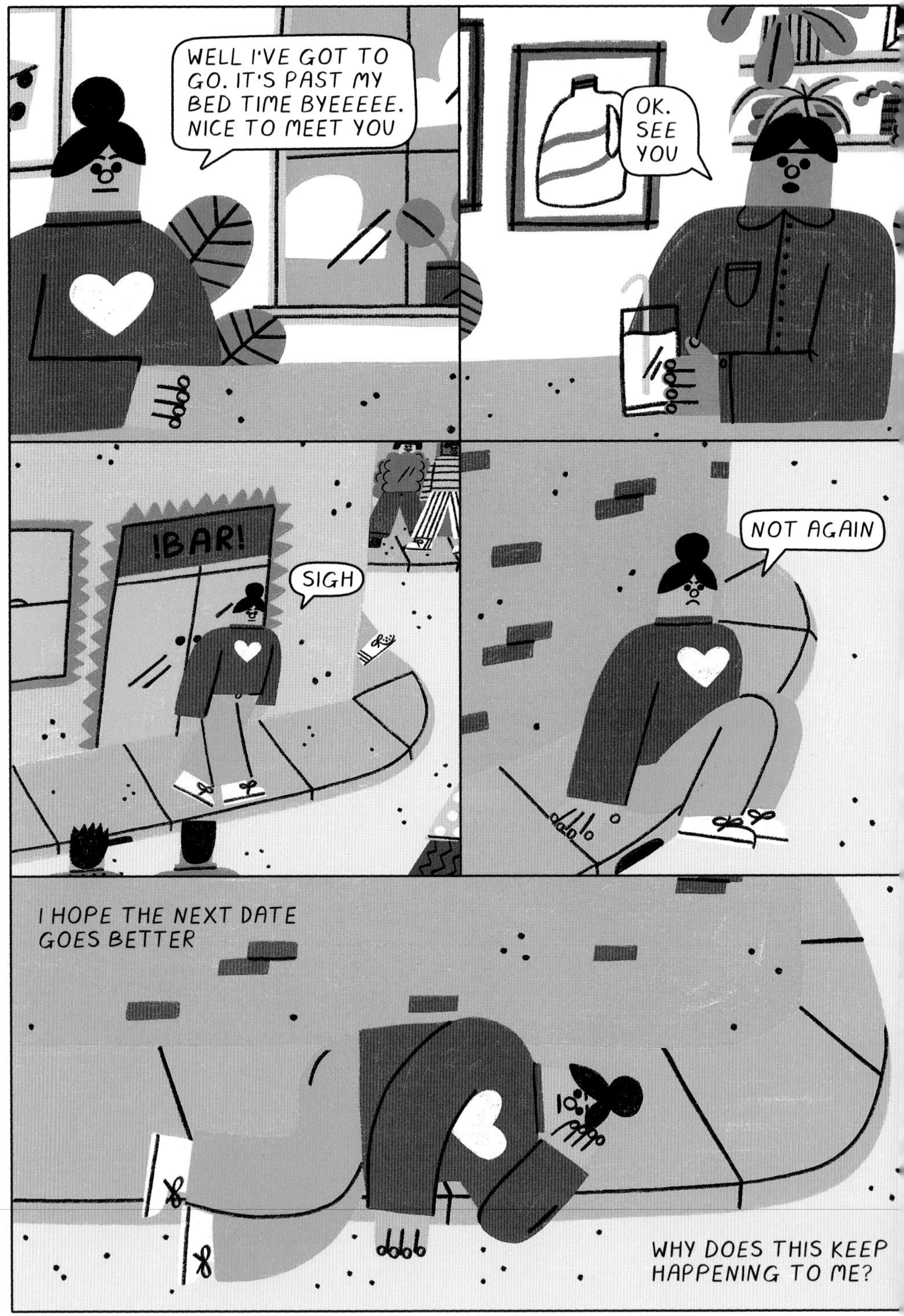
WELL I'VE GOT TO GO. IT'S PAST MY BED TIME BYEEEEE. NICE TO MEET YOU
OK. SEE YOU
!BAR!
SIGH
NOT AGAIN
I HOPE THE NEXT DATE GOES BETTER
WHY DOES THIS KEEP HAPPENING TO ME?

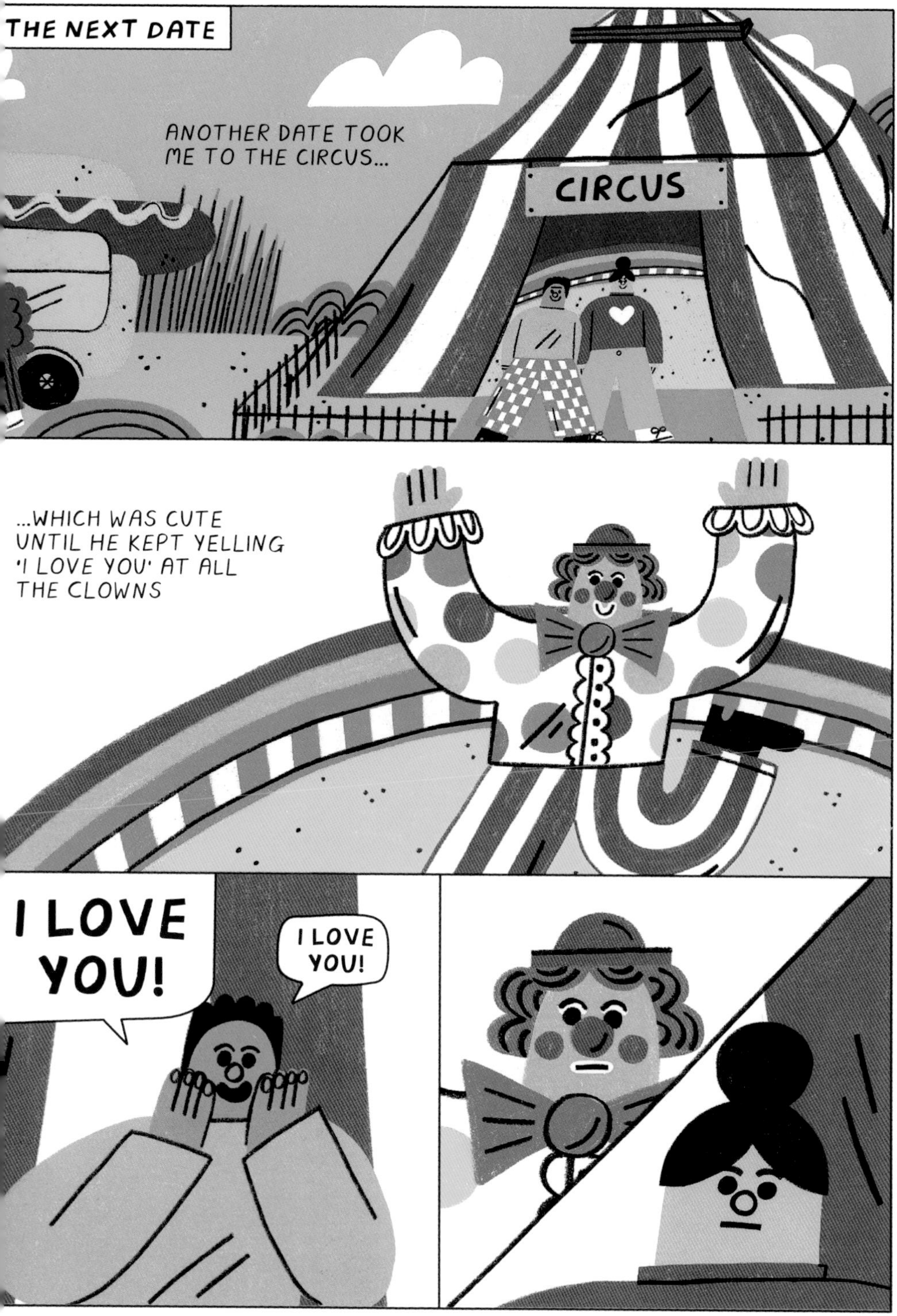
THE NEXT DATE
ANOTHER DATE TOOK ME TO THE CIRCUS...
CIRCUS
...WHICH WAS CUTE UNTIL HE KEPT YELLING 'I LOVE YOU' AT ALL THE CLOWNS
I LOVE YOU!
I LOVE YOU!

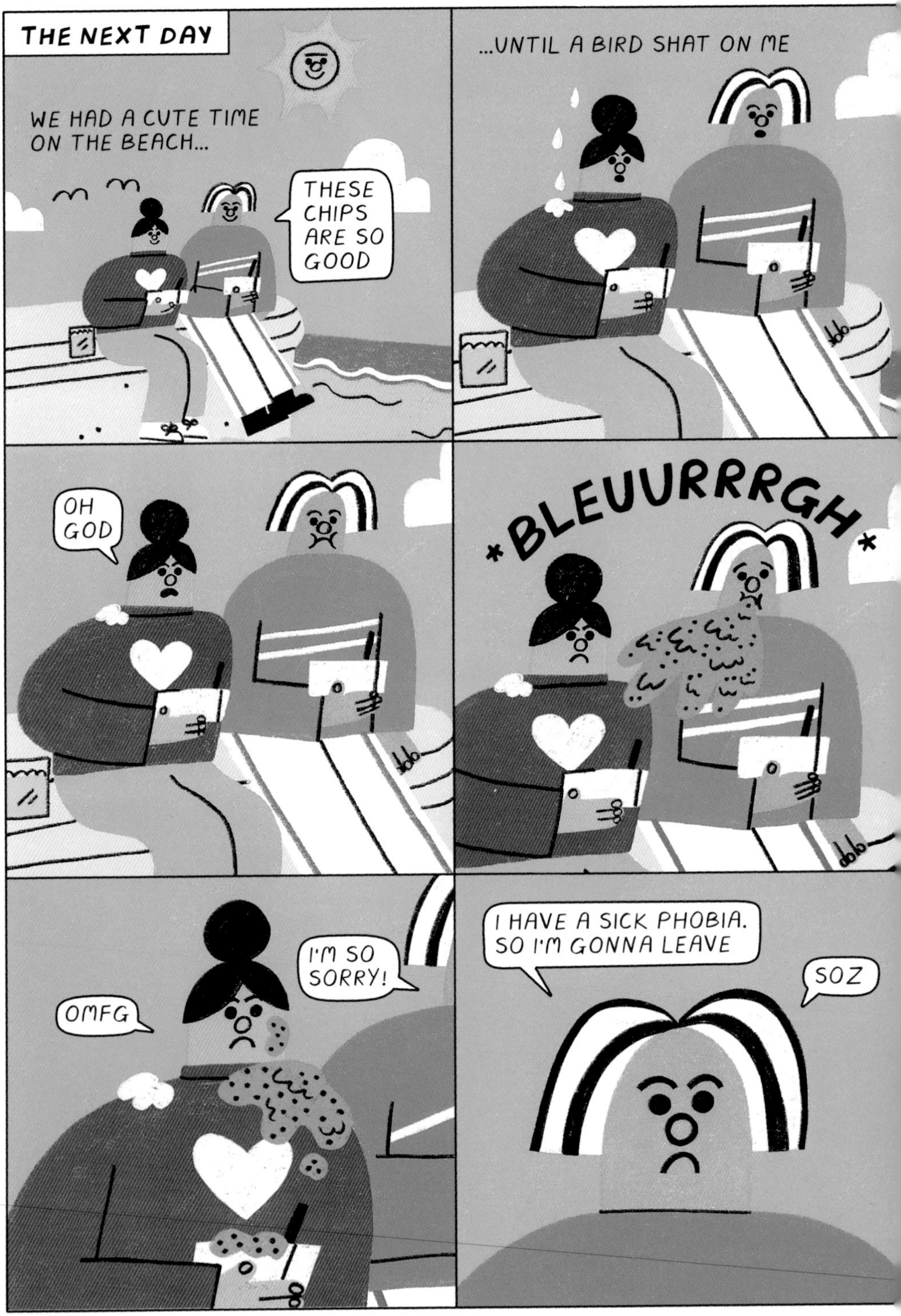
THE NEXT DAY
WE HAD A CUTE TIME ON THE BEACH...
THESE CHIPS ARE SO GOOD
...UNTIL A BIRD SHAT ON ME
OH GOD
BLEUURRRGH
OMFG
I'M SO SORRY!
I HAVE A SICK PHOBIA. SO I'M GONNA LEAVE
SOZ

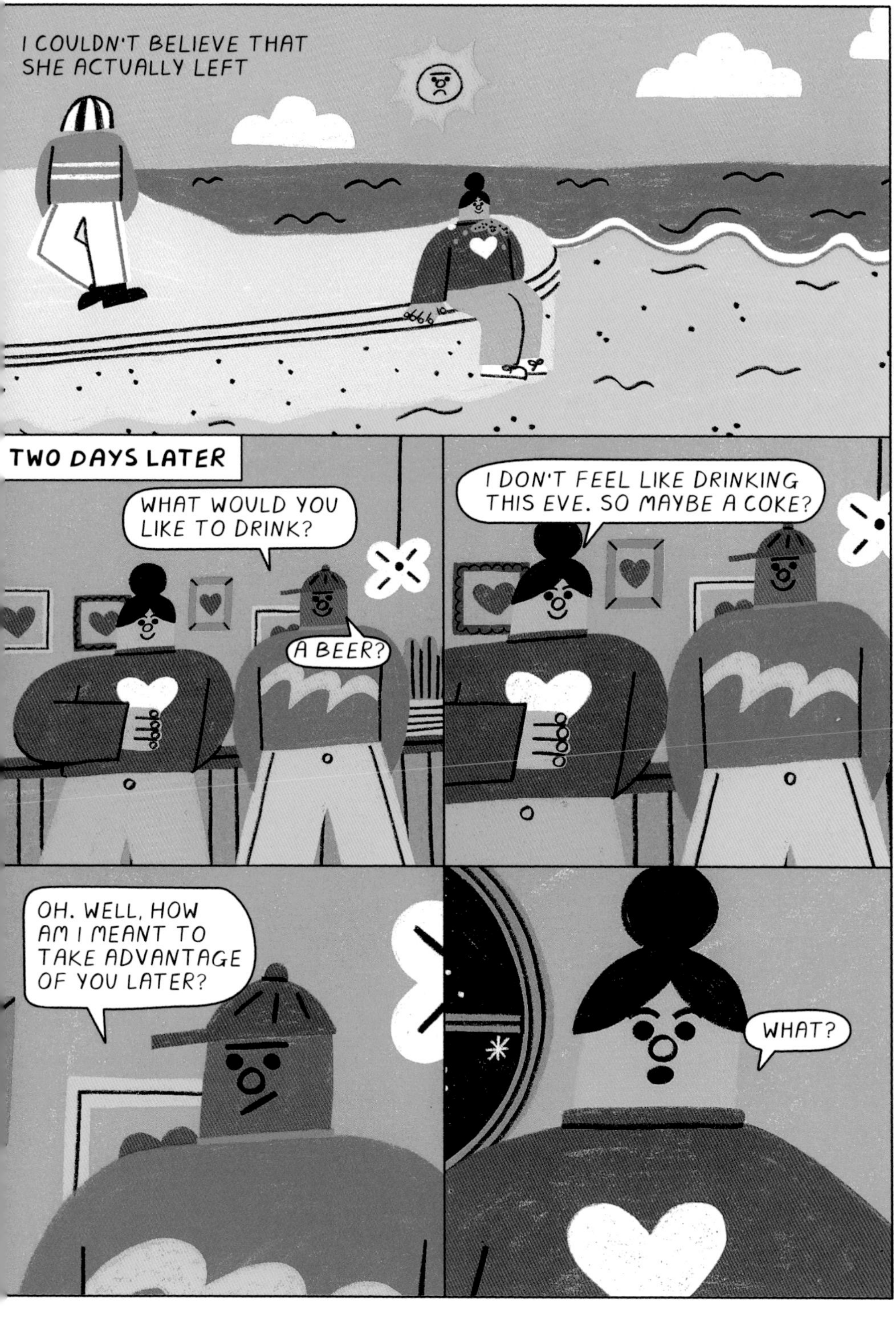
I COULDN'T BELIEVE THAT SHE ACTUALLY LEFT
TWO DAYS LATER
WHAT WOULD YOU LIKE TO DRINK?
A BEER?
I DON'T FEEL LIKE DRINKING THIS EVE. SO MAYBE A COKE?
OH. WELL, HOW AM I MEANT TO TAKE ADVANTAGE OF YOU LATER?
WHAT?

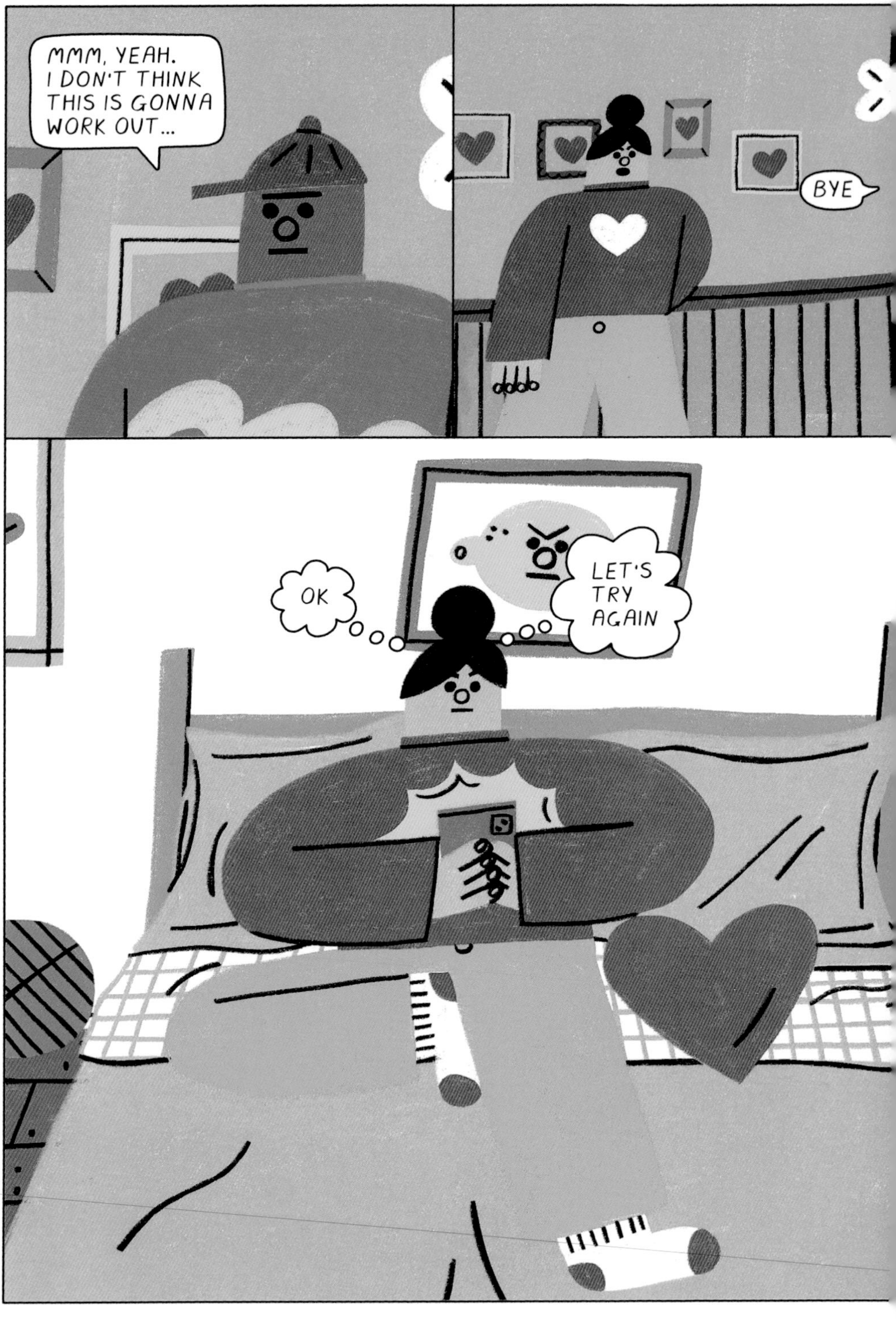
MMM, YEAH. I DON'T THINK THIS IS GONNA WORK OUT...
BYE
OK
LET'S TRY AGAIN

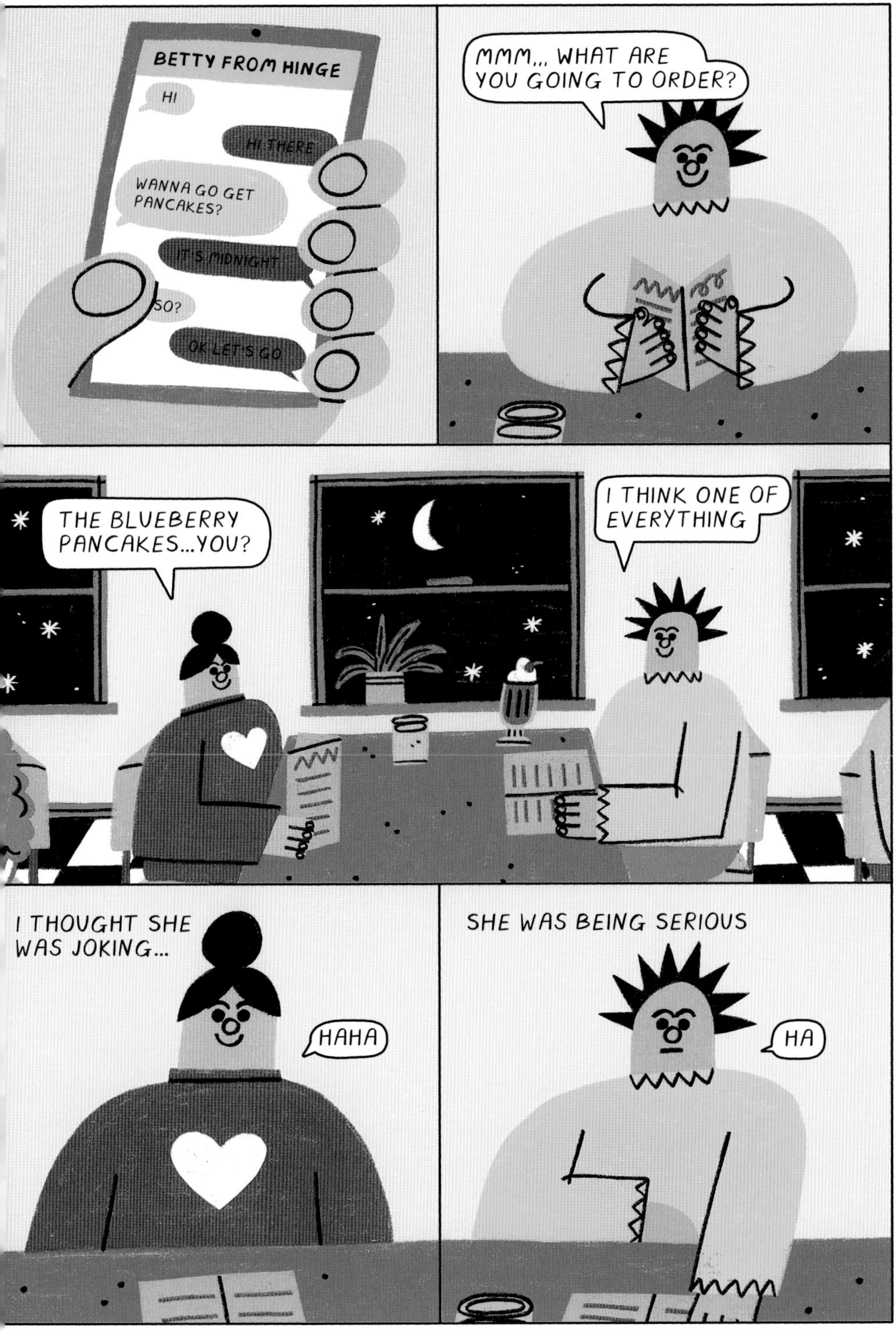
BETTY FROM HINGE
HI
HI THERE
WANNA GO GET PANCAKES?
IT'S MIDNIGHT
SO?
OK LET'S GO
MMM,,, WHAT ARE YOU GOING TO ORDER?
THE BLUEBERRY PANCAKES...YOU?
I THINK ONE OF EVERYTHING
I THOUGHT SHE WAS JOKING...
HAHA
SHE WAS BEING SERIOUS
HA

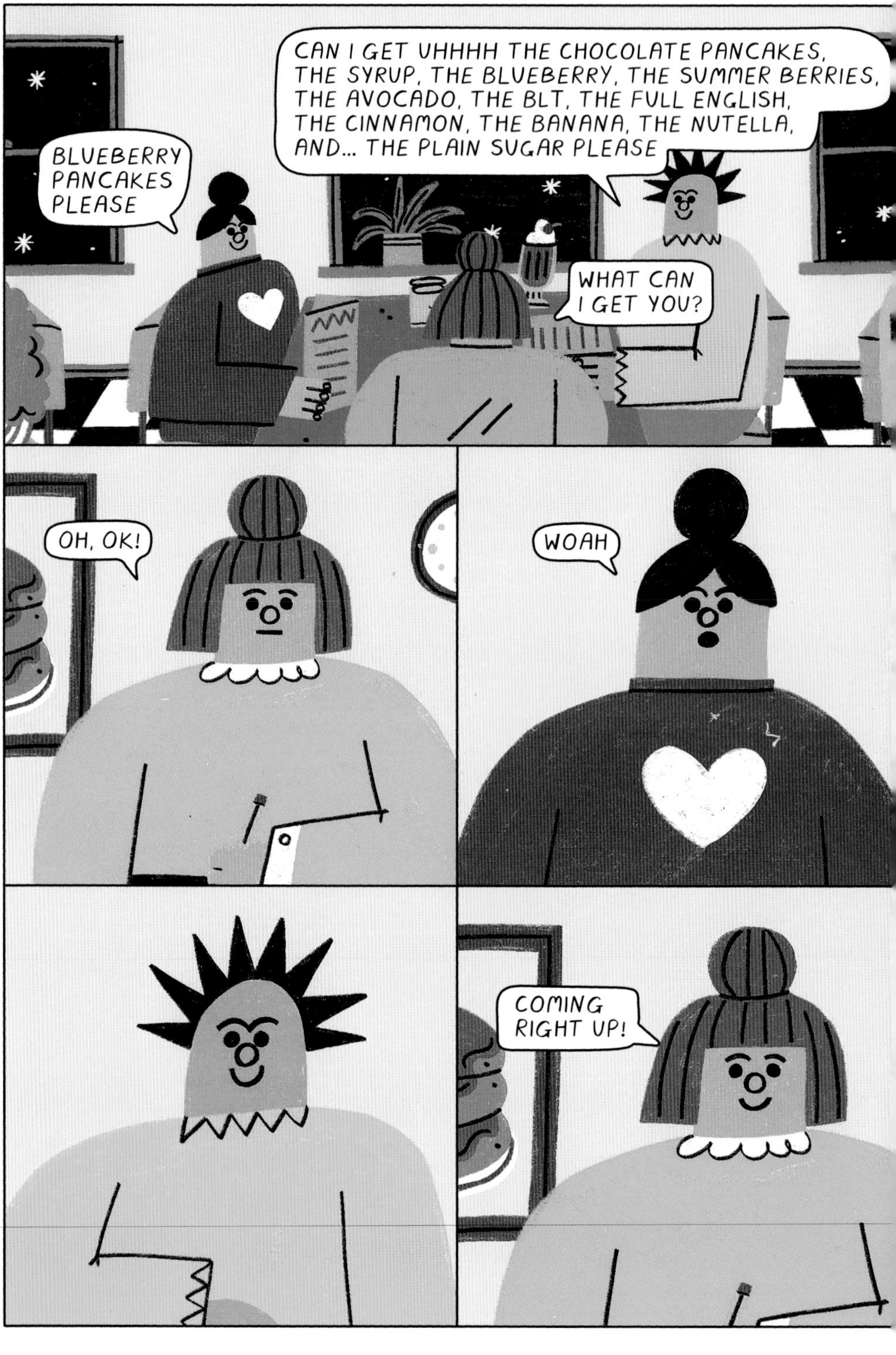
CAN I GET UHHHH THE CHOCOLATE PANCAKES, THE SYRUP, THE BLUEBERRY, THE SUMMER BERRIES, THE AVOCADO, THE BLT, THE FULL ENGLISH, THE CINNAMON, THE BANANA, THE NUTELLA, AND... THE PLAIN SUGAR PLEASE
BLUEBERRY PANCAKES PLEASE
WHAT CAN I GET YOU?
OH, OK!
WOAH
COMING RIGHT UP!

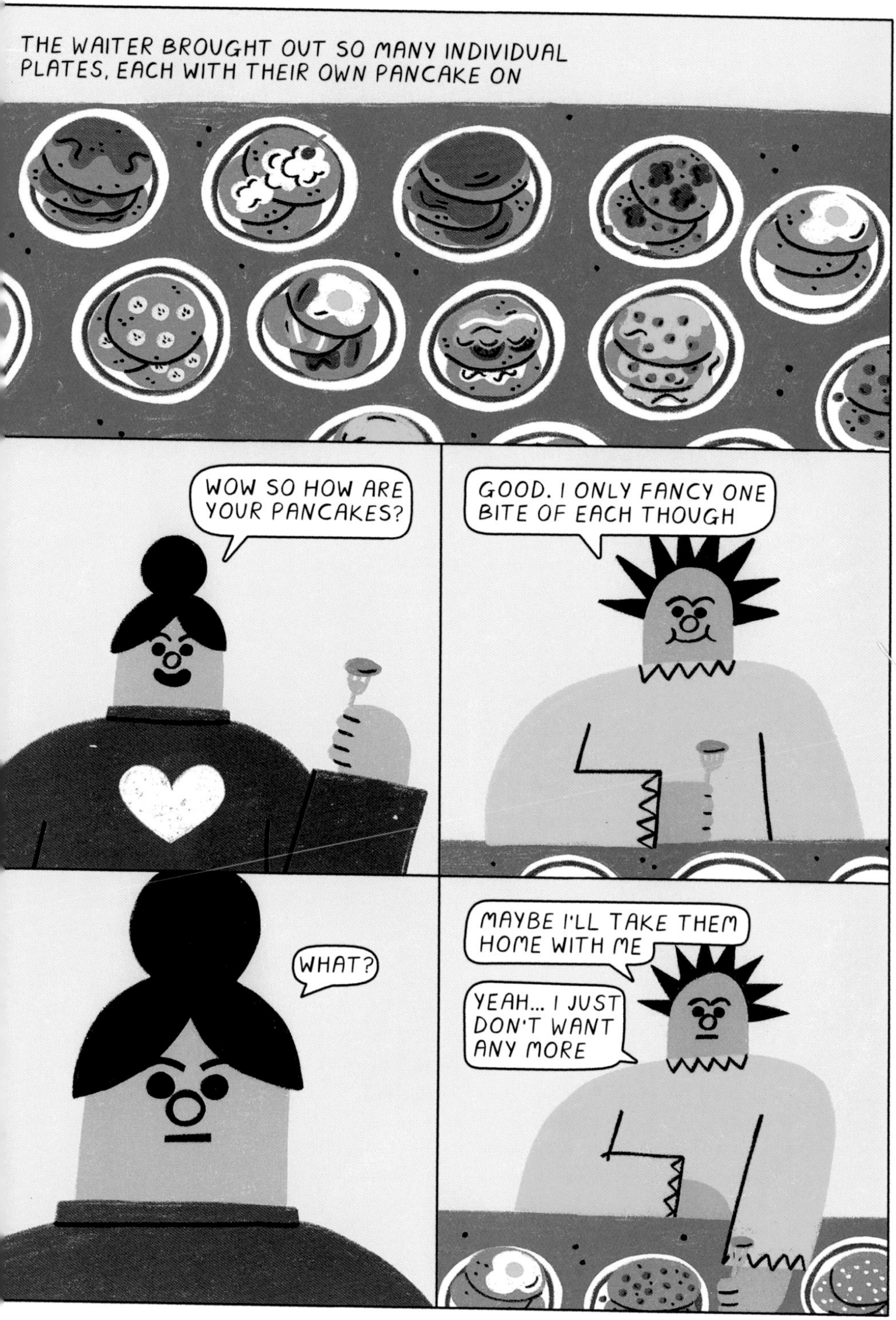
THE WAITER BROUGHT OUT SO MANY INDIVIDUAL PLATES, EACH WITH THEIR OWN PANCAKE ON
WOW SO HOW ARE YOUR PANCAKES?
GOOD. I ONLY FANCY ONE BITE OF EACH THOUGH
WHAT?
MAYBE I'LL TAKE THEM HOME WITH ME
YEAH... I JUST DON'T WANT ANY MORE

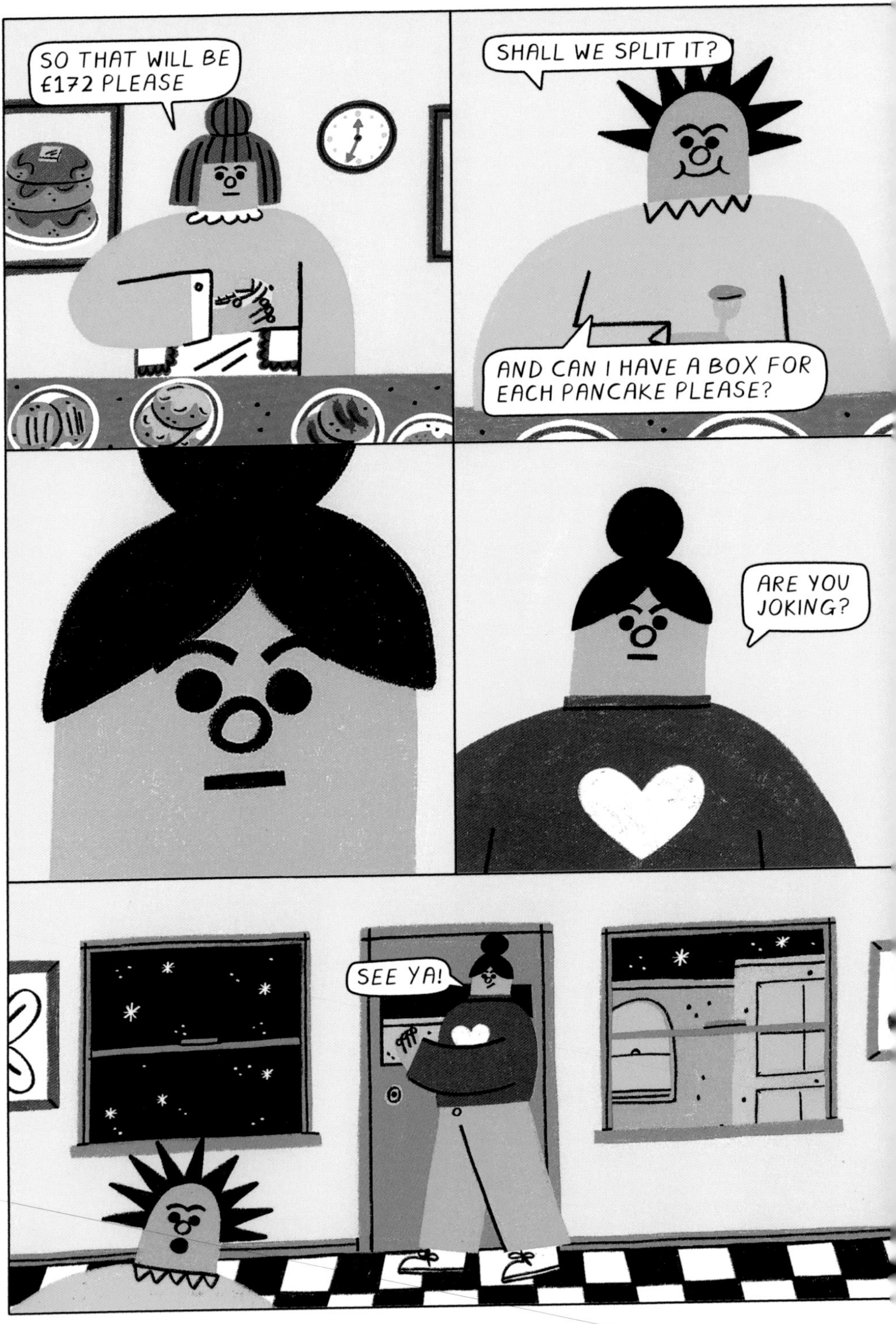
SO THAT WILL BE £172 PLEASE
SHALL WE SPLIT IT?
AND CAN I HAVE A BOX FOR EACH PANCAKE PLEASE?
ARE YOU JOKING?
SEE YA!

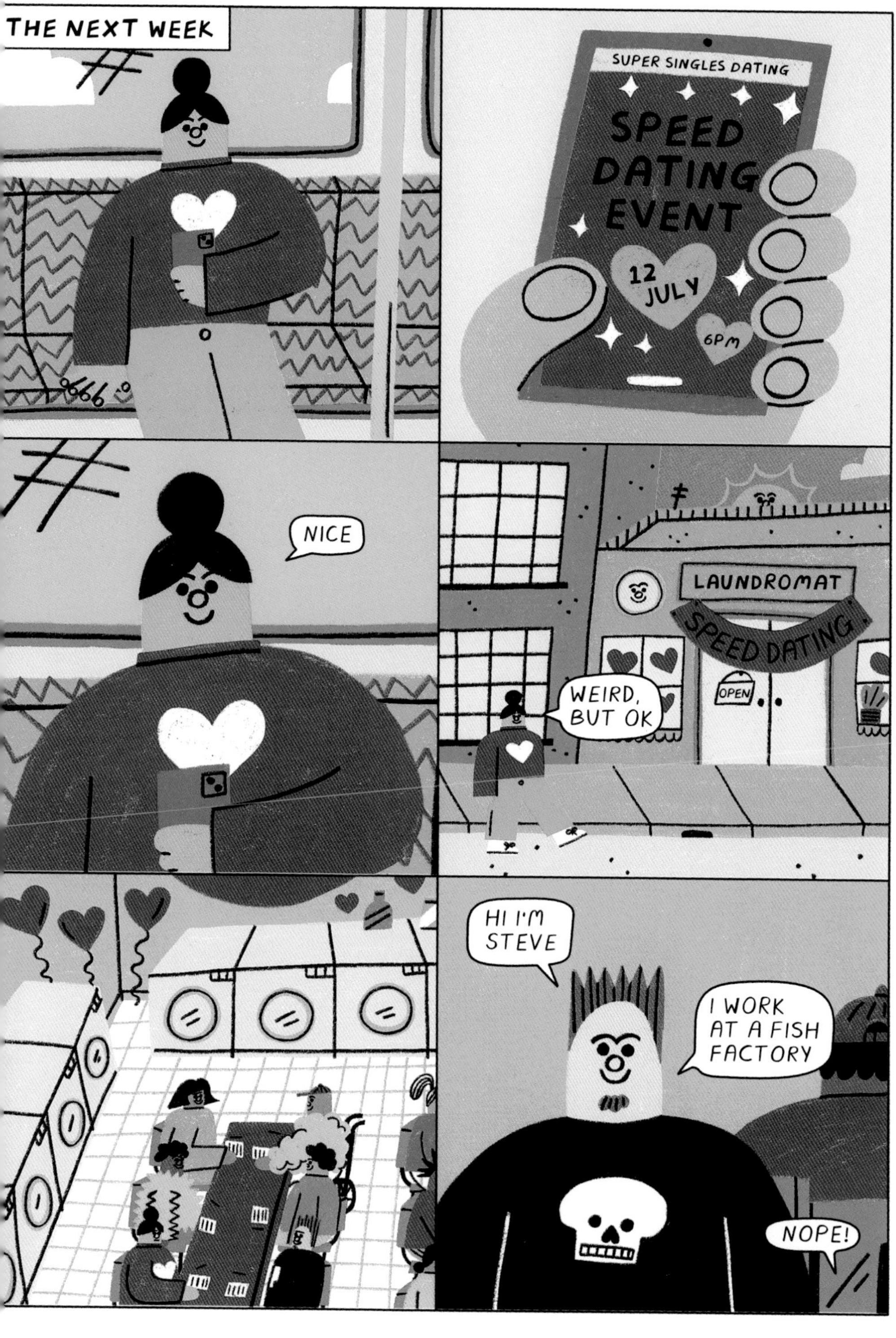
THE NEXT WEEK
SUPER SINGLES DATING
SPEED DATING EVENT
12 JULY
6PM
NICE
LAUNDROMAT
SPEED DATING
OPEN
WEIRD, BUT OK
HI I'M STEVE
I WORK AT A FISH FACTORY
NOPE!

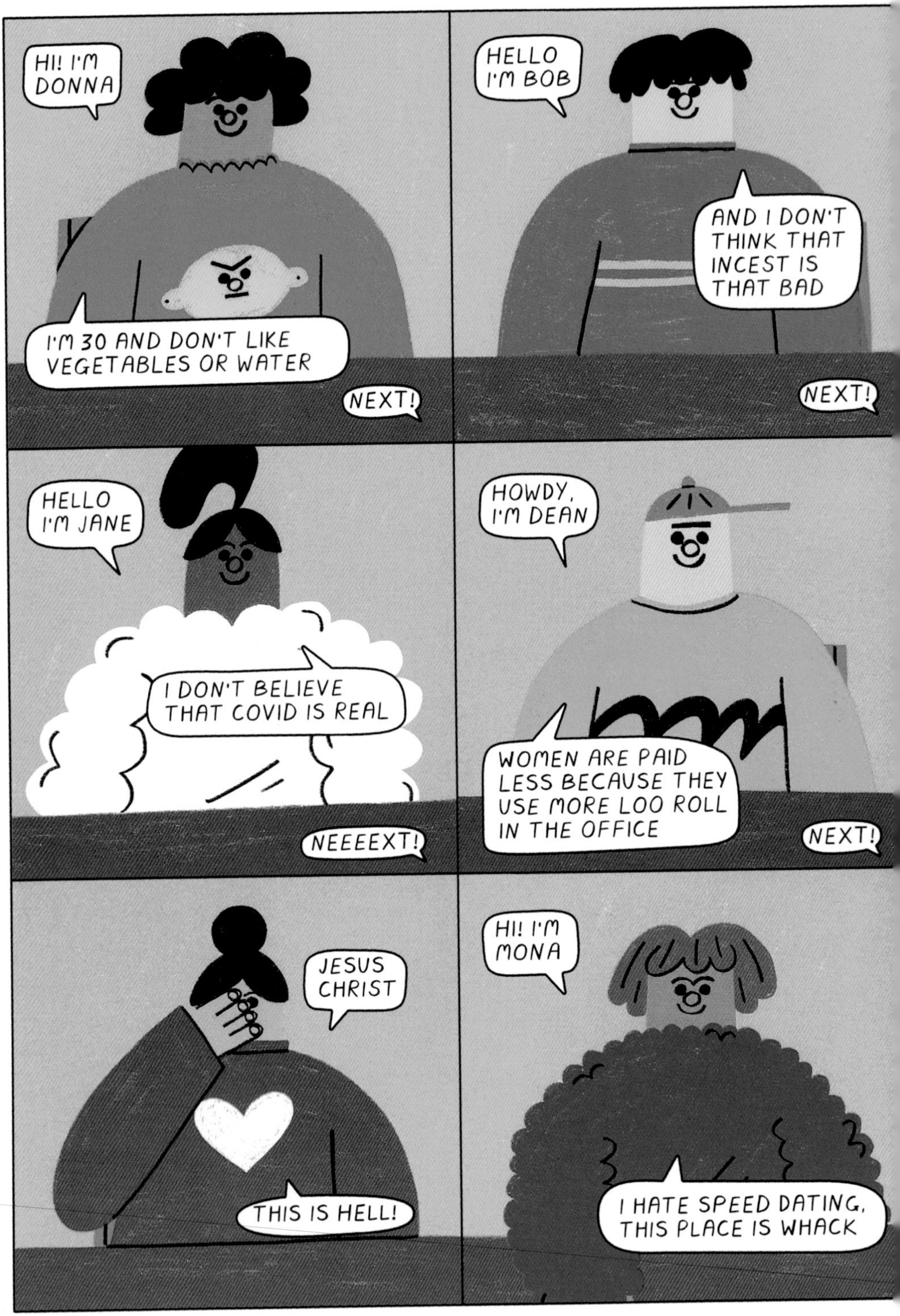
HI! I'M DONNA
I'M 30 AND DON'T LIKE VEGETABLES OR WATER
NEXT!
HELLO I'M BOB
AND I DON'T THINK THAT INCEST IS THAT BAD
NEXT!
HELLO I'M JANE
I DON'T BELIEVE THAT COVID IS REAL
NEEEEXT!
HOWDY, I'M DEAN
WOMEN ARE PAID LESS BECAUSE THEY USE MORE LOO ROLL IN THE OFFICE
NEXT!
JESUS CHRIST
THIS IS HELL!
HI! I'M MONA
I HATE SPEED DATING, THIS PLACE IS WHACK

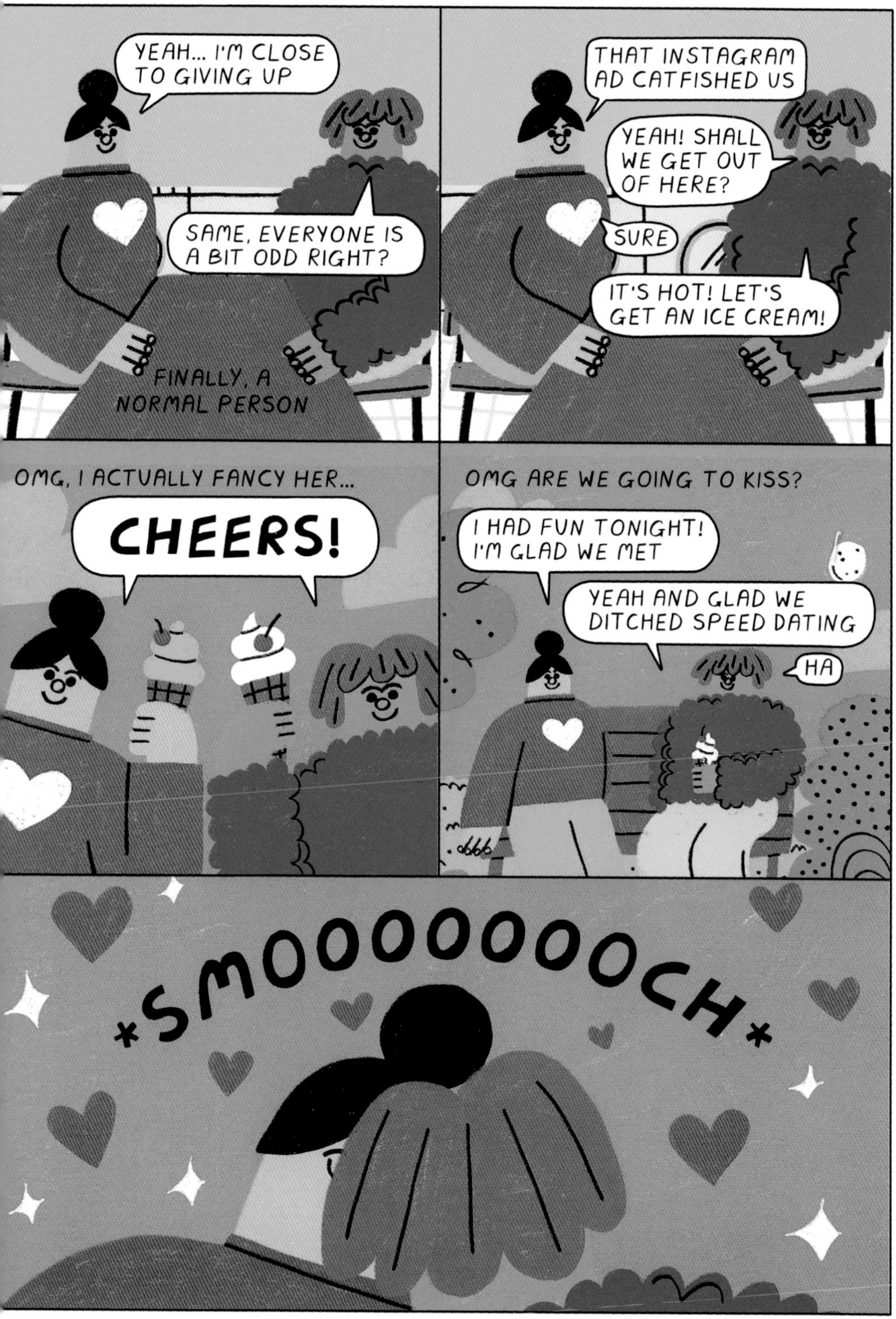
YEAH... I'M CLOSE TO GIVING UP
SAME, EVERYONE IS A BIT ODD RIGHT?
FINALLY, A NORMAL PERSON
THAT INSTAGRAM AD CATFISHED US
YEAH! SHALL WE GET OUT OF HERE?
SURE
IT'S HOT! LET'S GET AN ICE CREAM!
OMG, I ACTUALLY FANCY HER...
CHEERS!
OMG ARE WE GOING TO KISS?
I HAD FUN TONIGHT! I'M GLAD WE MET
YEAH AND GLAD WE DITCHED SPEED DATING
HA
SMOOOOOOOOCH

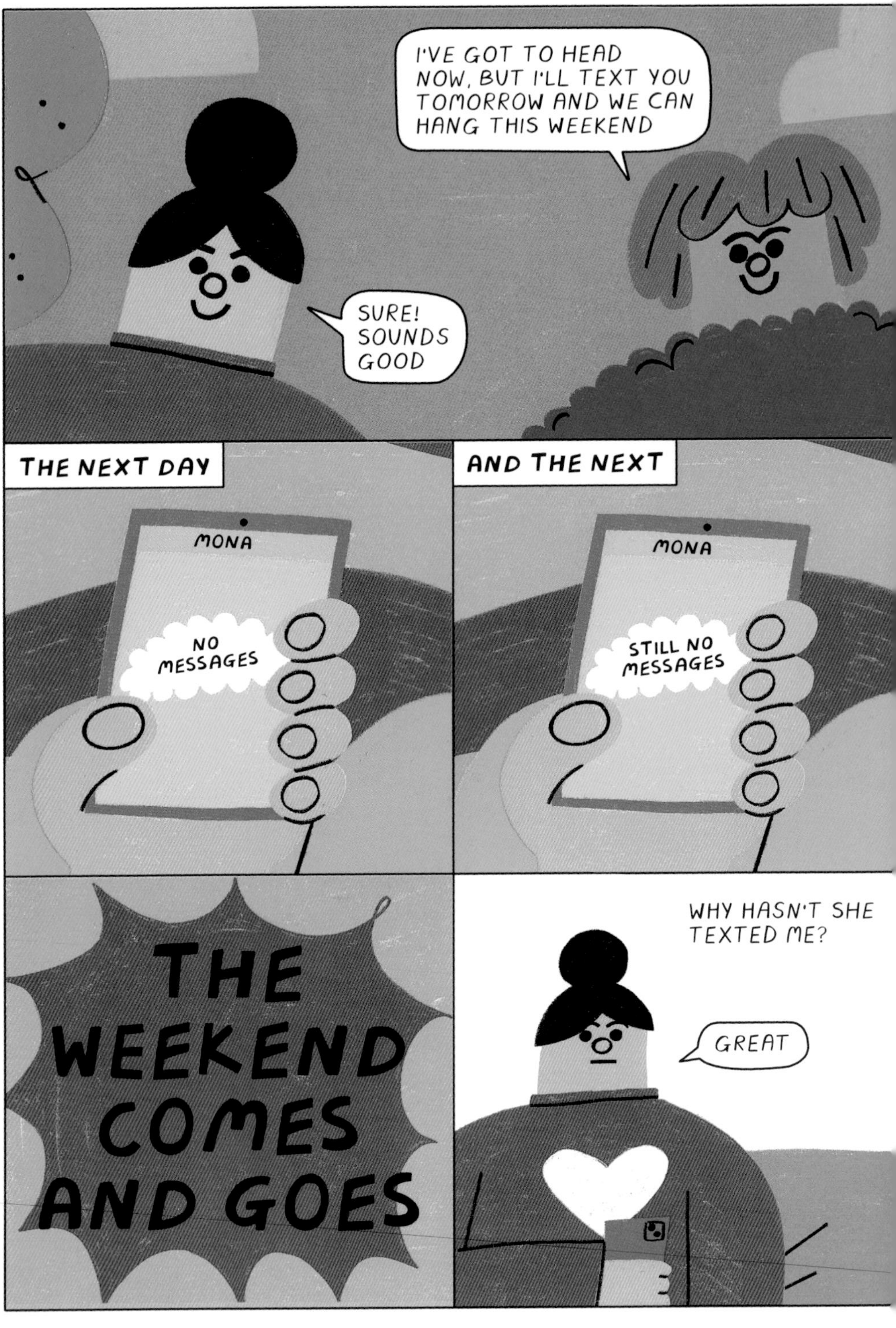
I'VE GOT TO HEAD NOW, BUT I'LL TEXT YOU TOMORROW AND WE CAN HANG THIS WEEKEND
SURE! SOUNDS GOOD
THE NEXT DAY
MONA
NO MESSAGES
AND THE NEXT
MONA
STILL NO MESSAGES
THE WEEKEND COMES AND GOES
WHY HASN'T SHE TEXTED ME?
GREAT

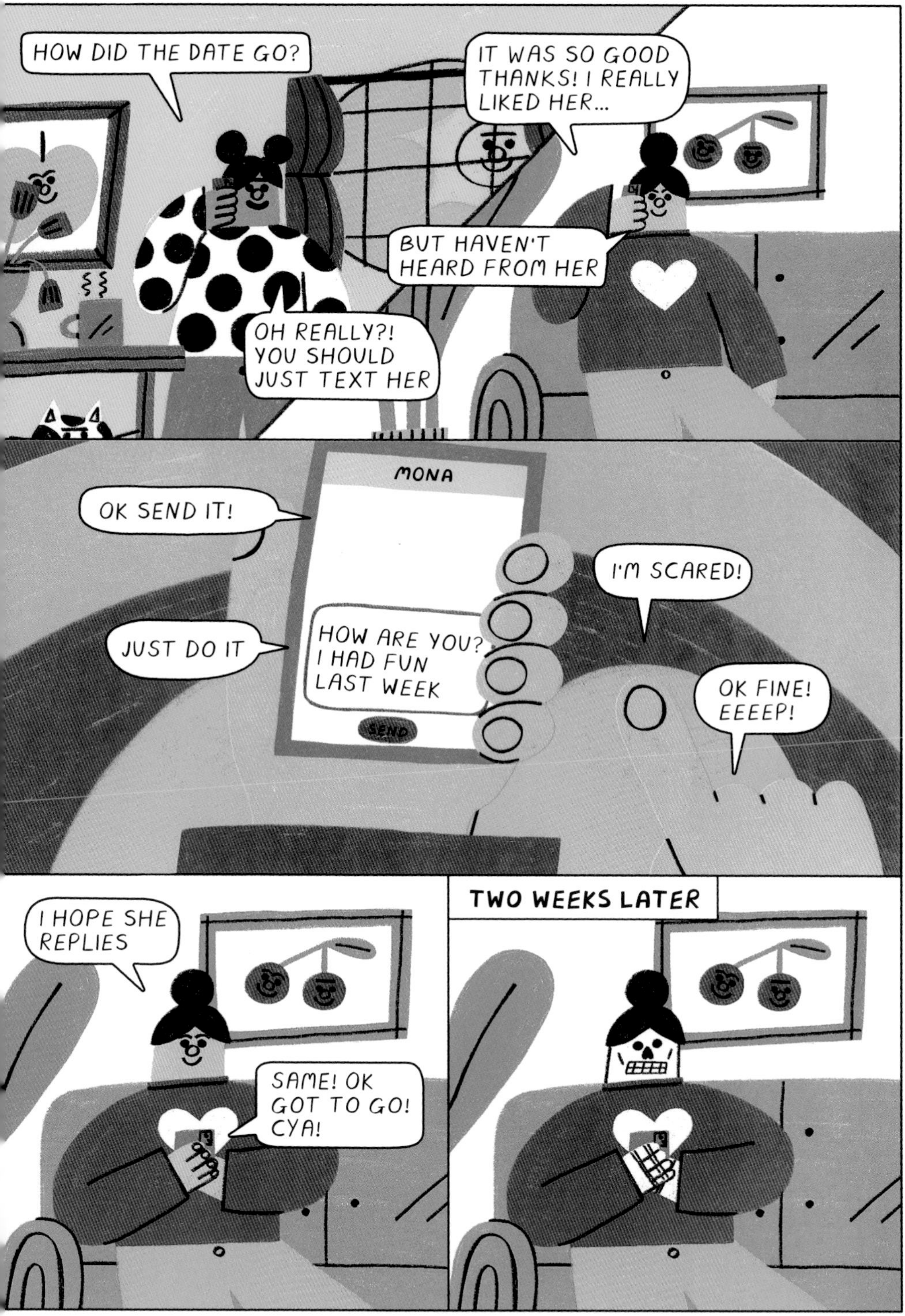
HOW DID THE DATE GO?
IT WAS SO GOOD THANKS! I REALLY LIKED HER...
BUT HAVEN'T HEARD FROM HER
OH REALLY?! YOU SHOULD JUST TEXT HER
MONA
OK SEND IT!
I'M SCARED!
JUST DO IT
HOW ARE YOU? I HAD FUN LAST WEEK
SEND
OK FINE! EEEEP!
I HOPE SHE REPLIES
SAME! OK GOT TO GO! CYA!
TWO WEEKS LATER

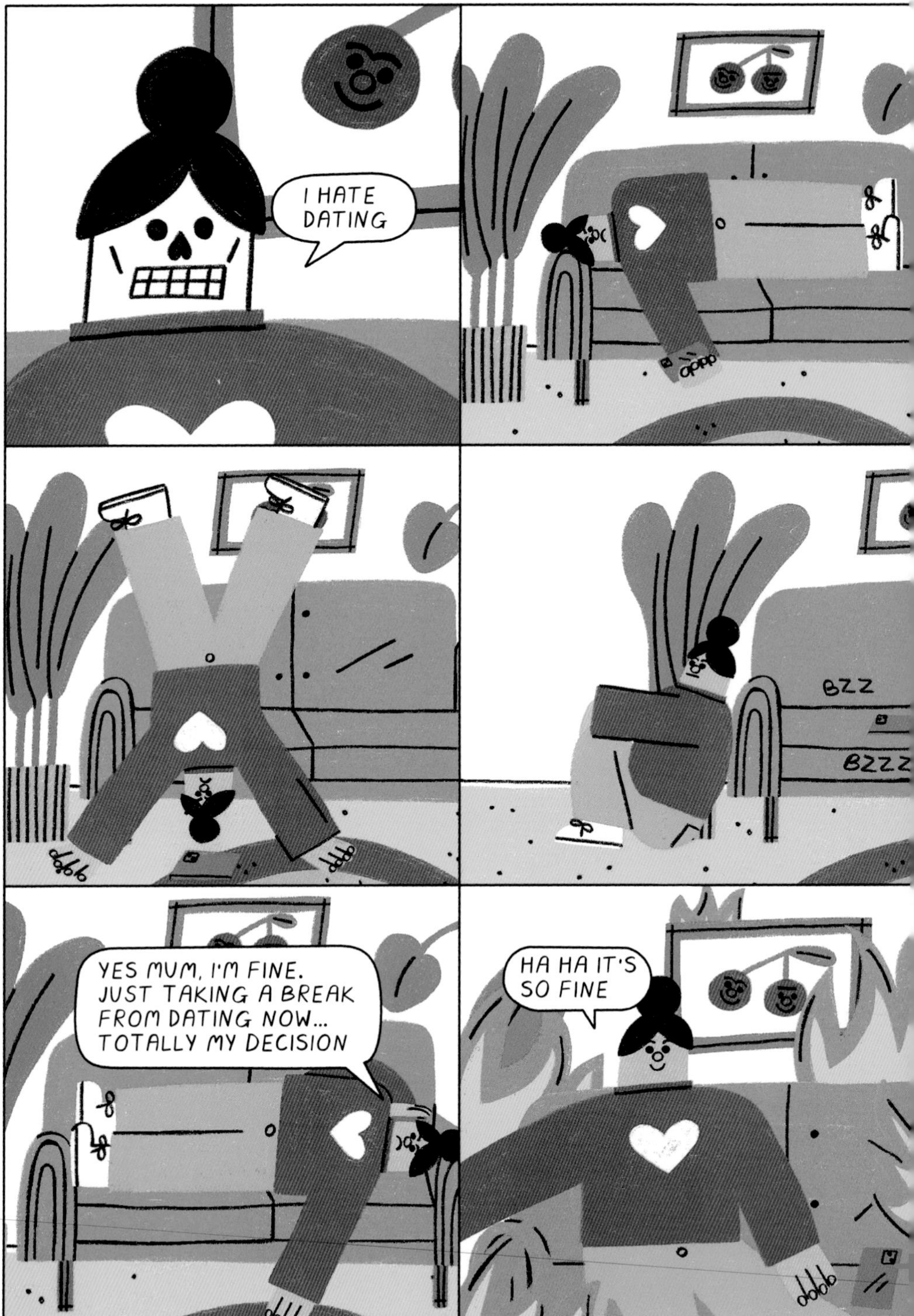
I HATE DATING
BZZ
BZZZ
YES MUM, I'M FINE. JUST TAKING A BREAK FROM DATING NOW... TOTALLY MY DECISION
HA HA IT'S SO FINE

EVERYTHING IS FINE

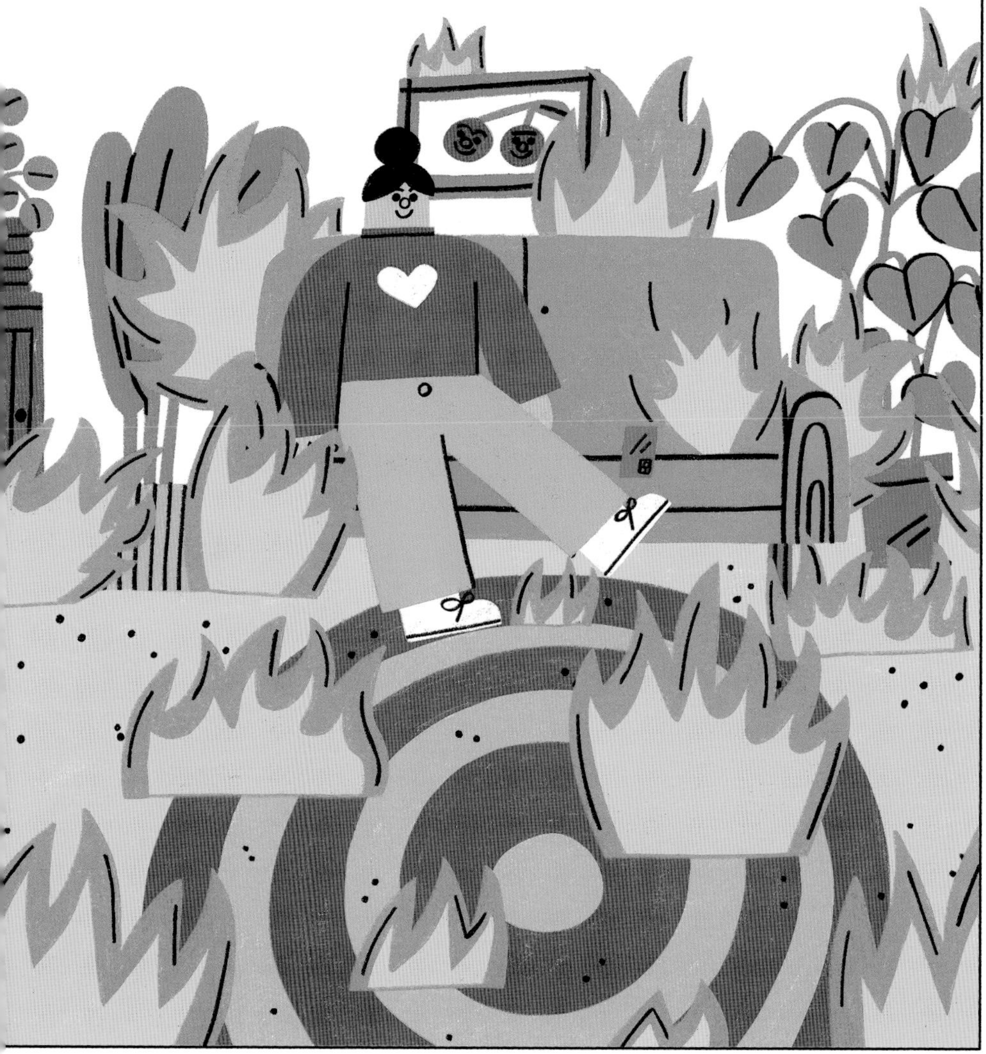

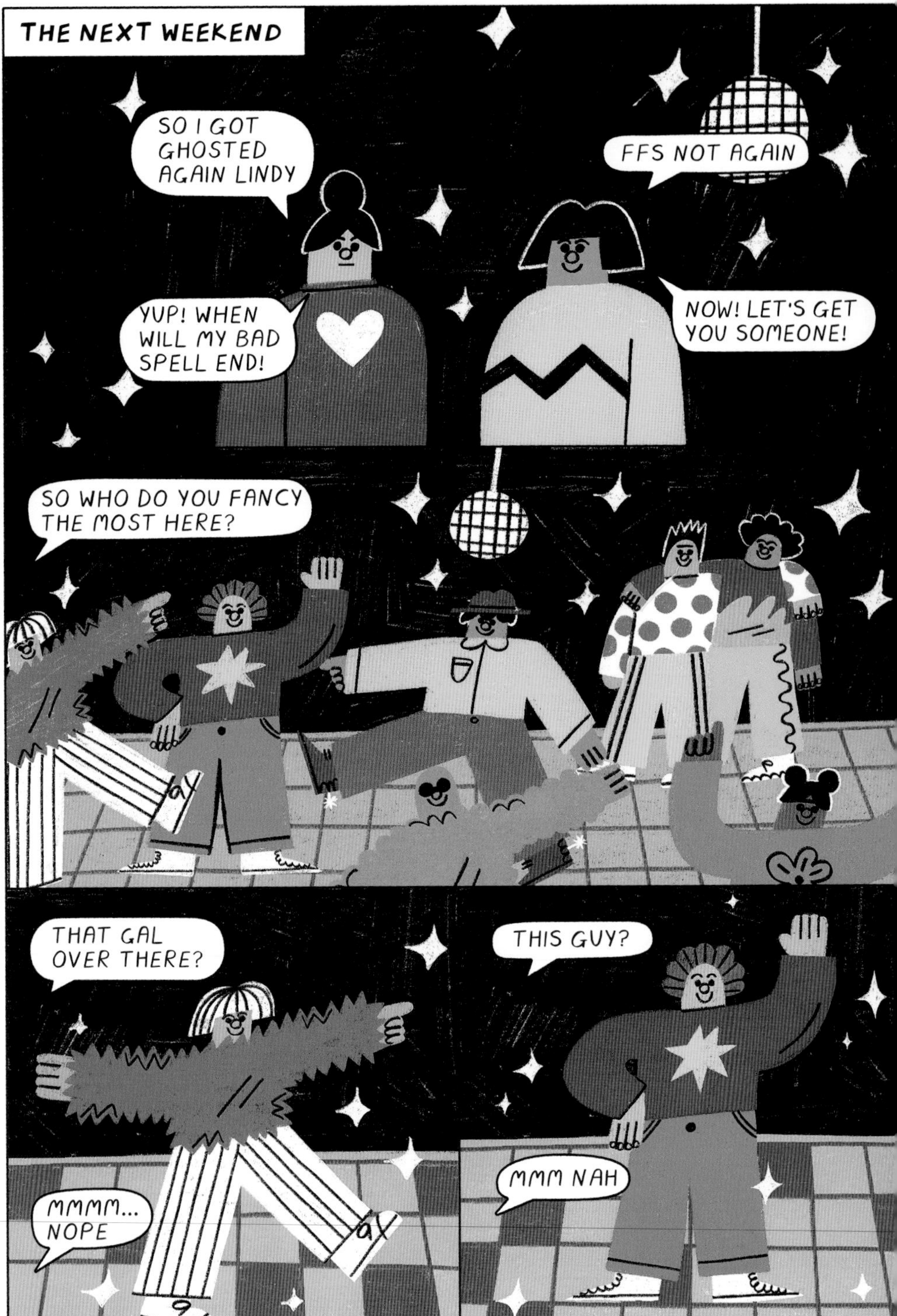
THE NEXT WEEKEND
SO I GOT GHOSTED AGAIN LINDY
FFS NOT AGAIN
YUP! WHEN WILL MY BAD SPELL END!
NOW! LET'S GET YOU SOMEONE!
SO WHO DO YOU FANCY THE MOST HERE?
THAT GAL OVER THERE?
MMMM... NOPE
THIS GUY?
MMM NAH

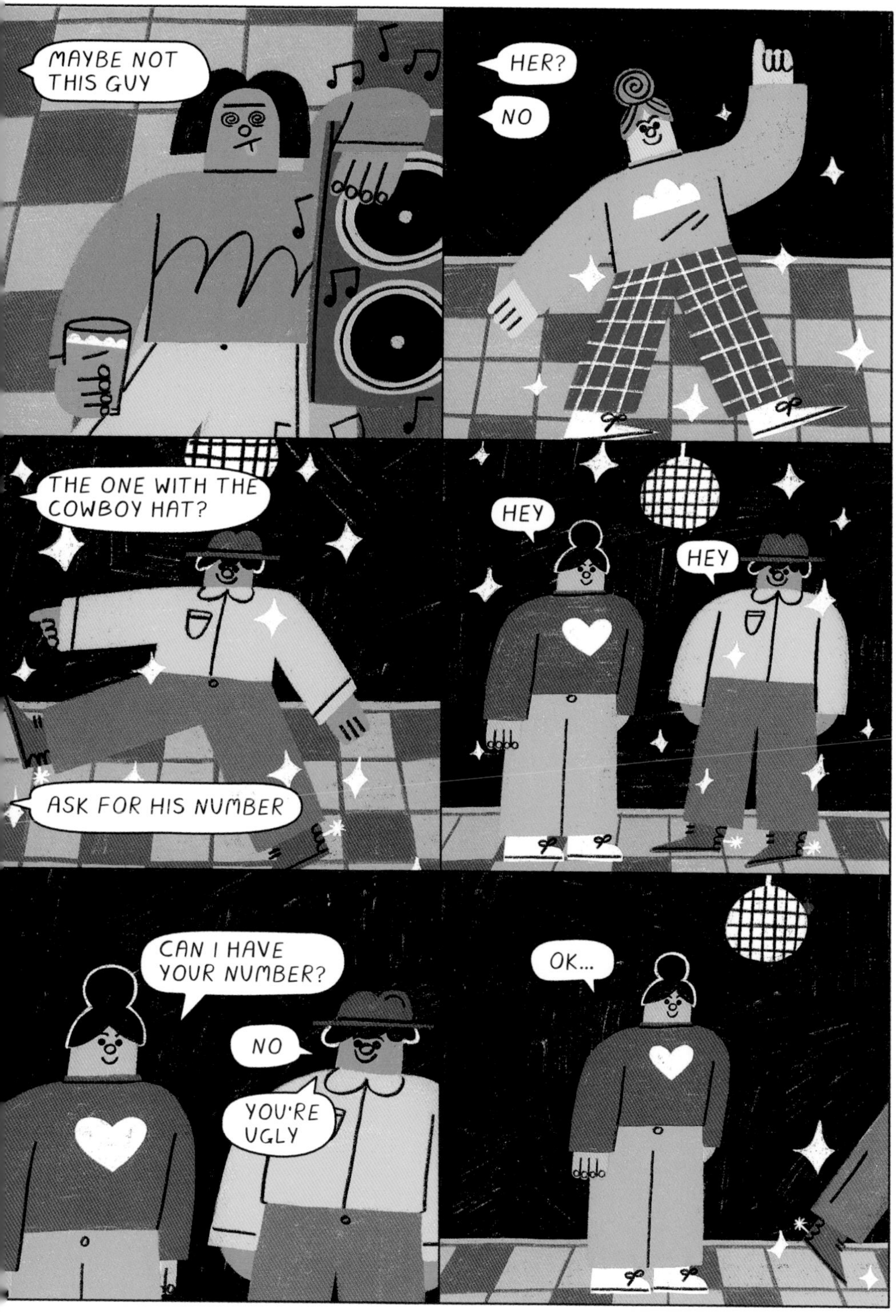
MAYBE NOT
THIS GUY
HER?
NO
THE ONE WITH THE
COWBOY HAT?
ASK FOR HIS NUMBER
HEY
HEY
CAN I HAVE
YOUR NUMBER?
NO
YOU'RE
UGLY
OK...

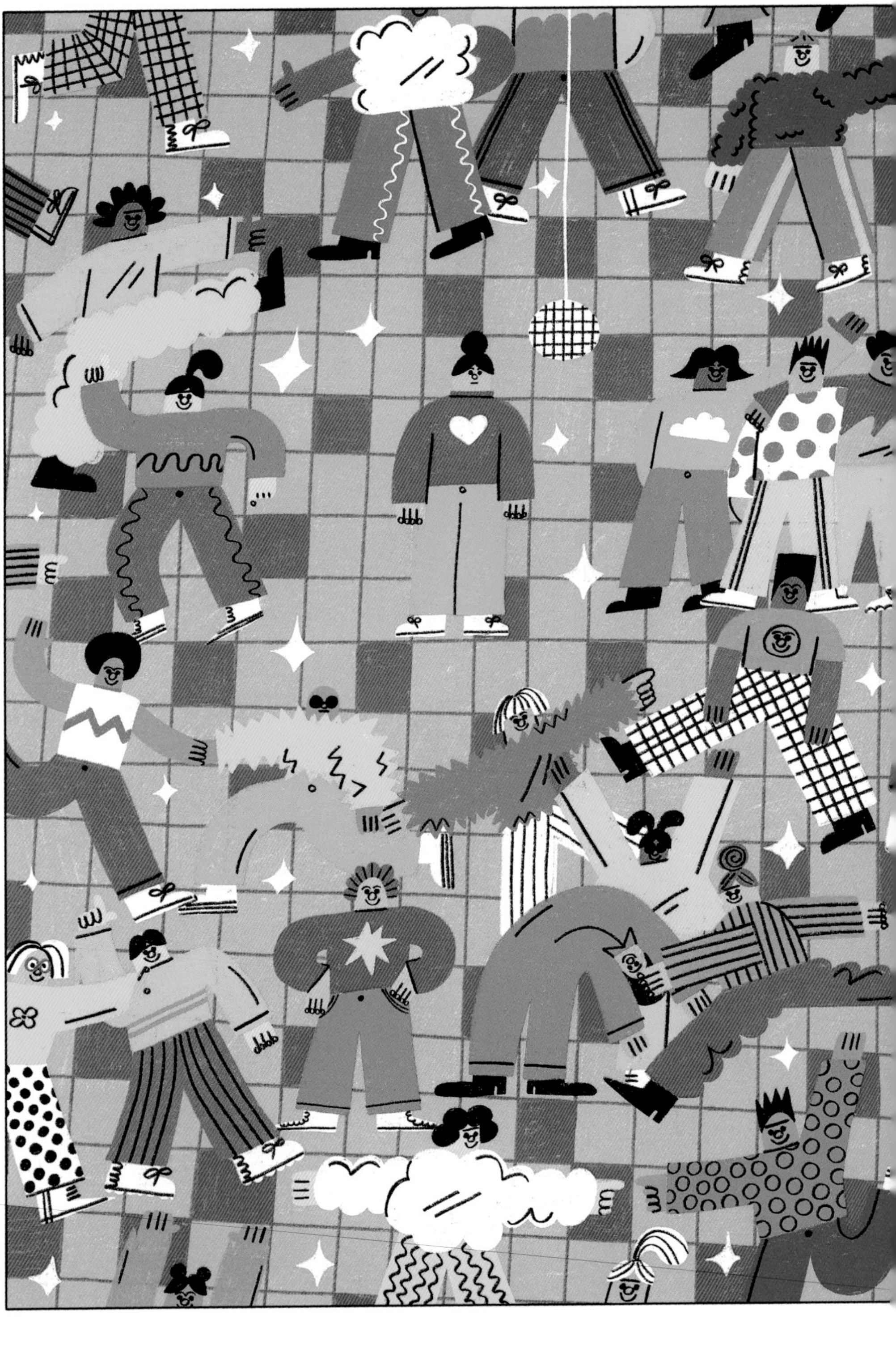

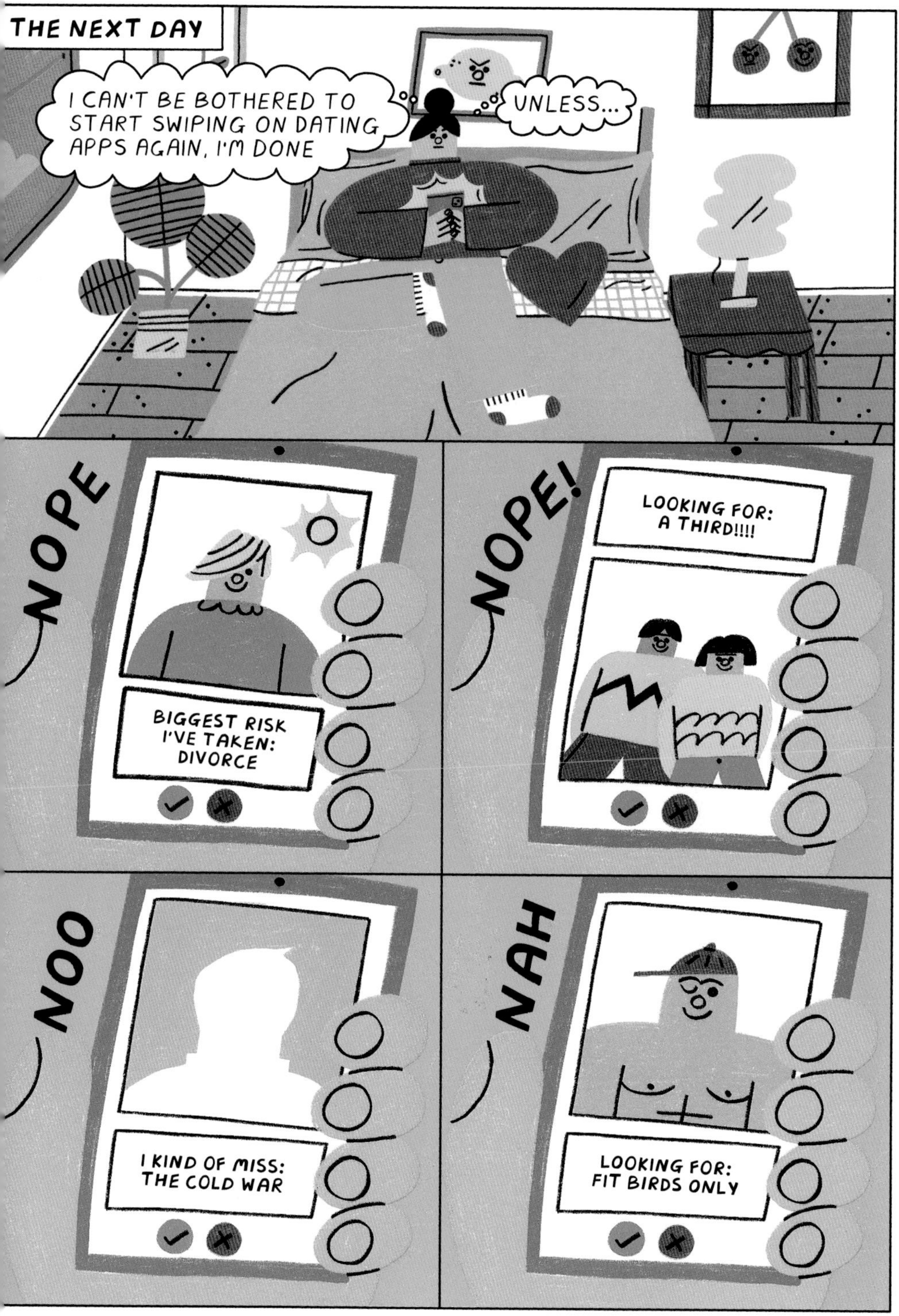
THE NEXT DAY
I CAN'T BE BOTHERED TO START SWIPING ON DATING APPS AGAIN, I'M DONE
UNLESS...
NOPE
BIGGEST RISK I'VE TAKEN: DIVORCE
NOPE!
LOOKING FOR: A THIRD!!!!
NOO
I KIND OF MISS: THE COLD WAR
NAH
LOOKING FOR: FIT BIRDS ONLY

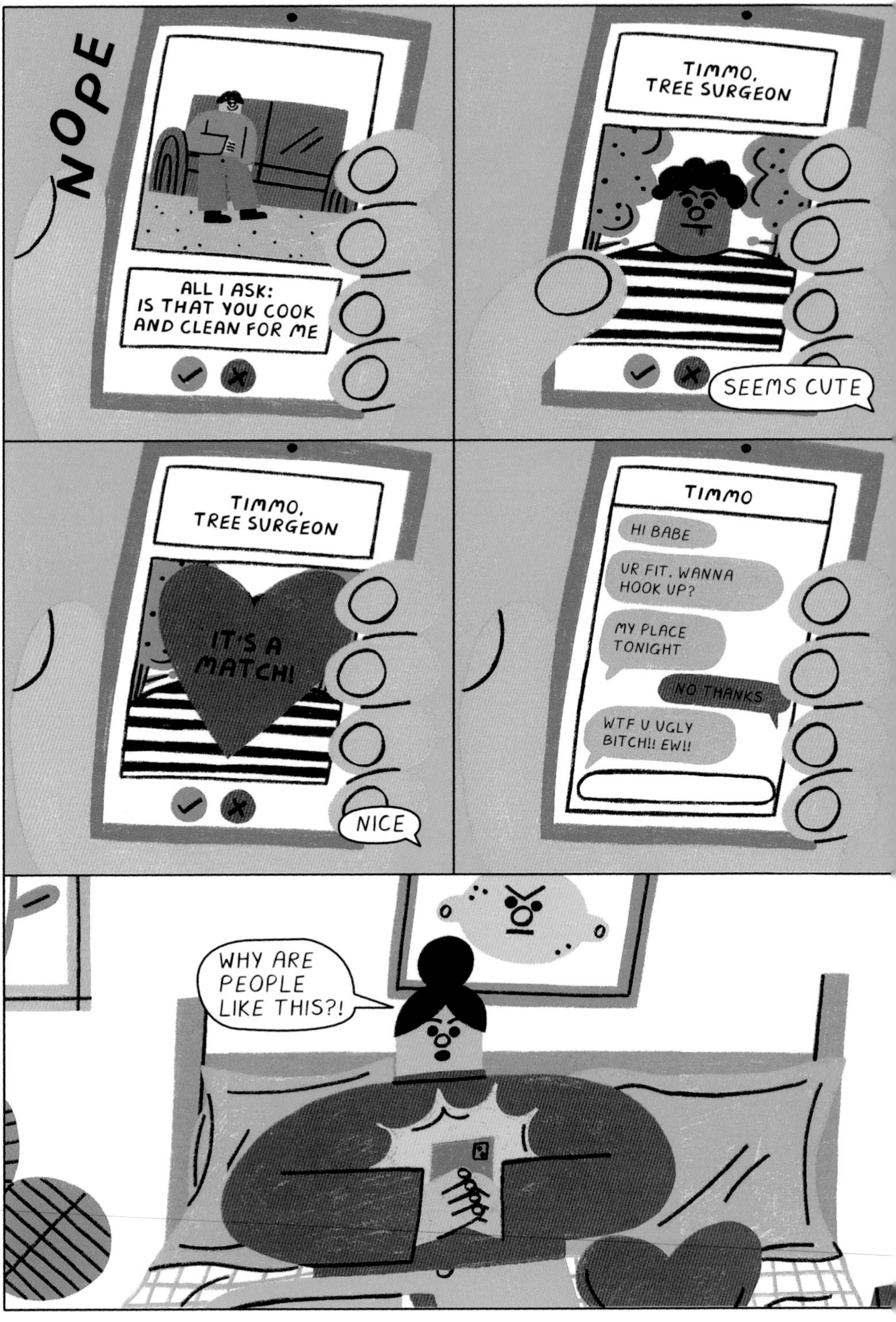
NOPE
ALL I ASK: IS THAT YOU COOK AND CLEAN FOR ME
TIMMO, TREE SURGEON
SEEMS CUTE
TIMMO, TREE SURGEON
IT'S A MATCH!
NICE
TIMMO
HI BABE
UR FIT. WANNA HOOK UP?
MY PLACE TONIGHT
NO THANKS
WTF U UGLY BITCH!! EW!!
WHY ARE PEOPLE LIKE THIS?!

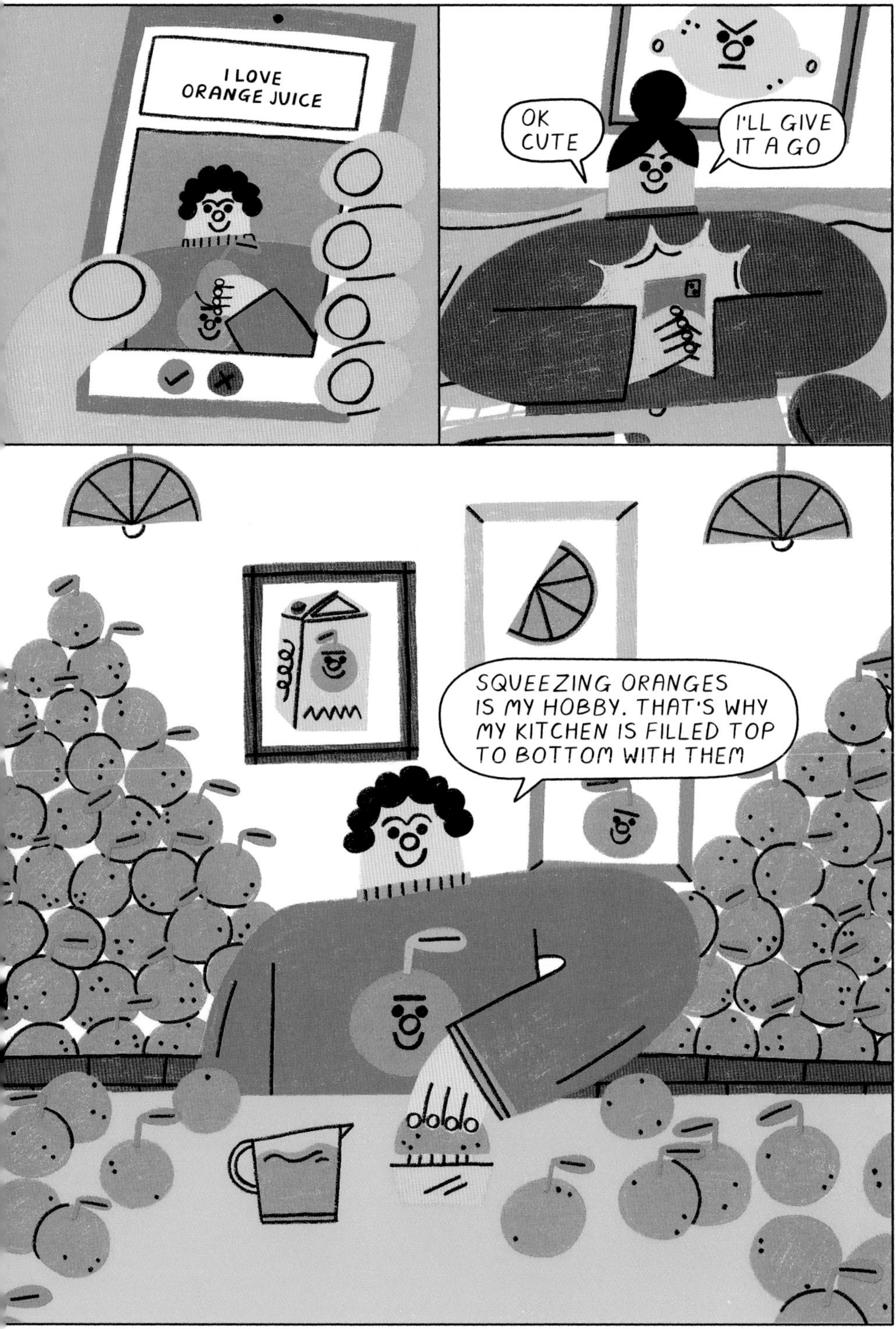
I LOVE
ORANGE JUICE
OK
CUTE
I'LL GIVE
IT A GO
SQUEEZING ORANGES
IS MY HOBBY. THAT'S WHY
MY KITCHEN IS FILLED TOP
TO BOTTOM WITH THEM

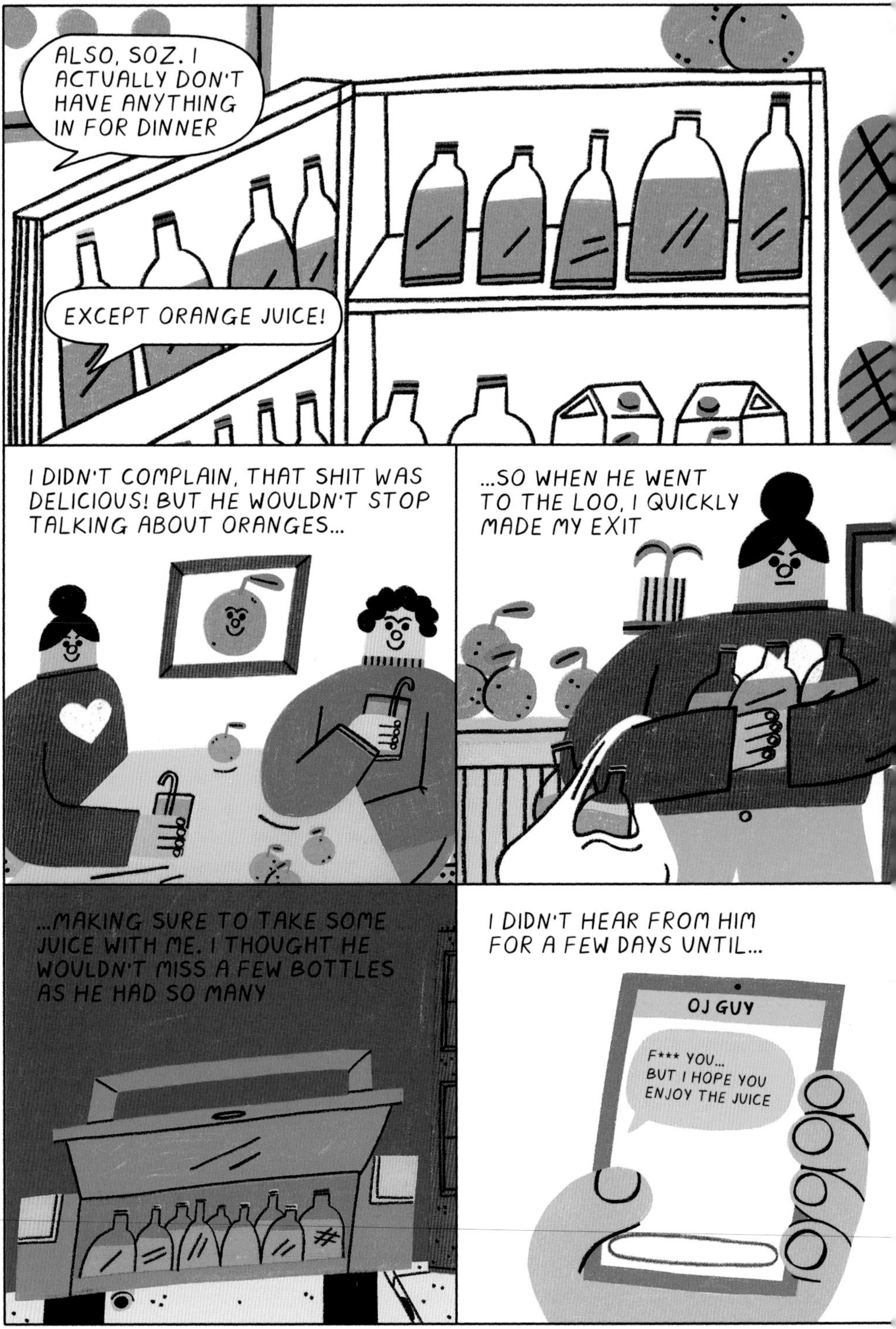
ALSO, SOZ. I ACTUALLY DON'T HAVE ANYTHING IN FOR DINNER
EXCEPT ORANGE JUICE!
I DIDN'T COMPLAIN, THAT SHIT WAS DELICIOUS! BUT HE WOULDN'T STOP TALKING ABOUT ORANGES...
...SO WHEN HE WENT TO THE LOO, I QUICKLY MADE MY EXIT
...MAKING SURE TO TAKE SOME JUICE WITH ME. I THOUGHT HE WOULDN'T MISS A FEW BOTTLES AS HE HAD SO MANY
I DIDN'T HEAR FROM HIM FOR A FEW DAYS UNTIL...
OJ GUY
F*** YOU... BUT I HOPE YOU ENJOY THE JUICE

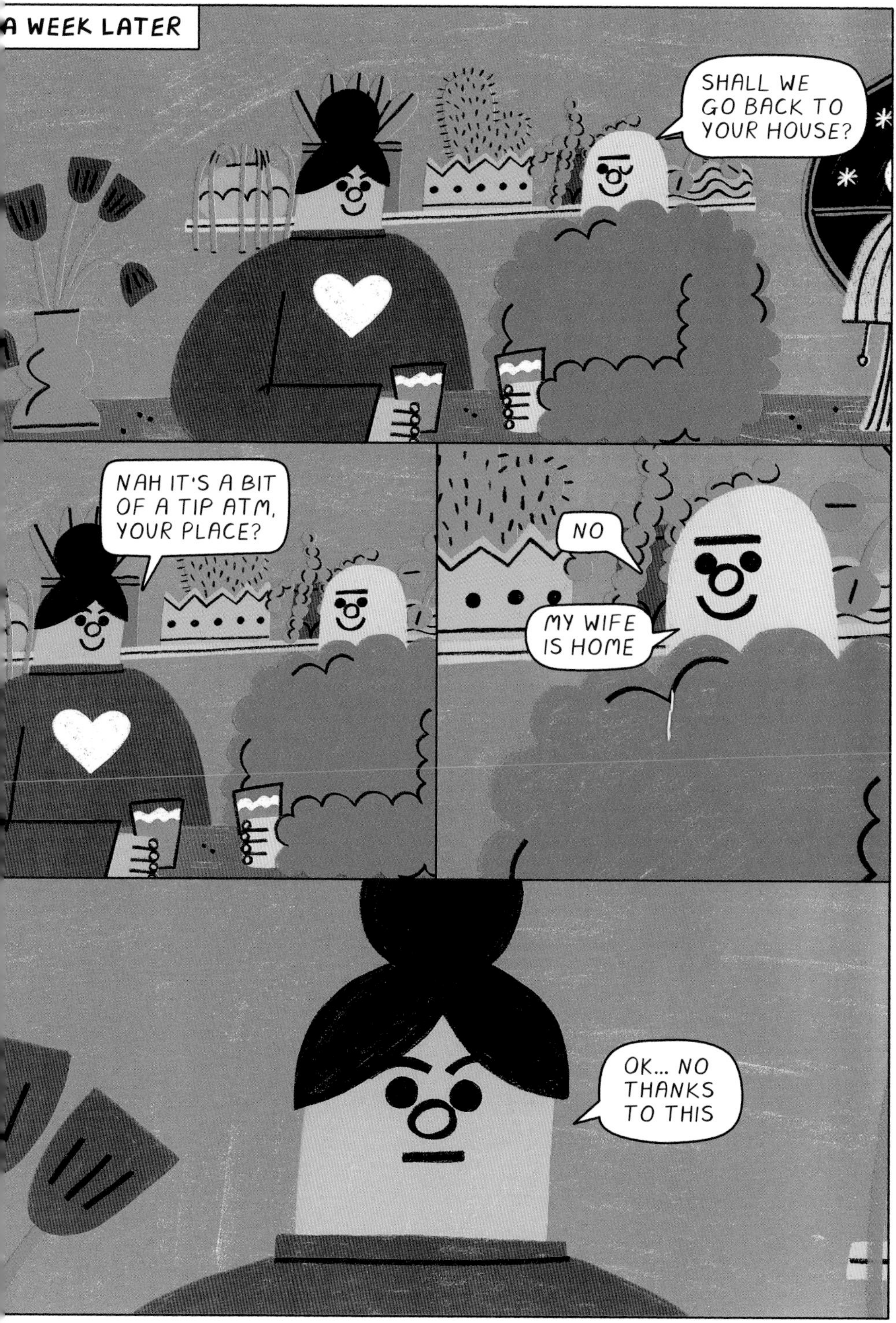
A WEEK LATER
SHALL WE GO BACK TO YOUR HOUSE?
NAH IT'S A BIT OF A TIP ATM, YOUR PLACE?
NO
MY WIFE IS HOME
OK... NO THANKS TO THIS

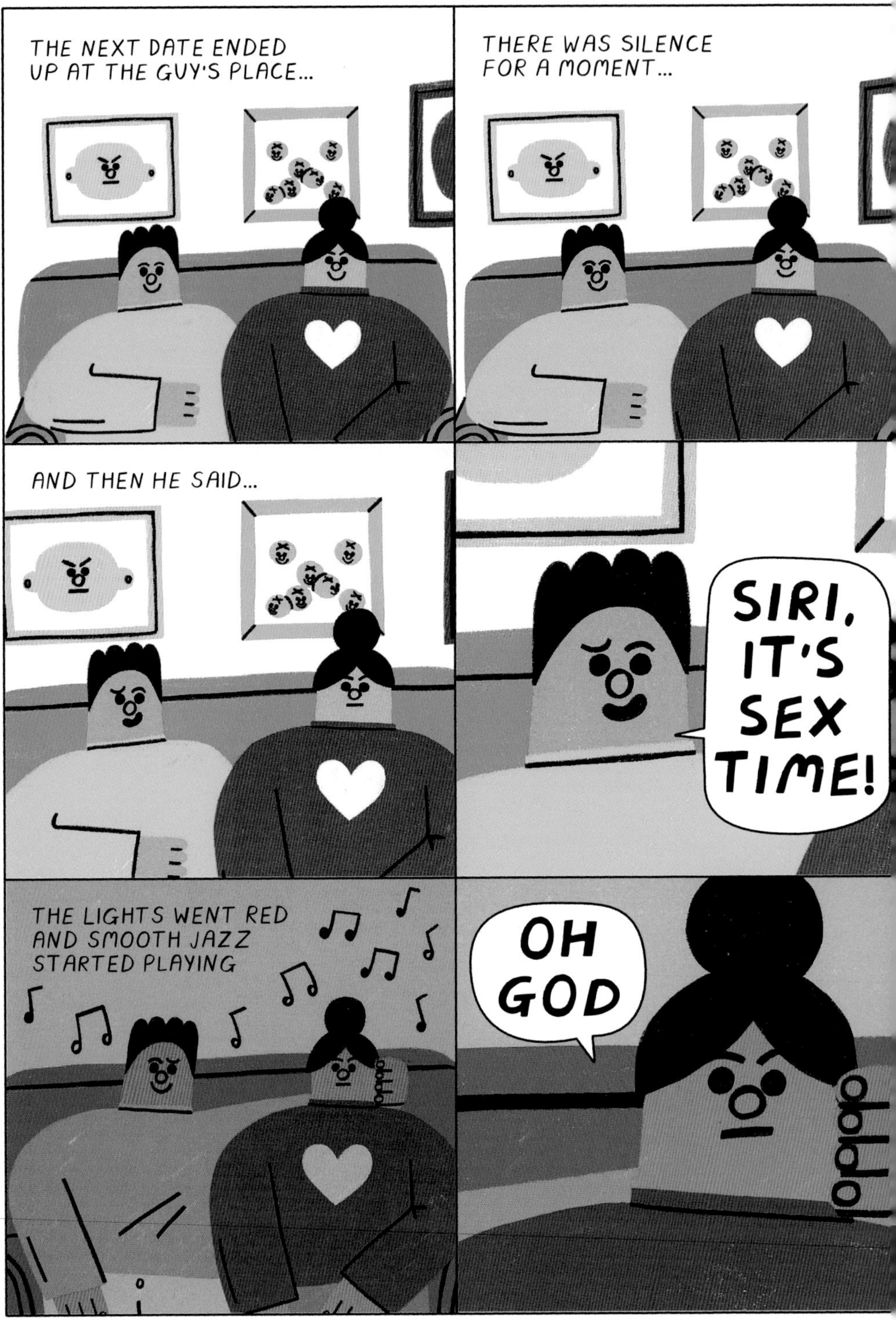
THE NEXT DATE ENDED UP AT THE GUY'S PLACE...
THERE WAS SILENCE FOR A MOMENT...
AND THEN HE SAID...
SIRI, IT'S SEX TIME!
THE LIGHTS WENT RED AND SMOOTH JAZZ STARTED PLAYING
OH GOD

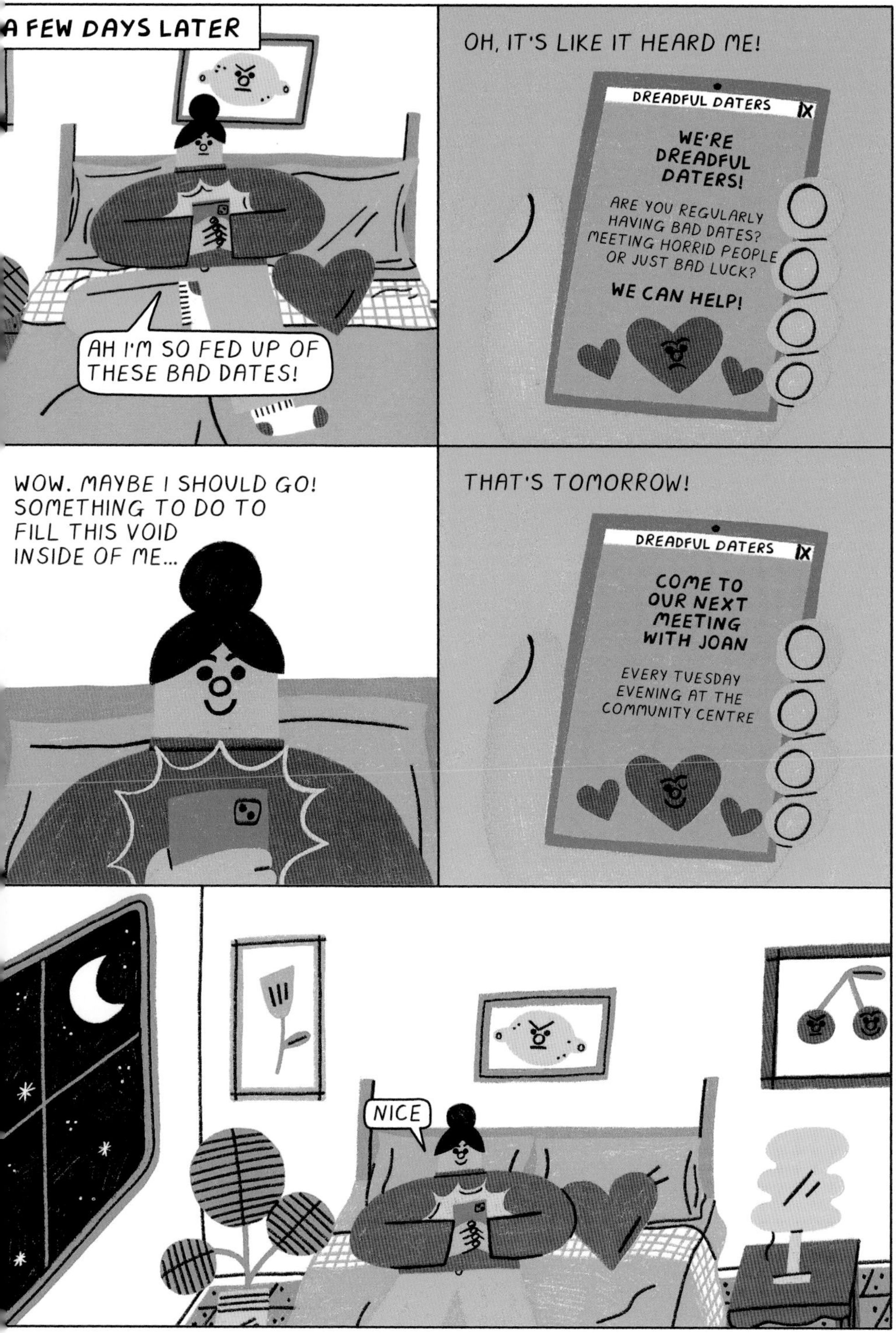
A FEW DAYS LATER
AH I'M SO FED UP OF THESE BAD DATES!
OH, IT'S LIKE IT HEARD ME!
DREADFUL DATERS
WE'RE DREADFUL DATERS!
ARE YOU REGULARLY HAVING BAD DATES? MEETING HORRID PEOPLE OR JUST BAD LUCK?
WE CAN HELP!
WOW. MAYBE I SHOULD GO! SOMETHING TO DO TO FILL THIS VOID INSIDE OF ME...
THAT'S TOMORROW!
DREADFUL DATERS
COME TO OUR NEXT MEETING WITH JOAN
EVERY TUESDAY EVENING AT THE COMMUNITY CENTRE
NICE

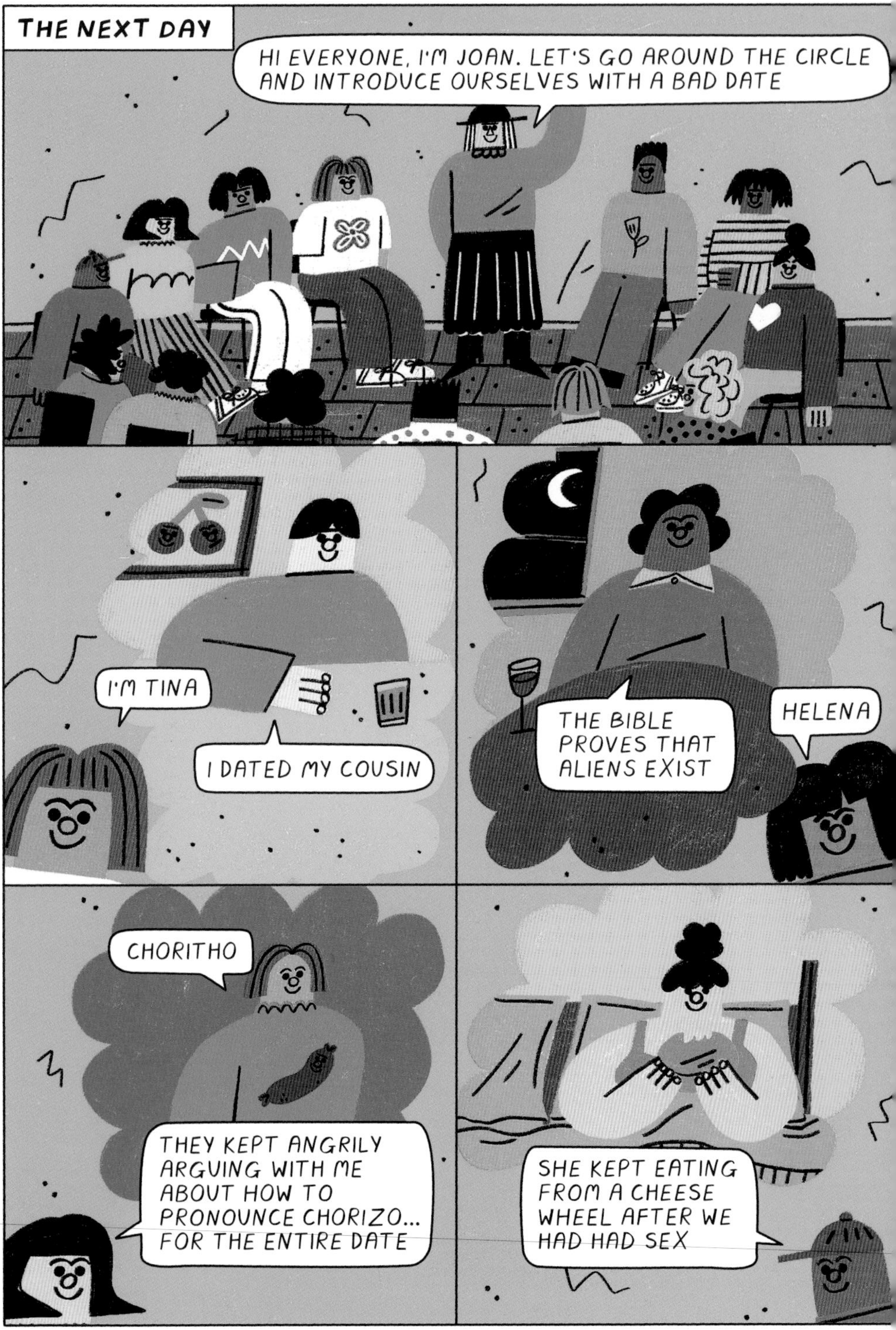
THE NEXT DAY
HI EVERYONE, I'M JOAN. LET'S GO AROUND THE CIRCLE AND INTRODUCE OURSELVES WITH A BAD DATE
I'M TINA
I DATED MY COUSIN
HELENA
THE BIBLE PROVES THAT ALIENS EXIST
CHORITHO
THEY KEPT ANGRILY ARGUING WITH ME ABOUT HOW TO PRONOUNCE CHORIZO... FOR THE ENTIRE DATE
SHE KEPT EATING FROM A CHEESE WHEEL AFTER WE HAD HAD SEX

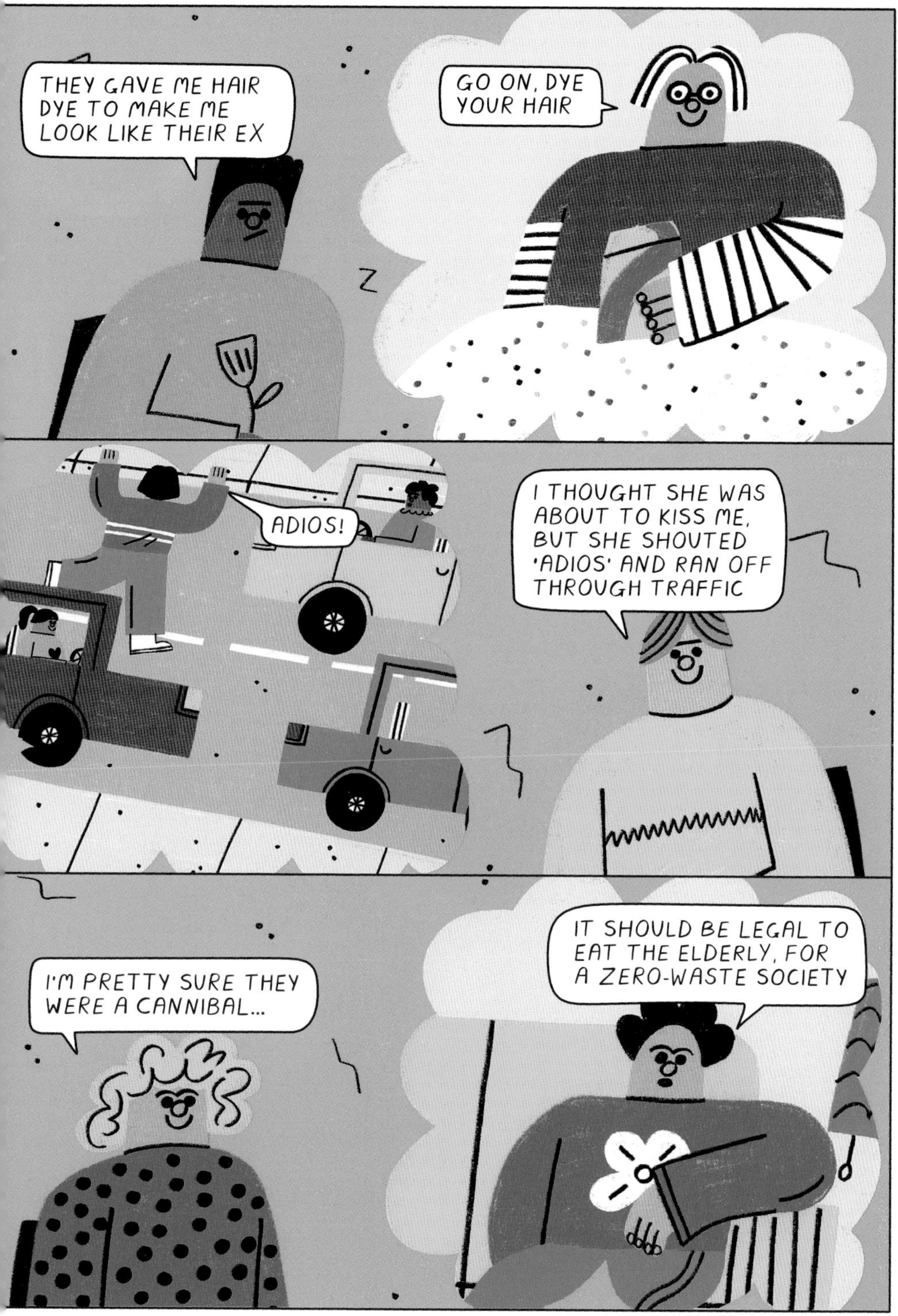
THEY GAVE ME HAIR DYE TO MAKE ME LOOK LIKE THEIR EX
GO ON, DYE YOUR HAIR
Z
ADIOS!
I THOUGHT SHE WAS ABOUT TO KISS ME, BUT SHE SHOUTED 'ADIOS' AND RAN OFF THROUGH TRAFFIC
I'M PRETTY SURE THEY WERE A CANNIBAL...
IT SHOULD BE LEGAL TO EAT THE ELDERLY, FOR A ZERO-WASTE SOCIETY

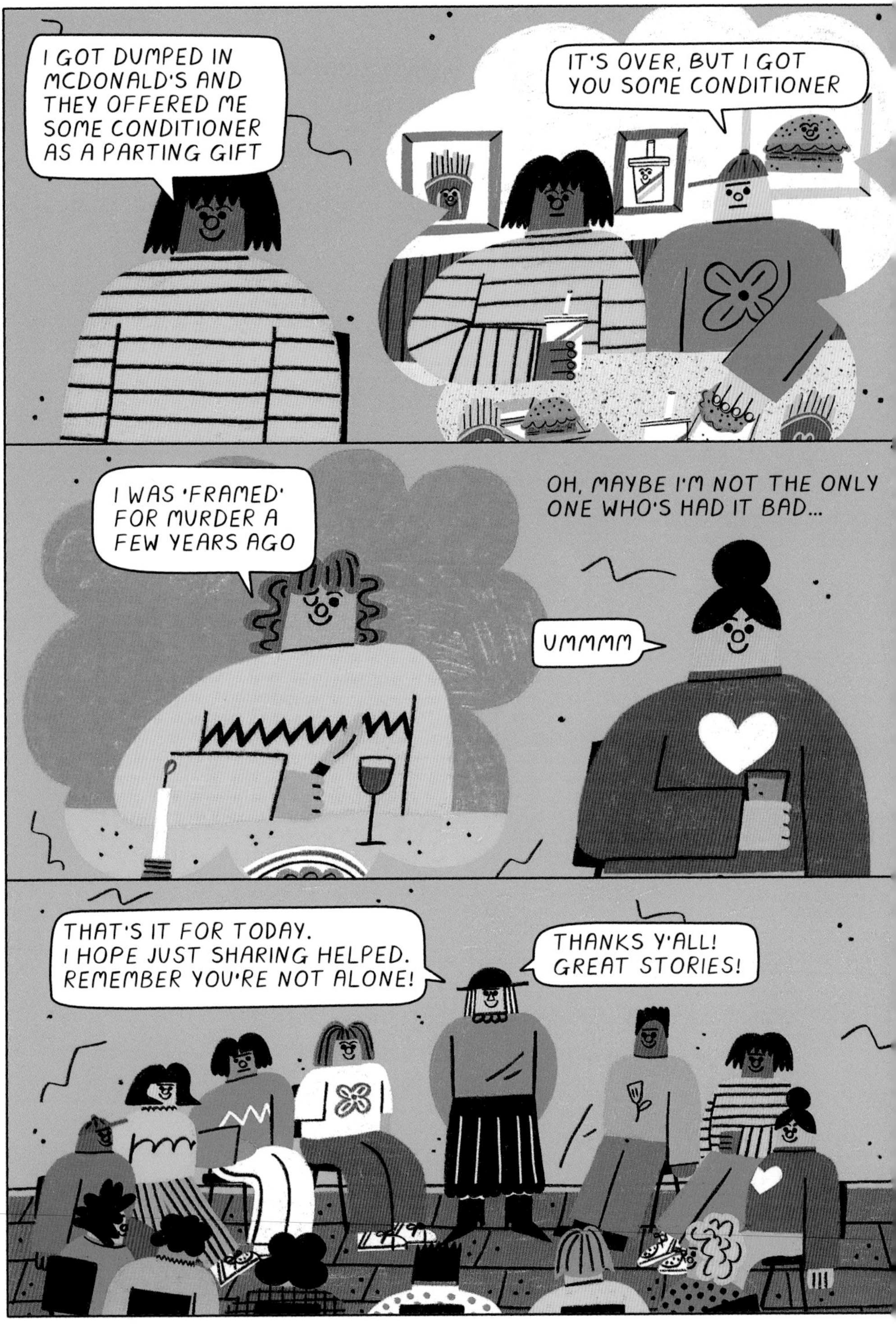
I GOT DUMPED IN MCDONALD'S AND THEY OFFERED ME SOME CONDITIONER AS A PARTING GIFT
IT'S OVER, BUT I GOT YOU SOME CONDITIONER
I WAS 'FRAMED' FOR MURDER A FEW YEARS AGO
OH, MAYBE I'M NOT THE ONLY ONE WHO'S HAD IT BAD...
UMMMM
THAT'S IT FOR TODAY. I HOPE JUST SHARING HELPED. REMEMBER YOU'RE NOT ALONE!
THANKS Y'ALL! GREAT STORIES!

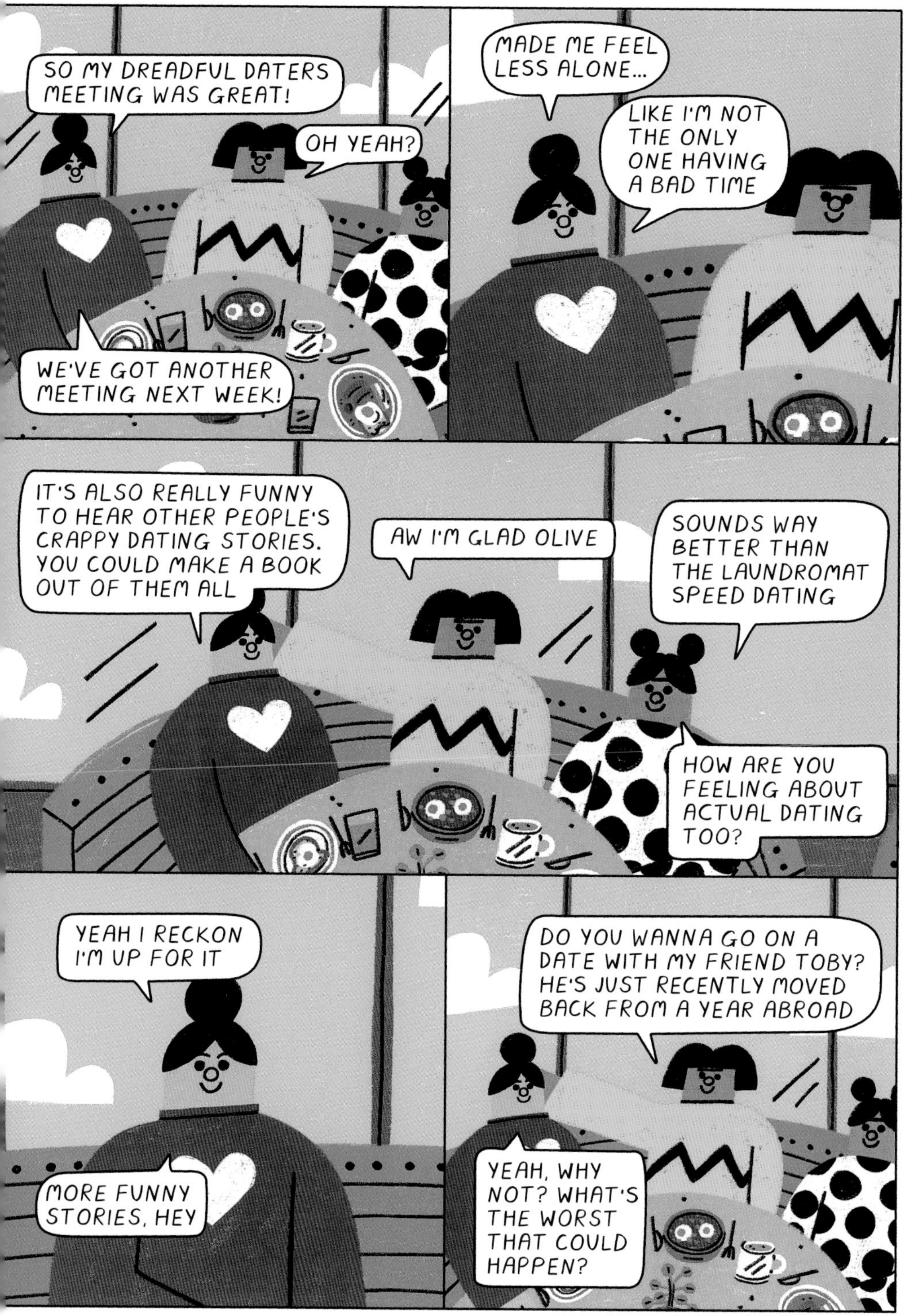
SO MY DREADFUL DATERS MEETING WAS GREAT!
OH YEAH?
WE'VE GOT ANOTHER MEETING NEXT WEEK!
MADE ME FEEL LESS ALONE...
LIKE I'M NOT THE ONLY ONE HAVING A BAD TIME
IT'S ALSO REALLY FUNNY TO HEAR OTHER PEOPLE'S CRAPPY DATING STORIES. YOU COULD MAKE A BOOK OUT OF THEM ALL
AW I'M GLAD OLIVE
SOUNDS WAY BETTER THAN THE LAUNDROMAT SPEED DATING
HOW ARE YOU FEELING ABOUT ACTUAL DATING TOO?
YEAH I RECKON I'M UP FOR IT
MORE FUNNY STORIES, HEY
DO YOU WANNA GO ON A DATE WITH MY FRIEND TOBY? HE'S JUST RECENTLY MOVED BACK FROM A YEAR ABROAD
YEAH, WHY NOT? WHAT'S THE WORST THAT COULD HAPPEN?

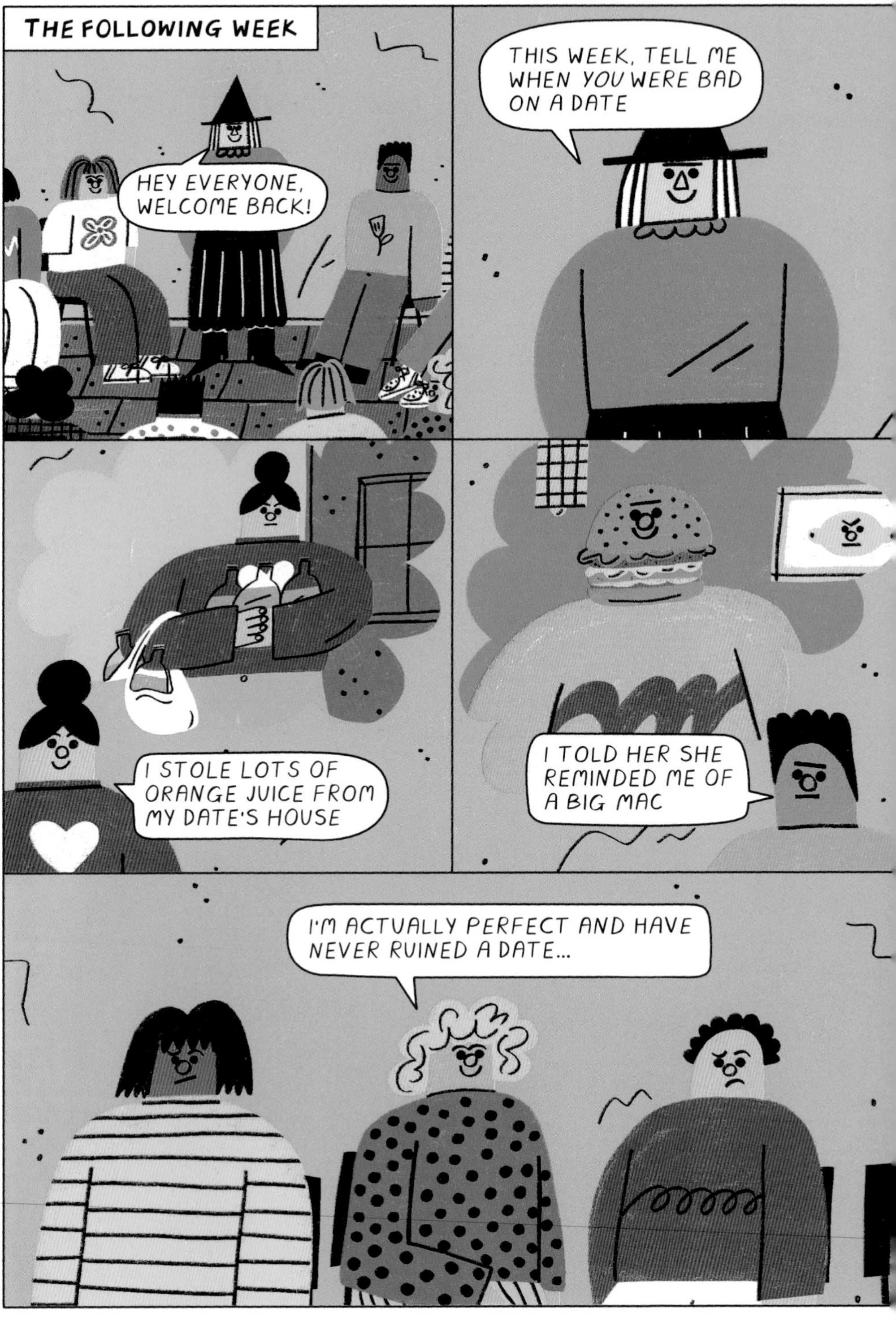
THE FOLLOWING WEEK
HEY EVERYONE, WELCOME BACK!
THIS WEEK, TELL ME WHEN YOU WERE BAD ON A DATE
I STOLE LOTS OF ORANGE JUICE FROM MY DATE'S HOUSE
I TOLD HER SHE REMINDED ME OF A BIG MAC
I'M ACTUALLY PERFECT AND HAVE NEVER RUINED A DATE...

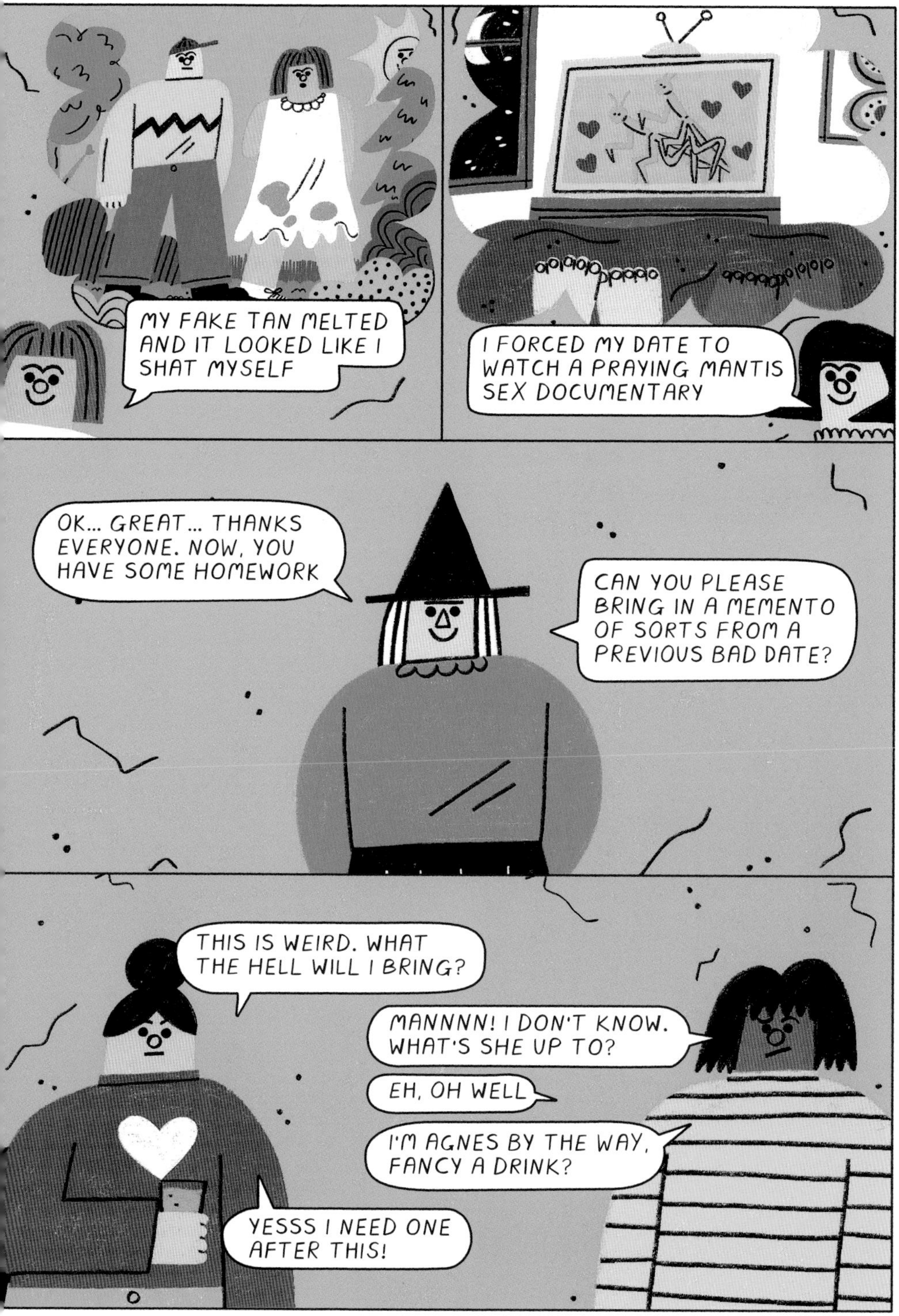
MY FAKE TAN MELTED AND IT LOOKED LIKE I SHAT MYSELF
I FORCED MY DATE TO WATCH A PRAYING MANTIS SEX DOCUMENTARY
OK... GREAT... THANKS EVERYONE. NOW, YOU HAVE SOME HOMEWORK
CAN YOU PLEASE BRING IN A MEMENTO OF SORTS FROM A PREVIOUS BAD DATE?
THIS IS WEIRD. WHAT THE HELL WILL I BRING?
MANNNN! I DON'T KNOW. WHAT'S SHE UP TO?
EH, OH WELL
I'M AGNES BY THE WAY, FANCY A DRINK?
YESSS I NEED ONE AFTER THIS!

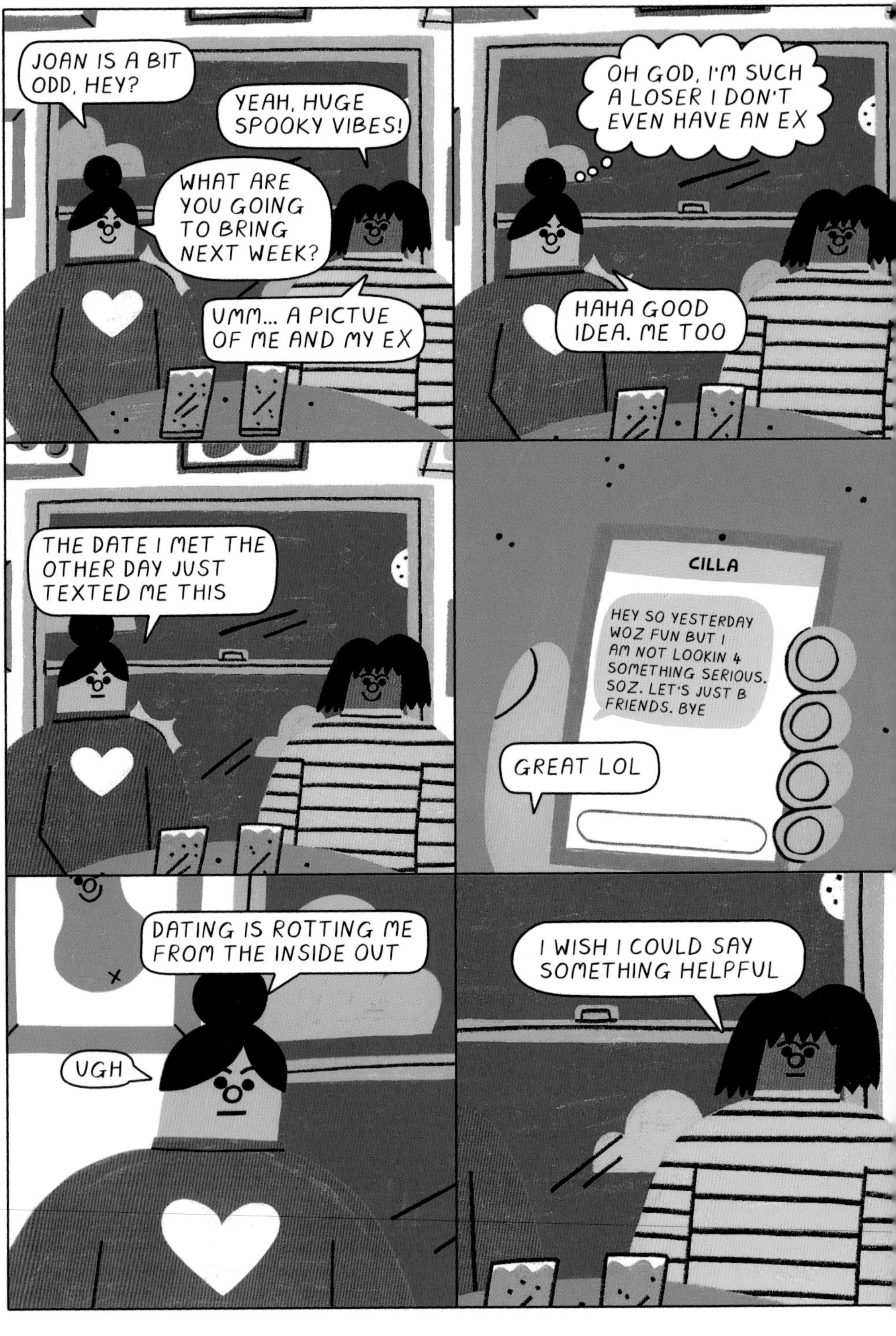
JOAN IS A BIT ODD, HEY?
YEAH, HUGE SPOOKY VIBES!
WHAT ARE YOU GOING TO BRING NEXT WEEK?
UMM... A PICTUE OF ME AND MY EX
OH GOD, I'M SUCH A LOSER I DON'T EVEN HAVE AN EX
HAHA GOOD IDEA. ME TOO
THE DATE I MET THE OTHER DAY JUST TEXTED ME THIS
CILLA
HEY SO YESTERDAY WOZ FUN BUT I AM NOT LOOKIN 4 SOMETHING SERIOUS. SOZ. LET'S JUST B FRIENDS. BYE
GREAT LOL
DATING IS ROTTING ME FROM THE INSIDE OUT
UGH
I WISH I COULD SAY SOMETHING HELPFUL

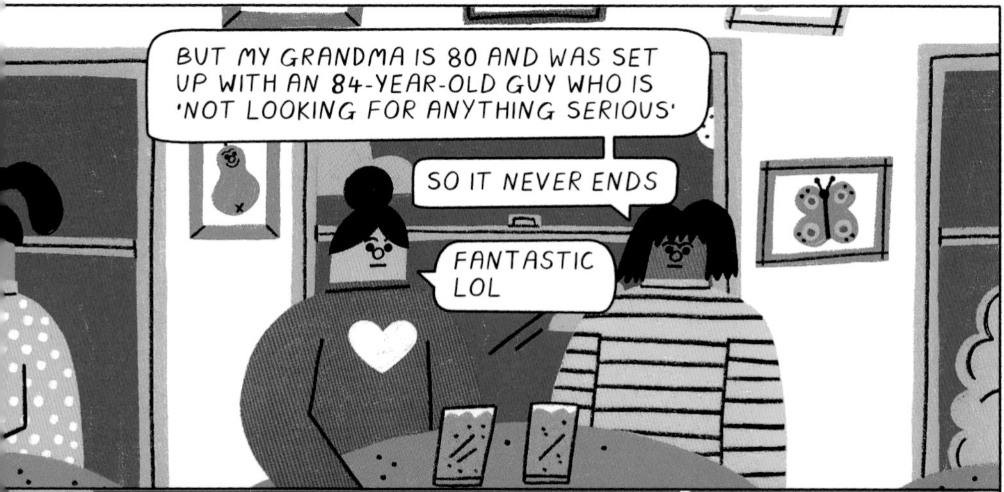
BUT MY GRANDMA IS 80 AND WAS SET UP WITH AN 84-YEAR-OLD GUY WHO IS 'NOT LOOKING FOR ANYTHING SERIOUS'
SO IT NEVER ENDS
FANTASTIC LOL

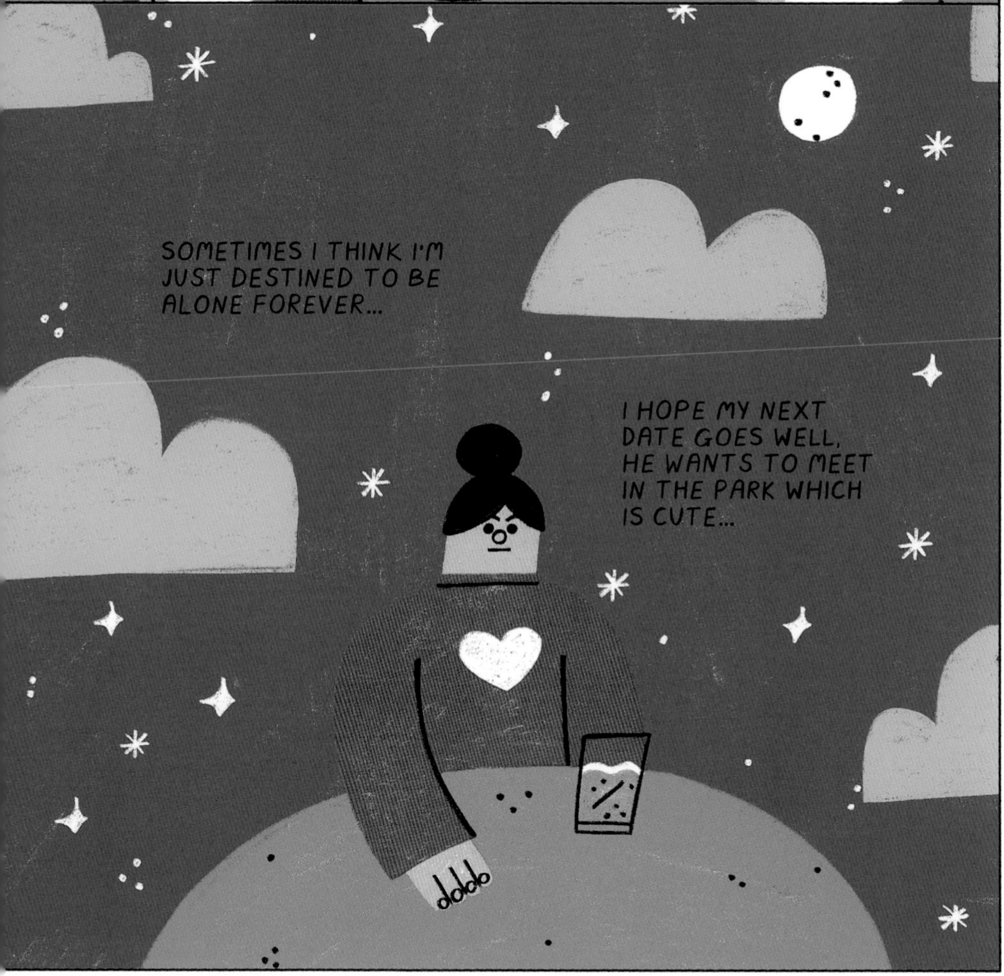
SOMETIMES I THINK I'M JUST DESTINED TO BE ALONE FOREVER...
I HOPE MY NEXT DATE GOES WELL, HE WANTS TO MEET IN THE PARK WHICH IS CUTE...

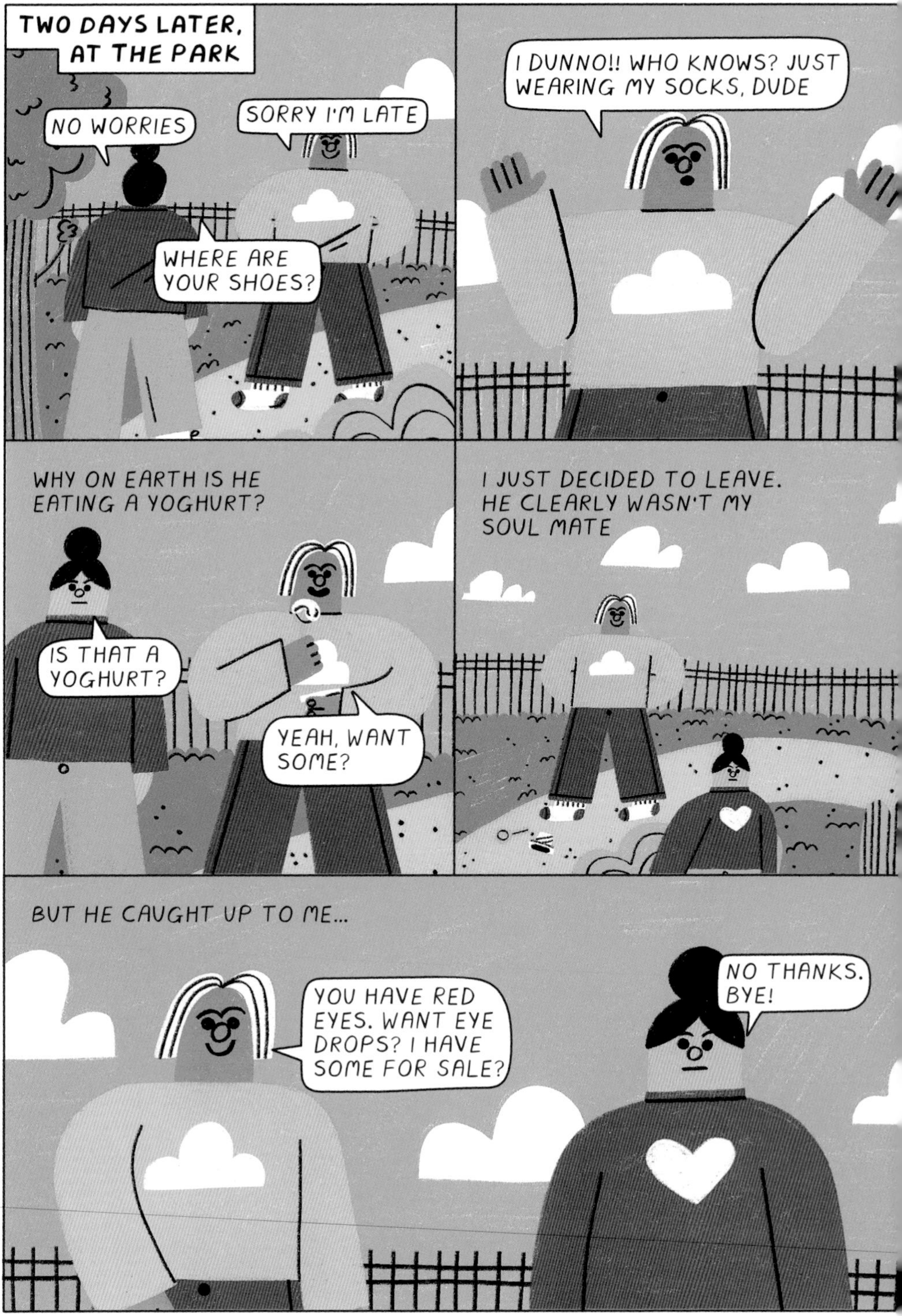
TWO DAYS LATER, AT THE PARK
SORRY I'M LATE
NO WORRIES
WHERE ARE YOUR SHOES?
I DUNNO!! WHO KNOWS? JUST WEARING MY SOCKS, DUDE
WHY ON EARTH IS HE EATING A YOGHURT?
IS THAT A YOGHURT?
YEAH, WANT SOME?
I JUST DECIDED TO LEAVE. HE CLEARLY WASN'T MY SOUL MATE
BUT HE CAUGHT UP TO ME...
YOU HAVE RED EYES. WANT EYE DROPS? I HAVE SOME FOR SALE?
NO THANKS. BYE!

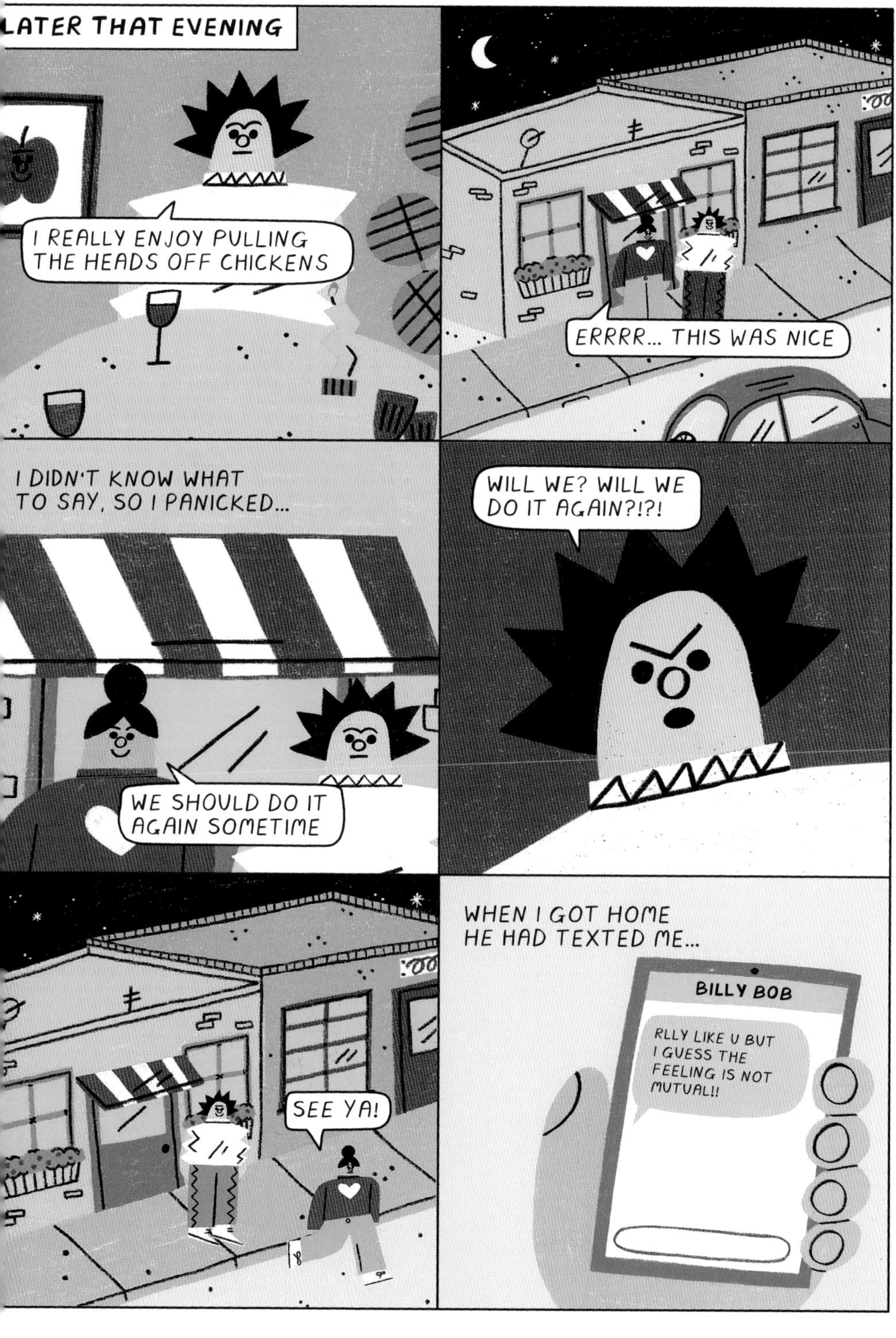
LATER THAT EVENING
I REALLY ENJOY PULLING THE HEADS OFF CHICKENS
ERRRR... THIS WAS NICE
I DIDN'T KNOW WHAT TO SAY, SO I PANICKED...
WE SHOULD DO IT AGAIN SOMETIME
WILL WE? WILL WE DO IT AGAIN?!?!
SEE YA!
WHEN I GOT HOME HE HAD TEXTED ME...
BILLY BOB
RLLY LIKE U BUT I GUESS THE FEELING IS NOT MUTUAL!!

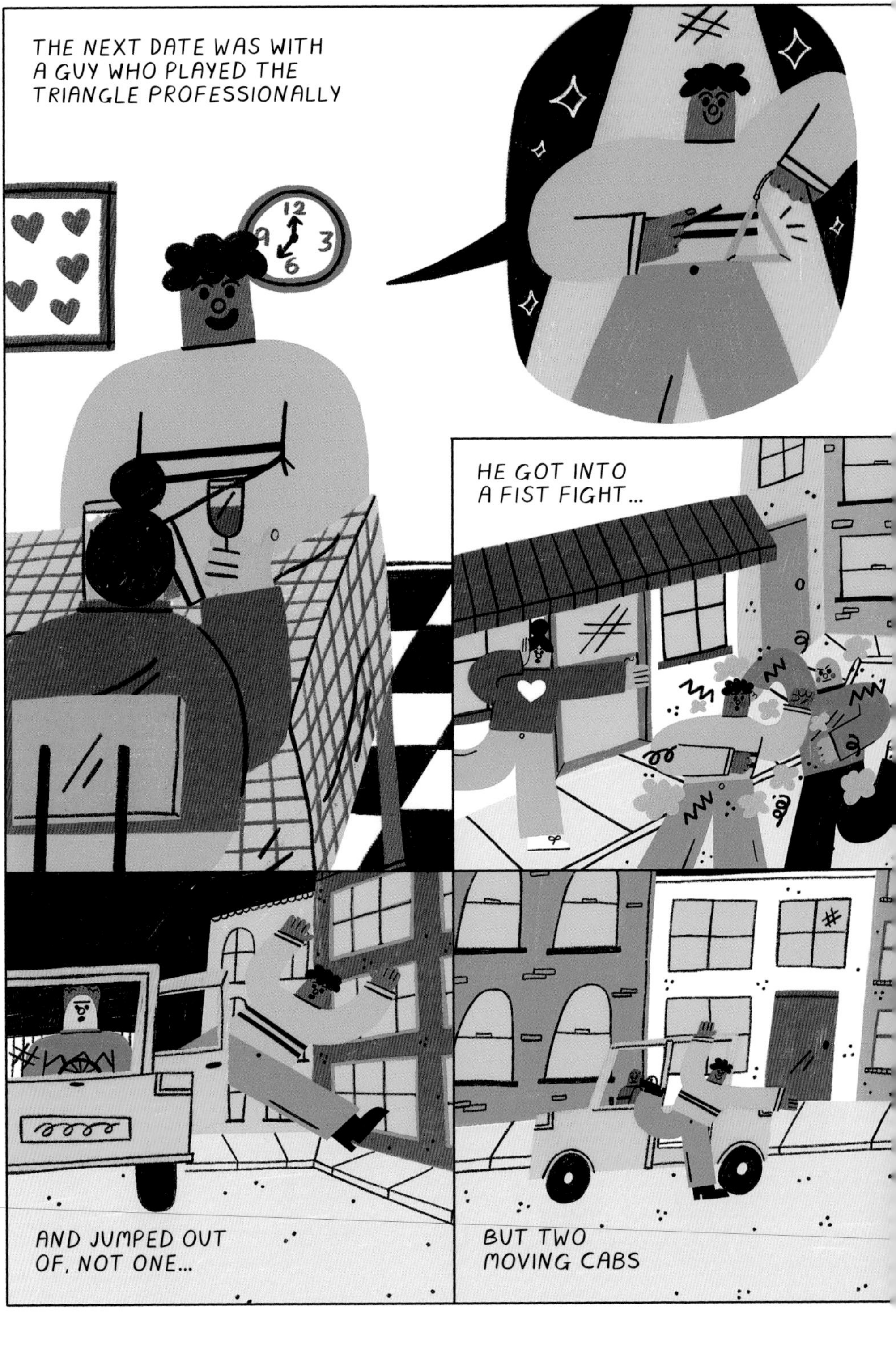
THE NEXT DATE WAS WITH A GUY WHO PLAYED THE TRIANGLE PROFESSIONALLY
HE GOT INTO A FIST FIGHT...
AND JUMPED OUT OF, NOT ONE...
BUT TWO MOVING CABS

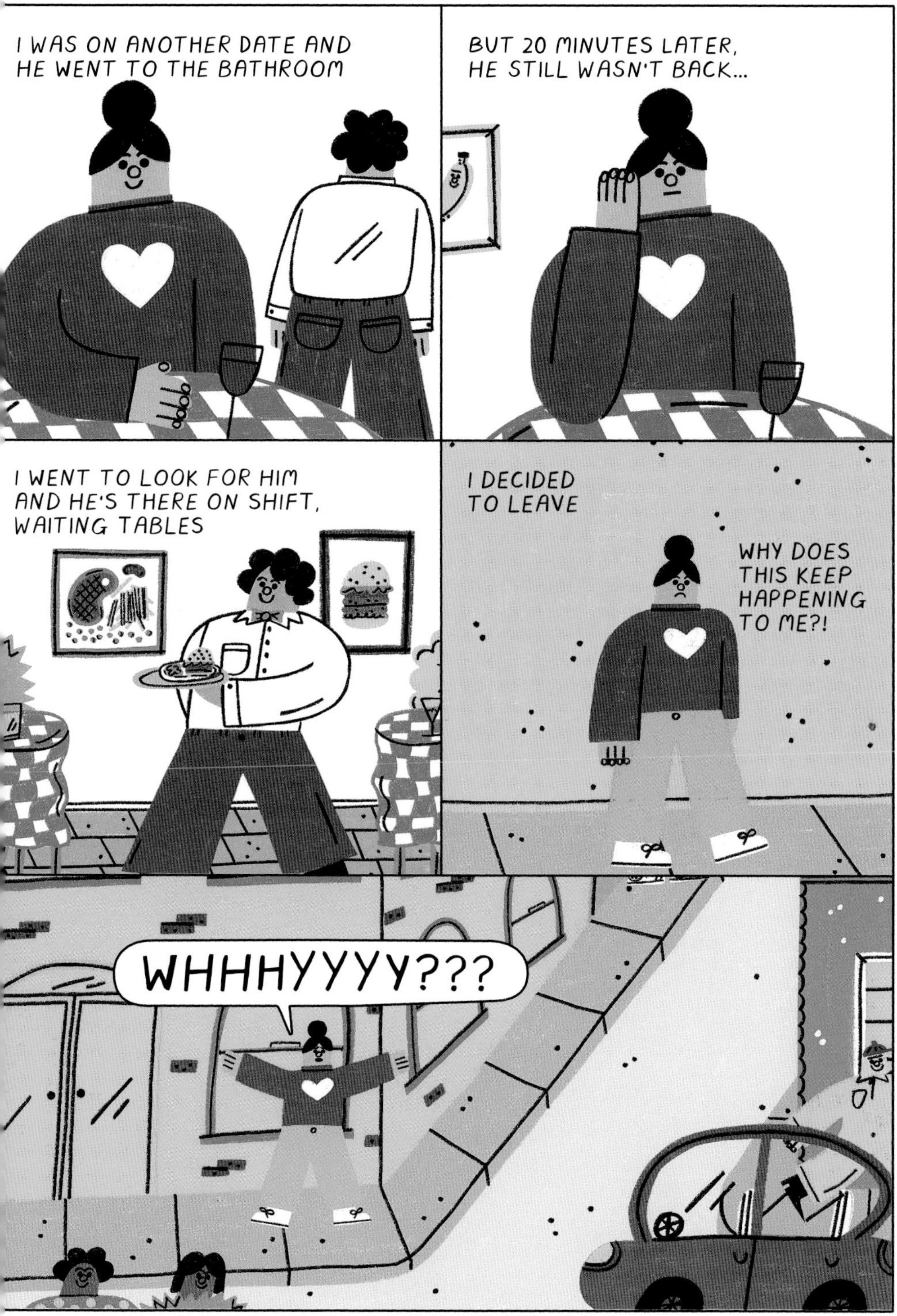
I WAS ON ANOTHER DATE AND HE WENT TO THE BATHROOM
BUT 20 MINUTES LATER, HE STILL WASN'T BACK...
I WENT TO LOOK FOR HIM AND HE'S THERE ON SHIFT, WAITING TABLES
I DECIDED TO LEAVE
WHY DOES THIS KEEP HAPPENING TO ME?!
WHHHYYYY???

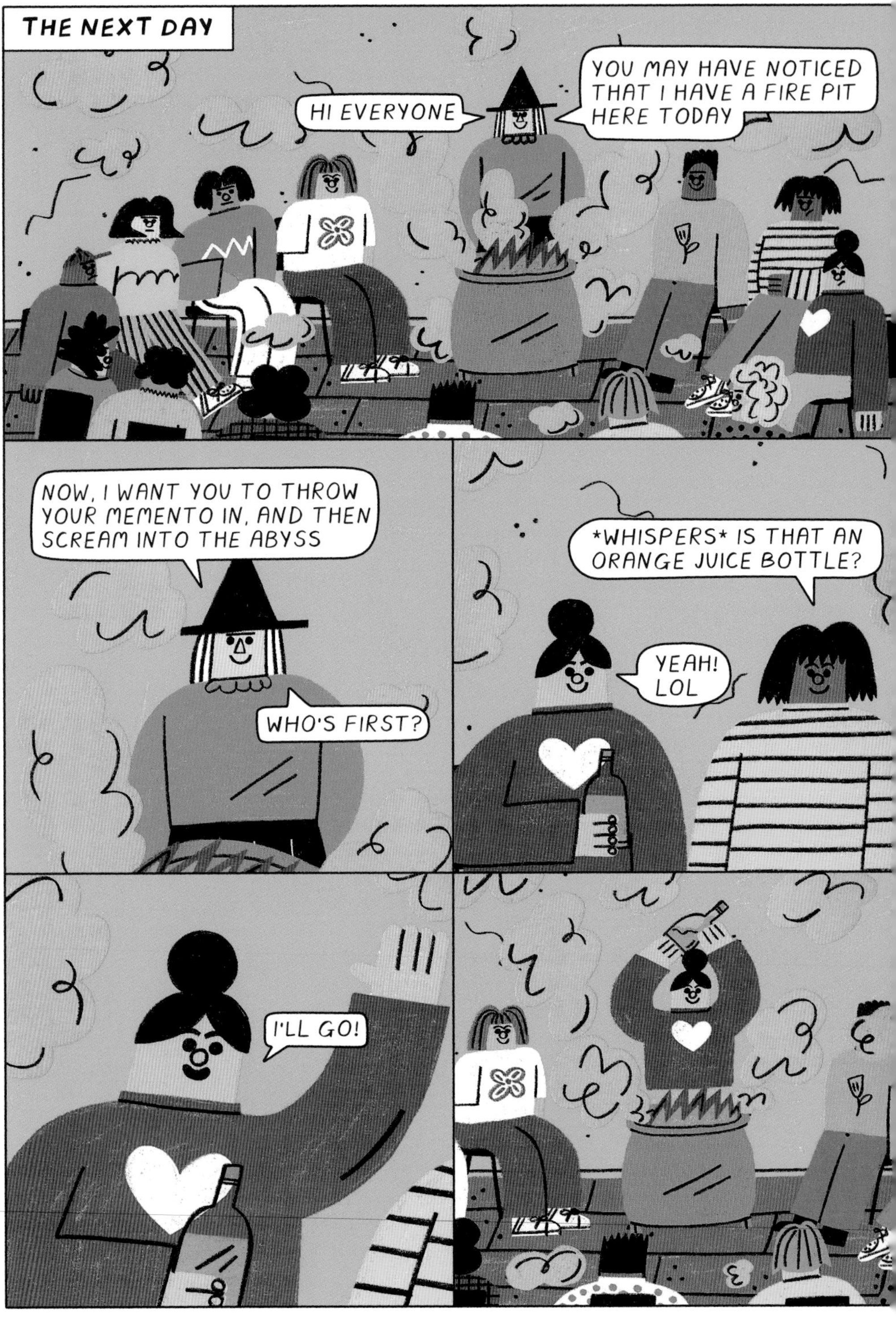
THE NEXT DAY
HI EVERYONE
YOU MAY HAVE NOTICED THAT I HAVE A FIRE PIT HERE TODAY
NOW, I WANT YOU TO THROW YOUR MEMENTO IN, AND THEN SCREAM INTO THE ABYSS
WHO'S FIRST?
WHISPERS IS THAT AN ORANGE JUICE BOTTLE?
YEAH! LOL
I'LL GO!

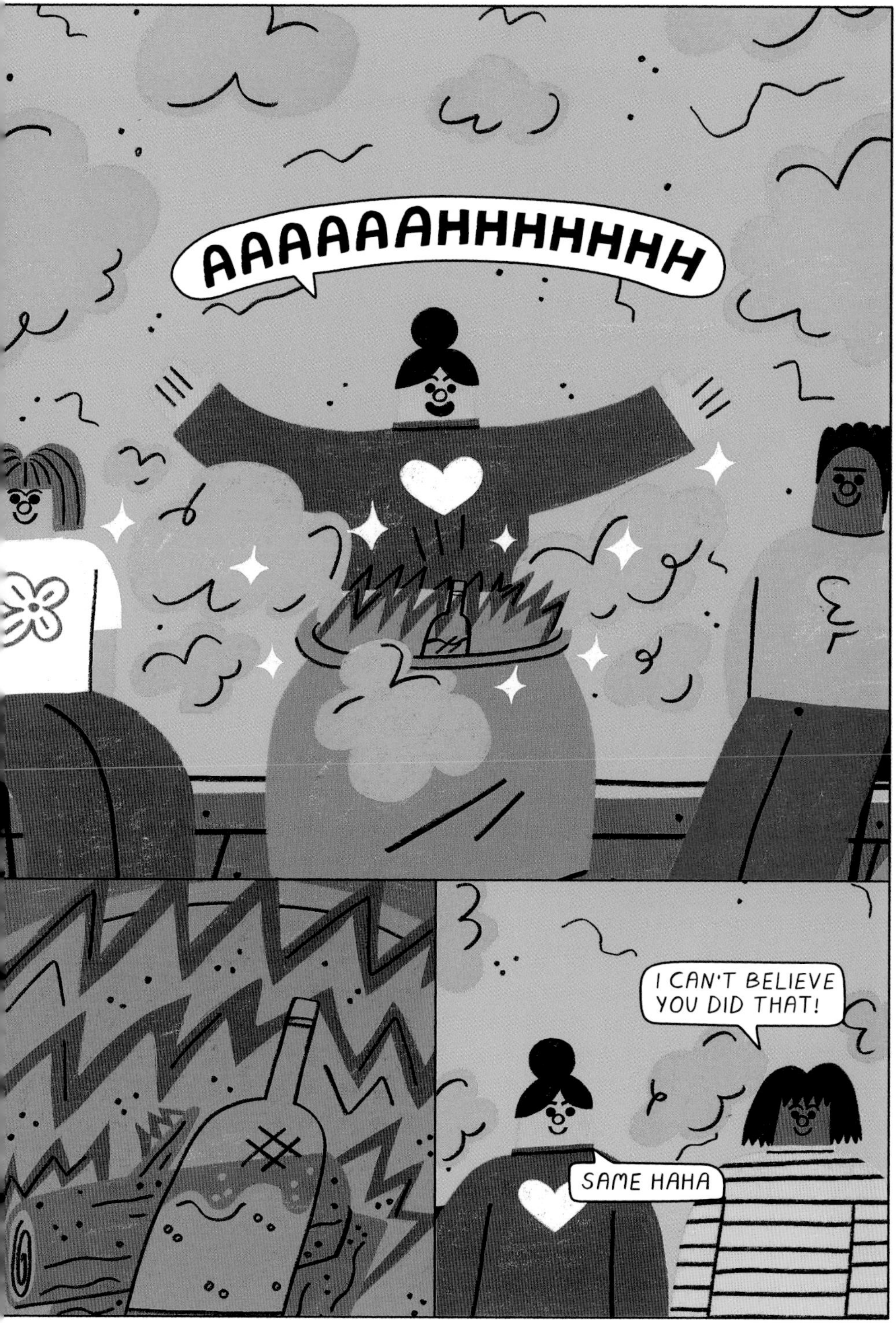
AAAAAAHHHHHHH
I CAN'T BELIEVE YOU DID THAT!
SAME HAHA

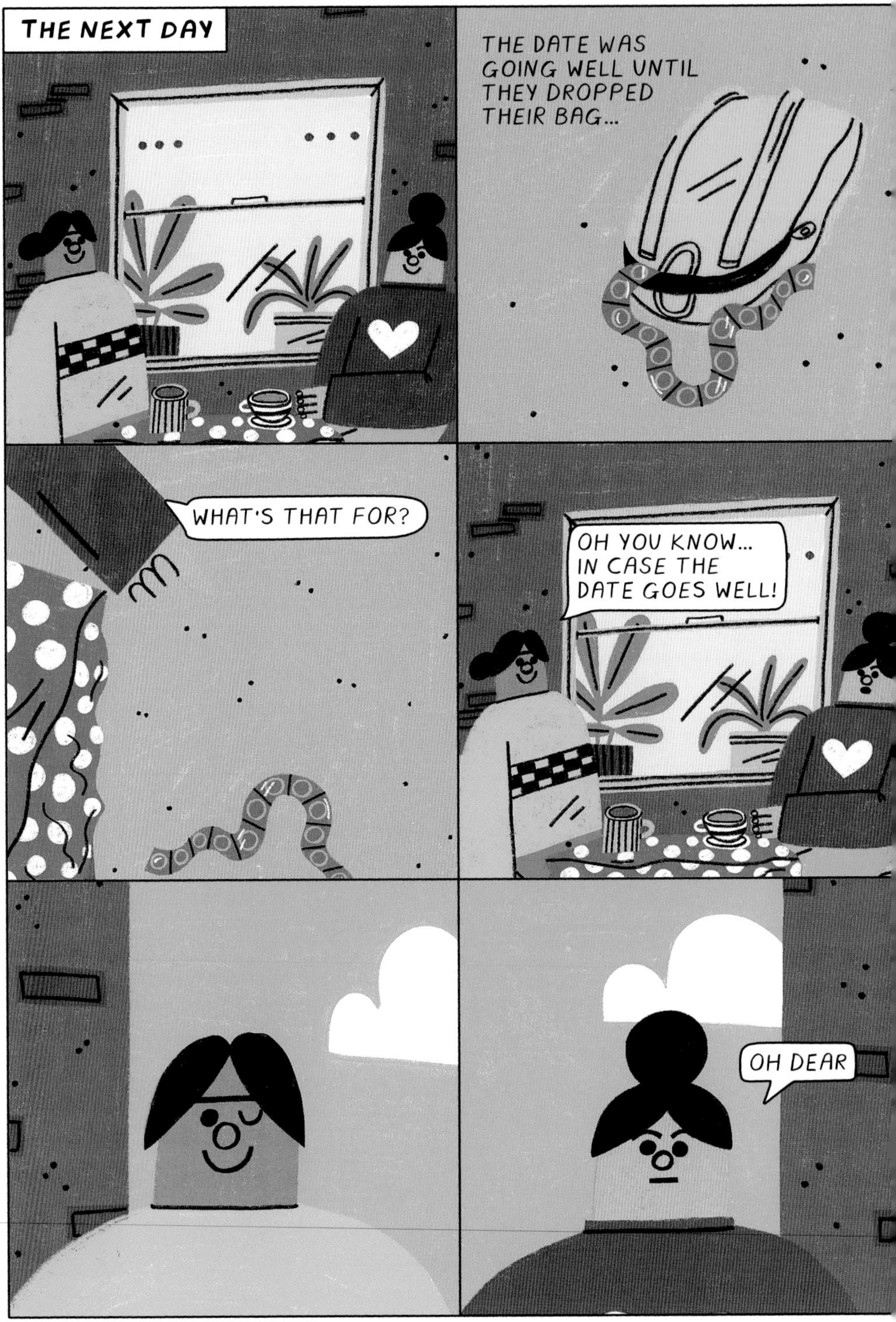
THE NEXT DAY
THE DATE WAS GOING WELL UNTIL THEY DROPPED THEIR BAG...
WHAT'S THAT FOR?
OH YOU KNOW... IN CASE THE DATE GOES WELL!
OH DEAR

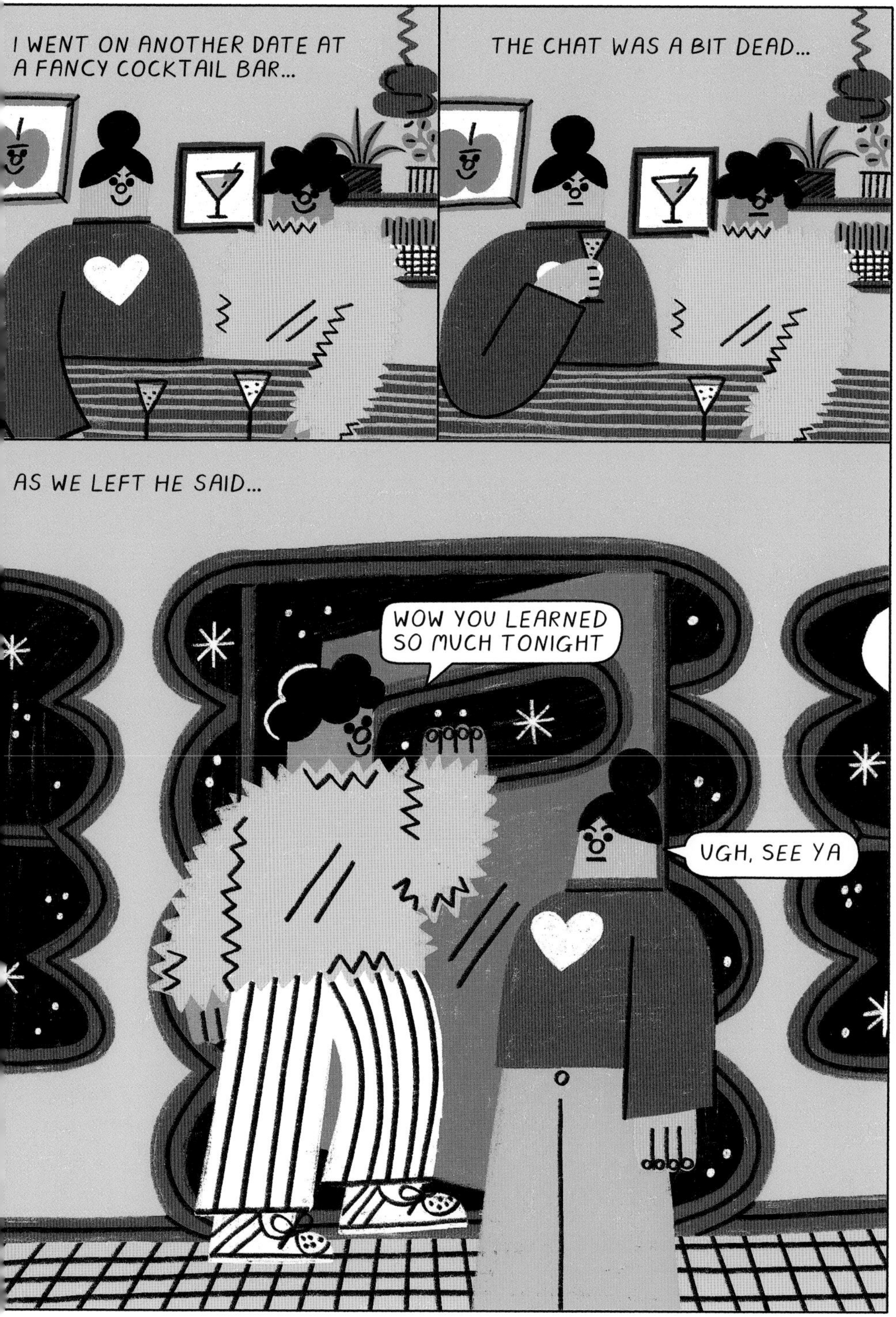
I WENT ON ANOTHER DATE AT A FANCY COCKTAIL BAR...
THE CHAT WAS A BIT DEAD...
AS WE LEFT HE SAID...
WOW YOU LEARNED SO MUCH TONIGHT
UGH, SEE YA

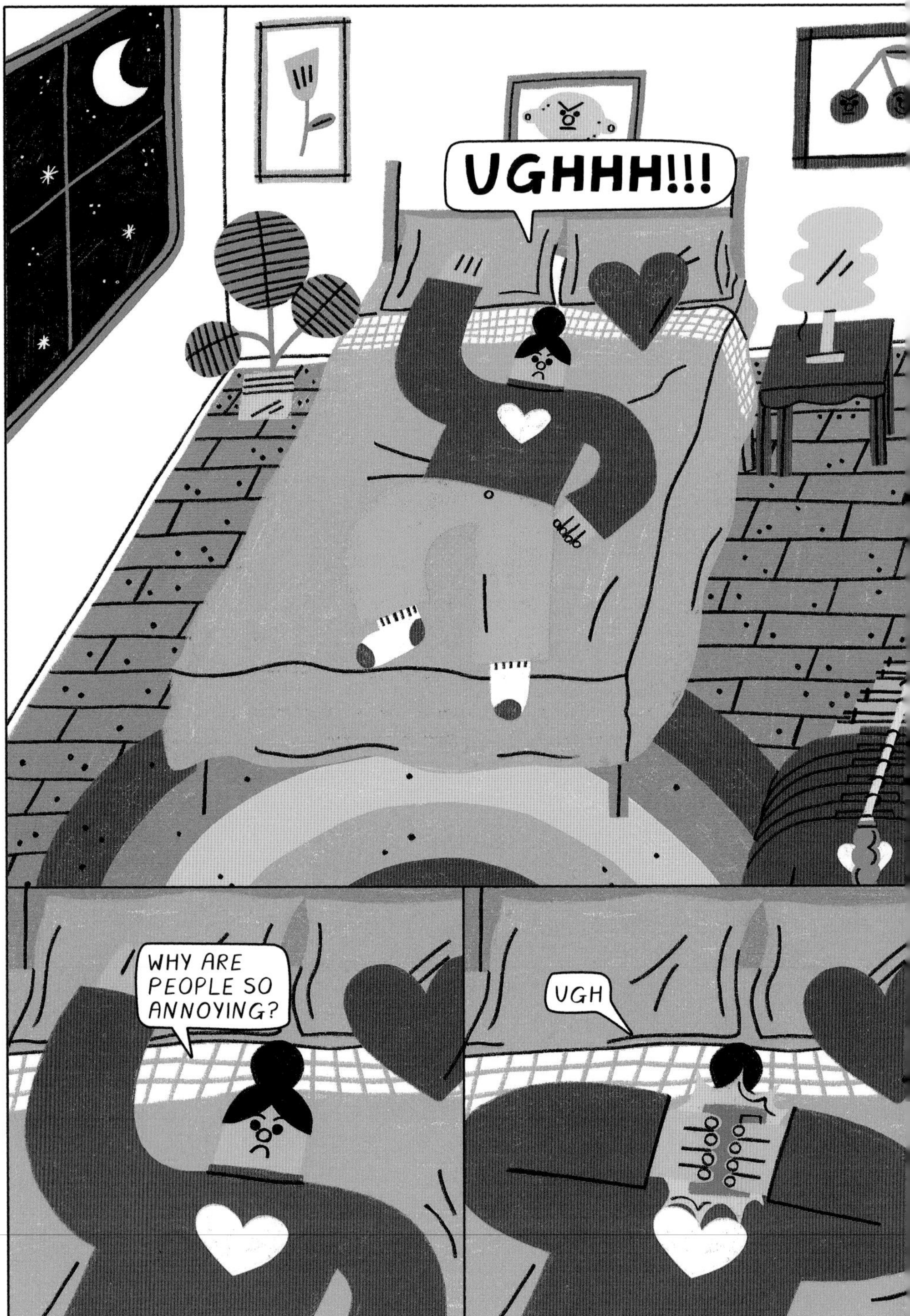
UGHHH!!!
WHY ARE PEOPLE SO ANNOYING?
UGH

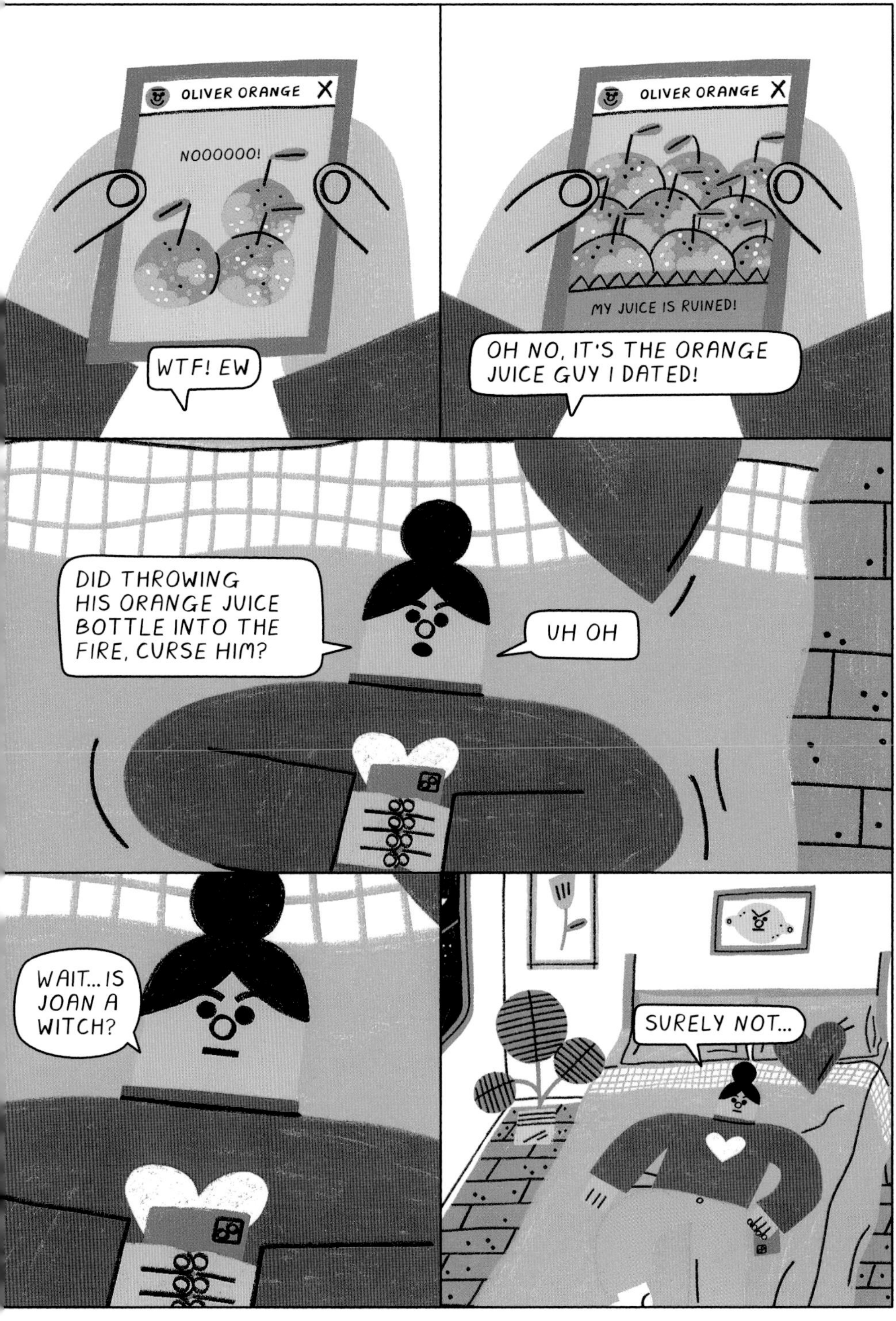
OLIVER ORANGE
NOOOOOO!
WTF! EW
OLIVER ORANGE
MY JUICE IS RUINED!
OH NO, IT'S THE ORANGE JUICE GUY I DATED!
DID THROWING HIS ORANGE JUICE BOTTLE INTO THE FIRE, CURSE HIM?
UH OH
WAIT... IS JOAN A WITCH?
SURELY NOT...

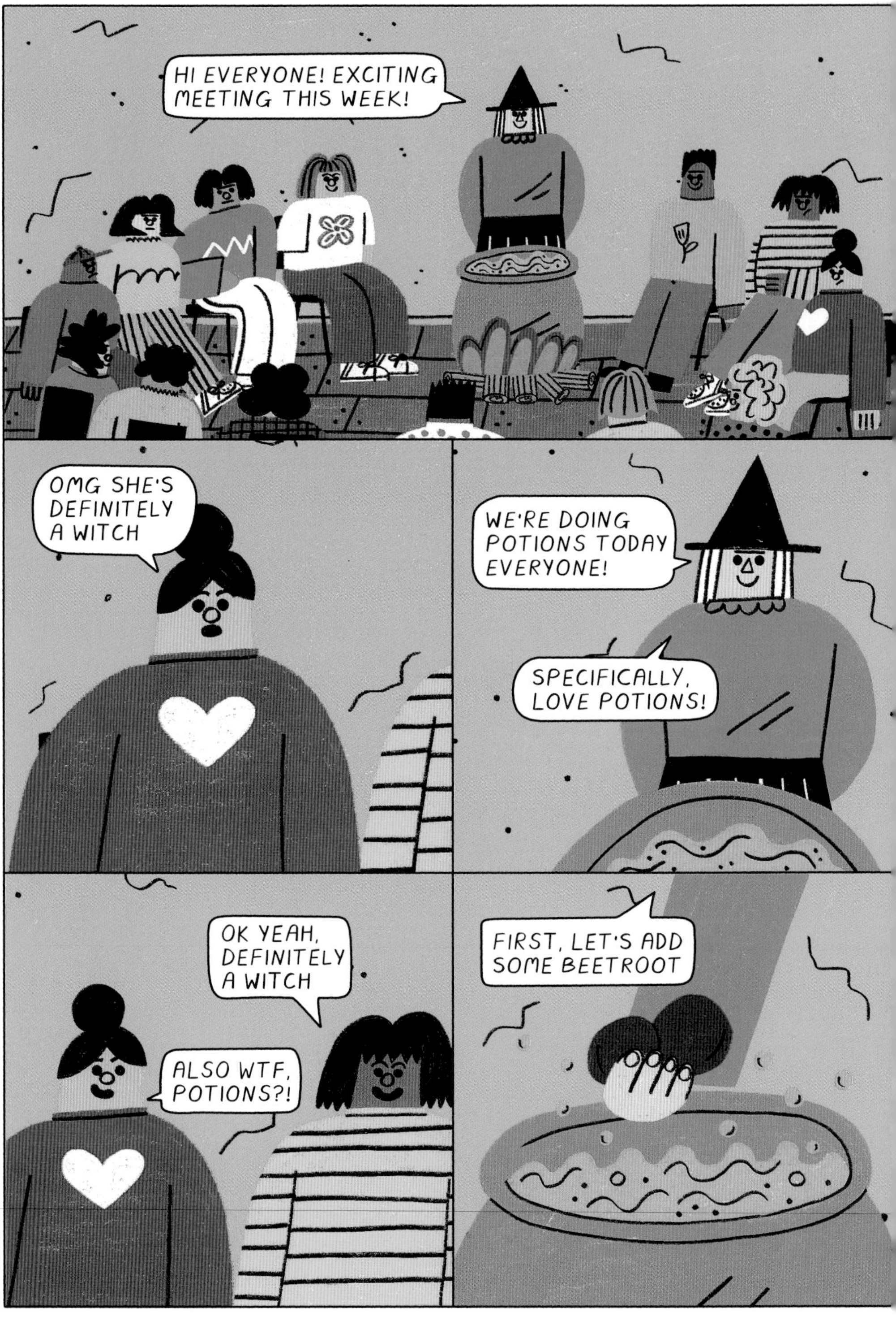
HI EVERYONE! EXCITING MEETING THIS WEEK!
OMG SHE'S DEFINITELY A WITCH
WE'RE DOING POTIONS TODAY EVERYONE!
SPECIFICALLY, LOVE POTIONS!
OK YEAH, DEFINITELY A WITCH
ALSO WTF, POTIONS?!
FIRST, LET'S ADD SOME BEETROOT

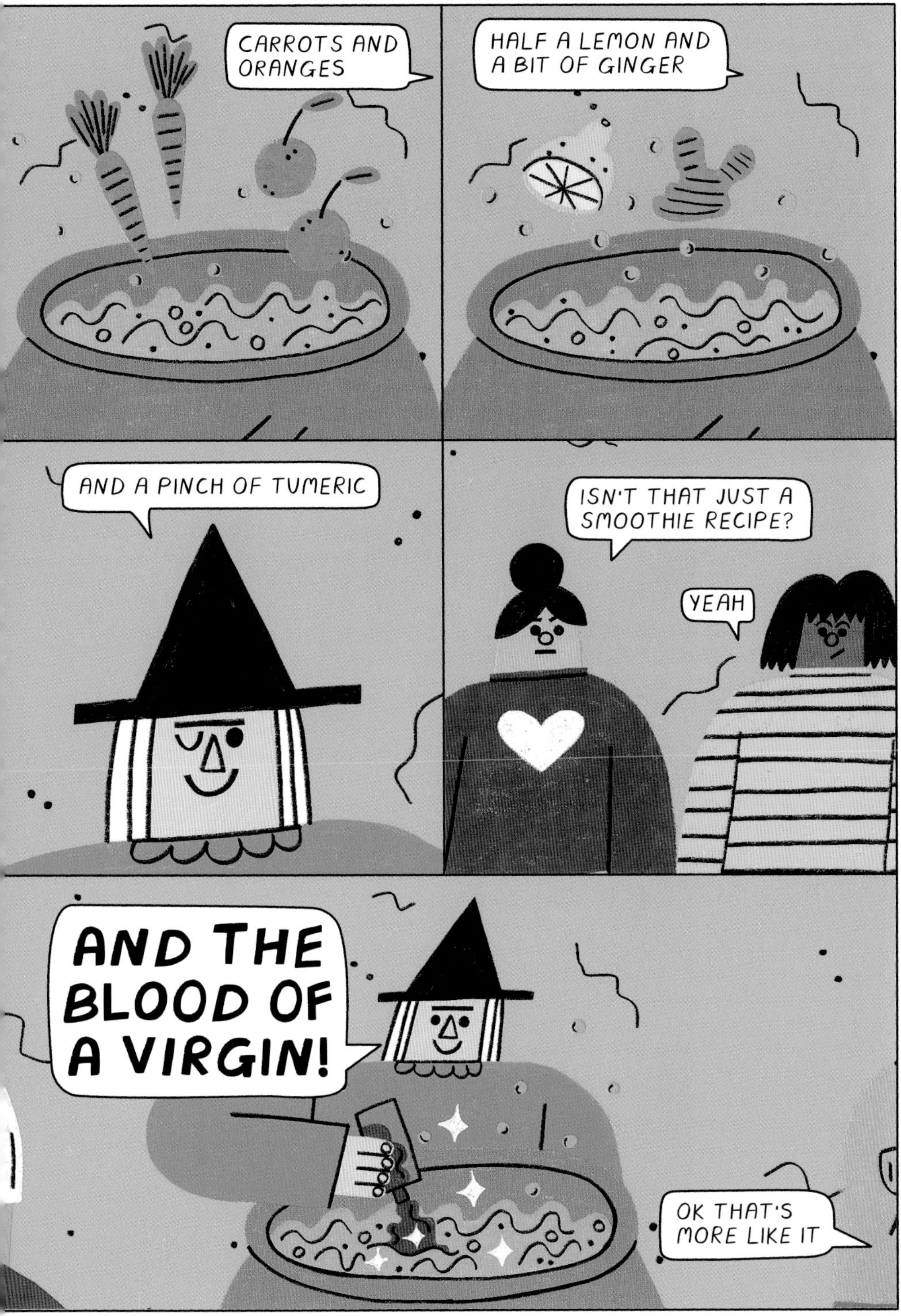
CARROTS AND ORANGES
HALF A LEMON AND A BIT OF GINGER
AND A PINCH OF TUMERIC
ISN'T THAT JUST A SMOOTHIE RECIPE?
YEAH
AND THE BLOOD OF A VIRGIN!
OK THAT'S MORE LIKE IT

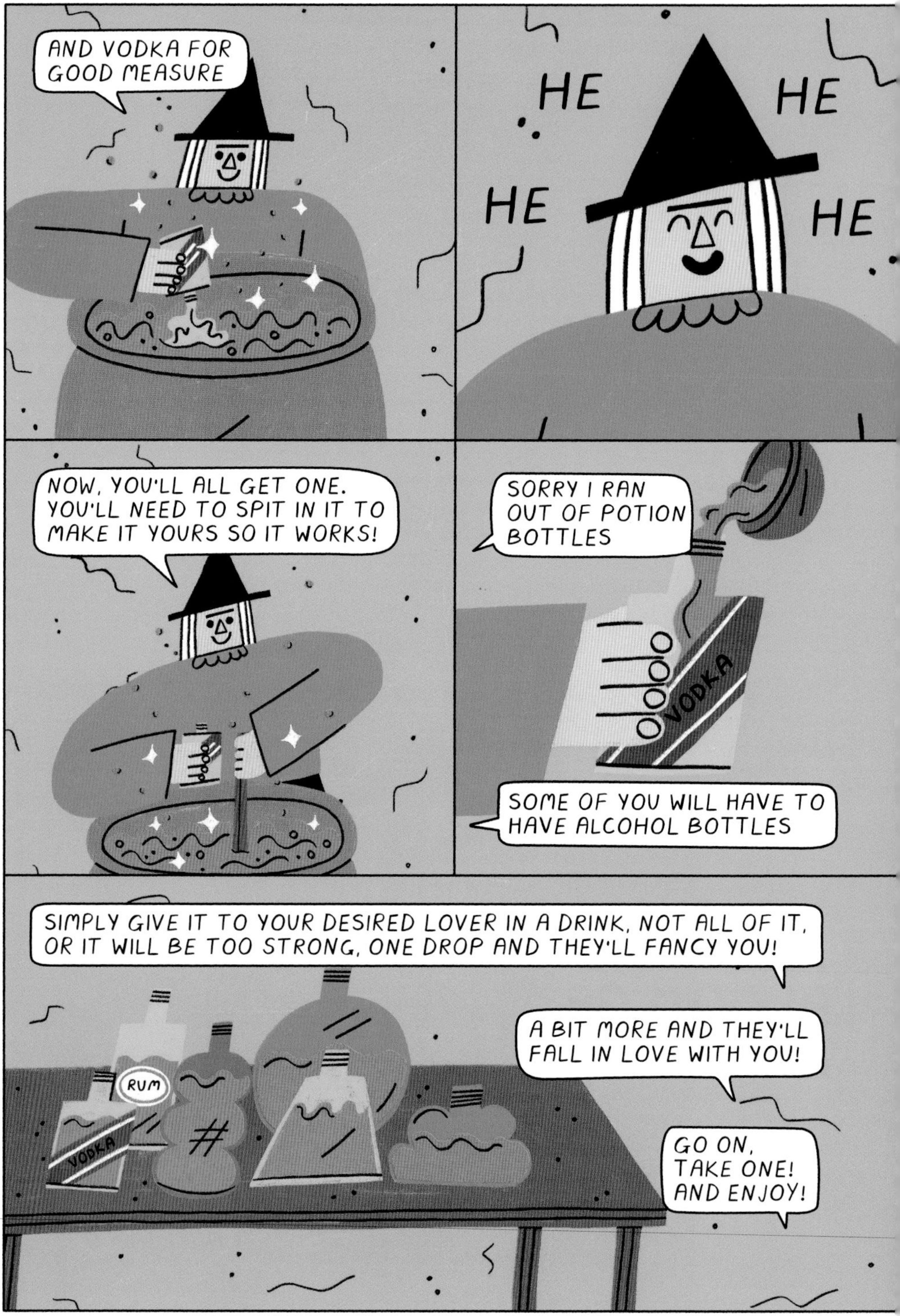
AND VODKA FOR GOOD MEASURE
HE
HE
HE
HE
NOW, YOU'LL ALL GET ONE. YOU'LL NEED TO SPIT IN IT TO MAKE IT YOURS SO IT WORKS!
SORRY I RAN OUT OF POTION BOTTLES
VODKA
SOME OF YOU WILL HAVE TO HAVE ALCOHOL BOTTLES
SIMPLY GIVE IT TO YOUR DESIRED LOVER IN A DRINK, NOT ALL OF IT, OR IT WILL BE TOO STRONG, ONE DROP AND THEY'LL FANCY YOU!
RUM
VODKA
A BIT MORE AND THEY'LL FALL IN LOVE WITH YOU!
GO ON, TAKE ONE! AND ENJOY!

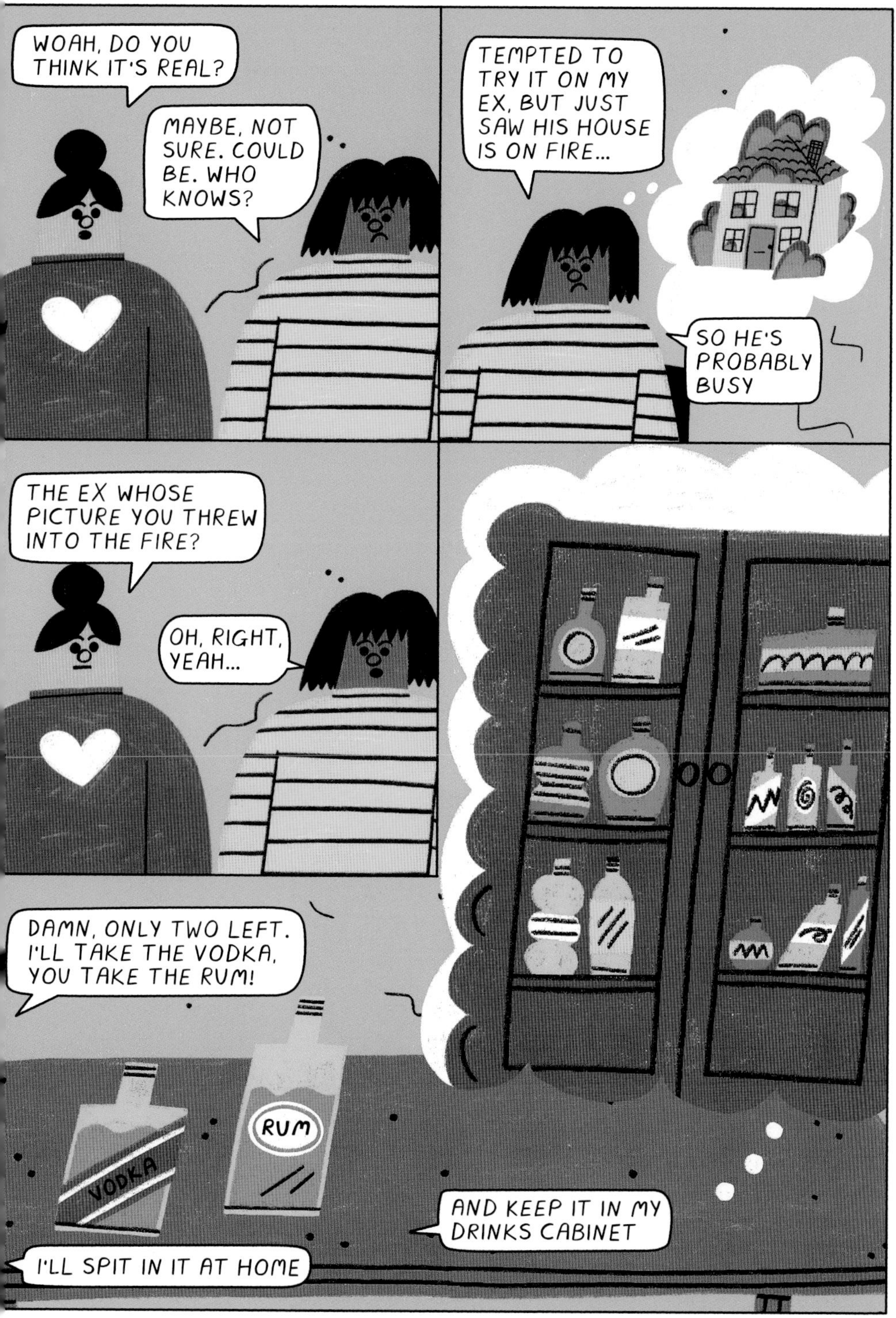
WOAH, DO YOU THINK IT'S REAL?
MAYBE, NOT SURE. COULD BE. WHO KNOWS?
TEMPTED TO TRY IT ON MY EX, BUT JUST SAW HIS HOUSE IS ON FIRE...
SO HE'S PROBABLY BUSY
THE EX WHOSE PICTURE YOU THREW INTO THE FIRE?
OH, RIGHT, YEAH...
DAMN, ONLY TWO LEFT. I'LL TAKE THE VODKA, YOU TAKE THE RUM!
VODKA
RUM
I'LL SPIT IN IT AT HOME
AND KEEP IT IN MY DRINKS CABINET

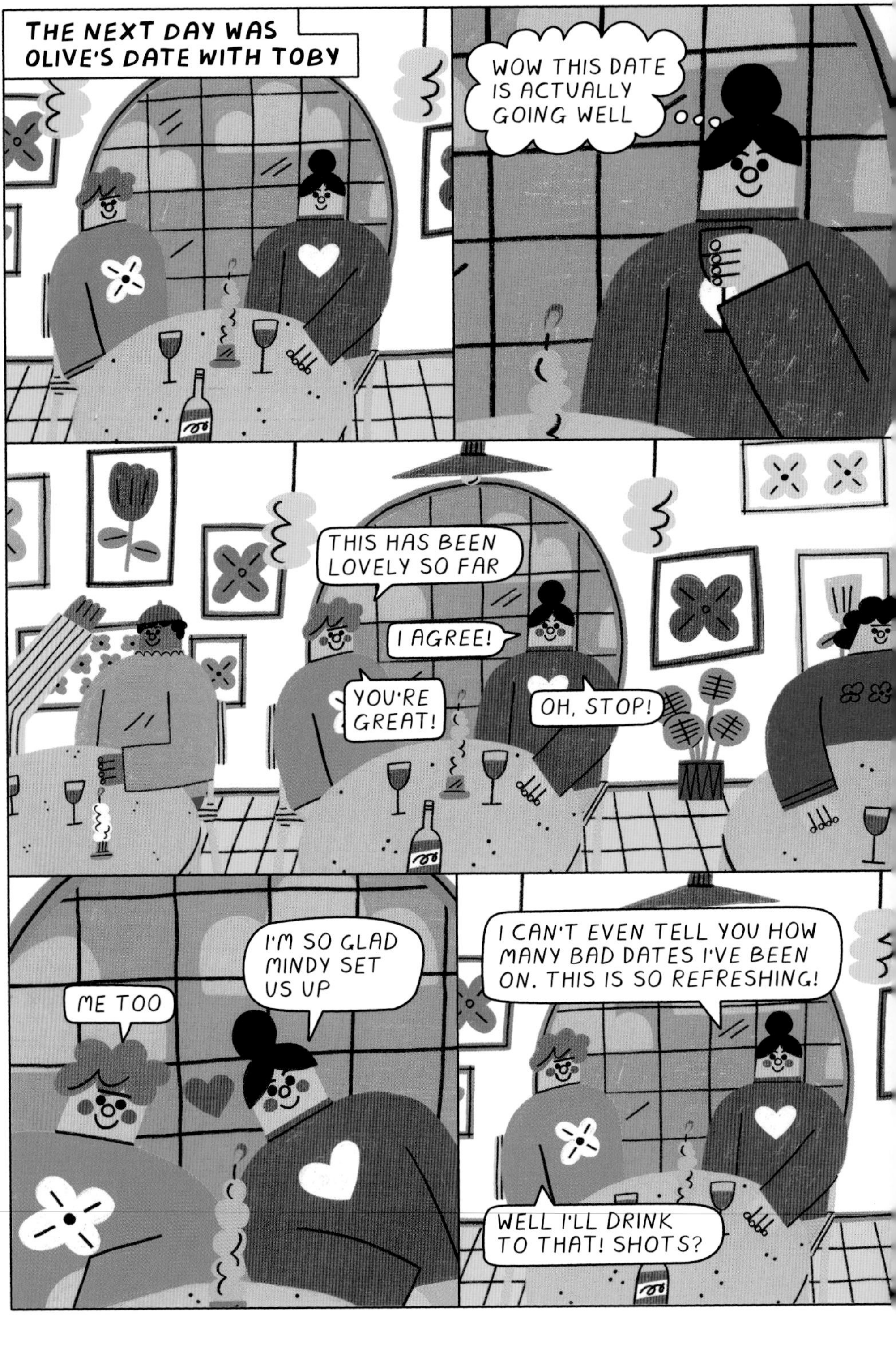
THE NEXT DAY WAS OLIVE'S DATE WITH TOBY
WOW THIS DATE IS ACTUALLY GOING WELL
THIS HAS BEEN LOVELY SO FAR
I AGREE!
YOU'RE GREAT!
OH, STOP!
ME TOO
I'M SO GLAD MINDY SET US UP
I CAN'T EVEN TELL YOU HOW MANY BAD DATES I'VE BEEN ON. THIS IS SO REFRESHING!
WELL I'LL DRINK TO THAT! SHOTS?

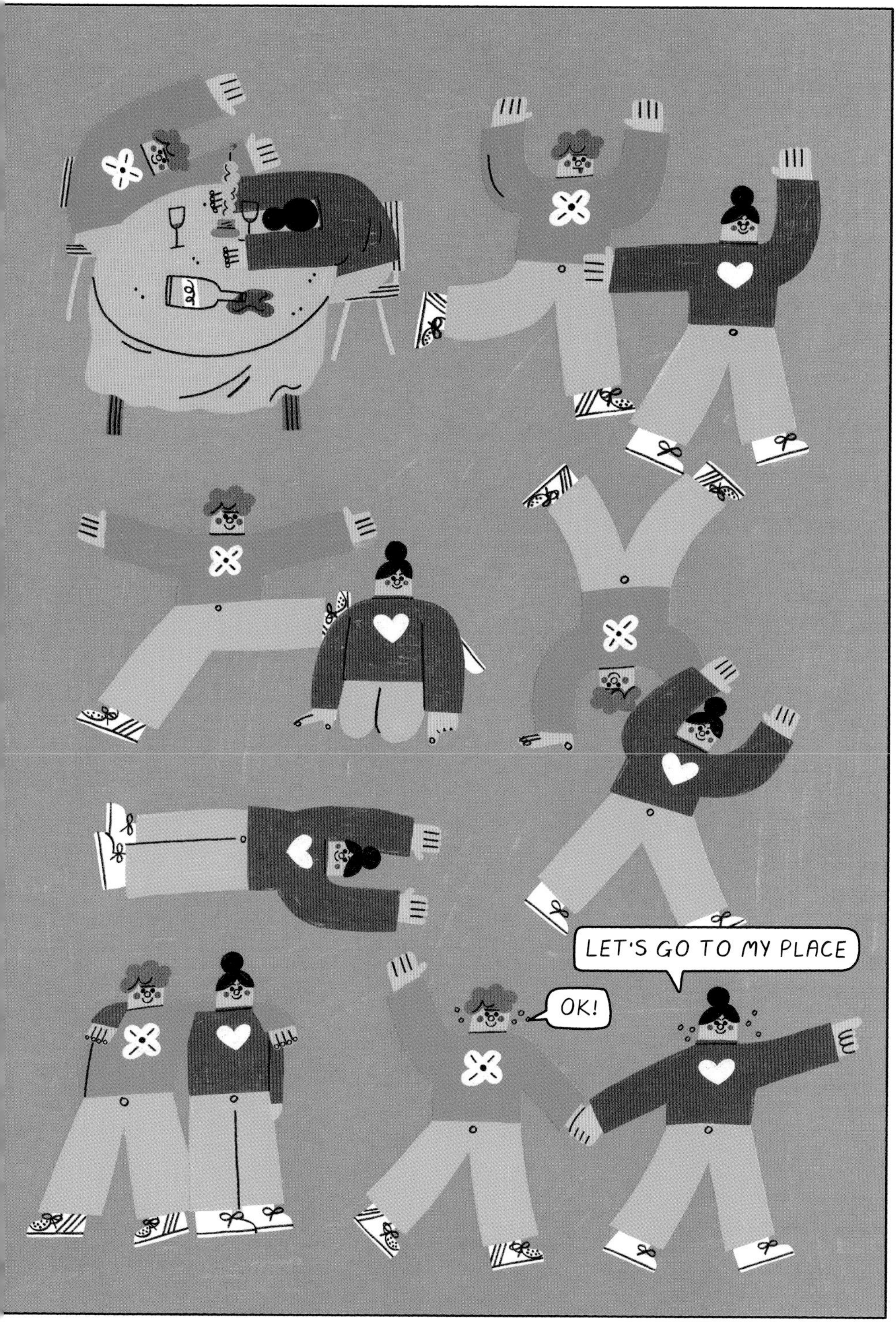
OK!
LET'S GO TO MY PLACE

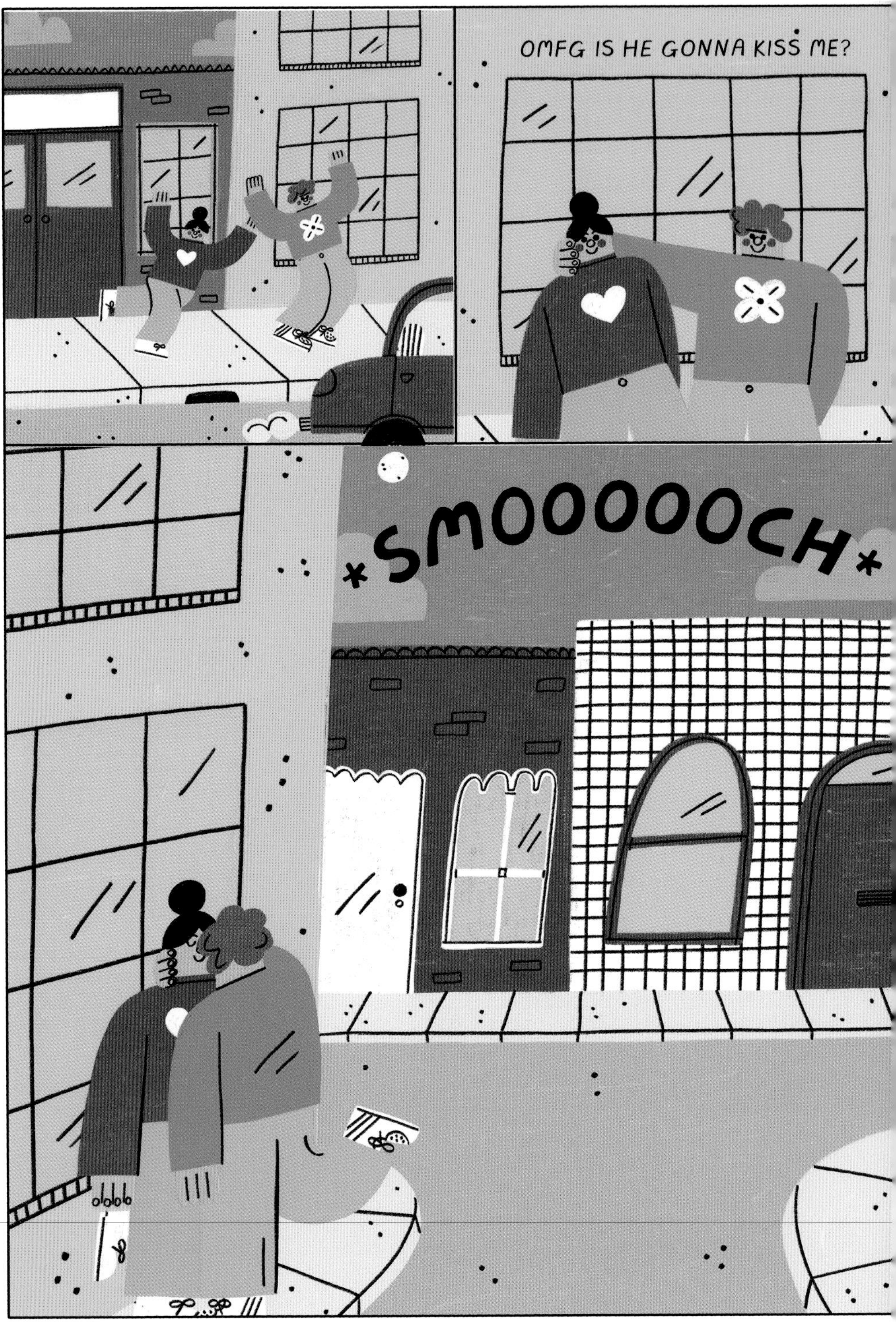
OMFG IS HE GONNA KISS ME?
SMOOOOOCH

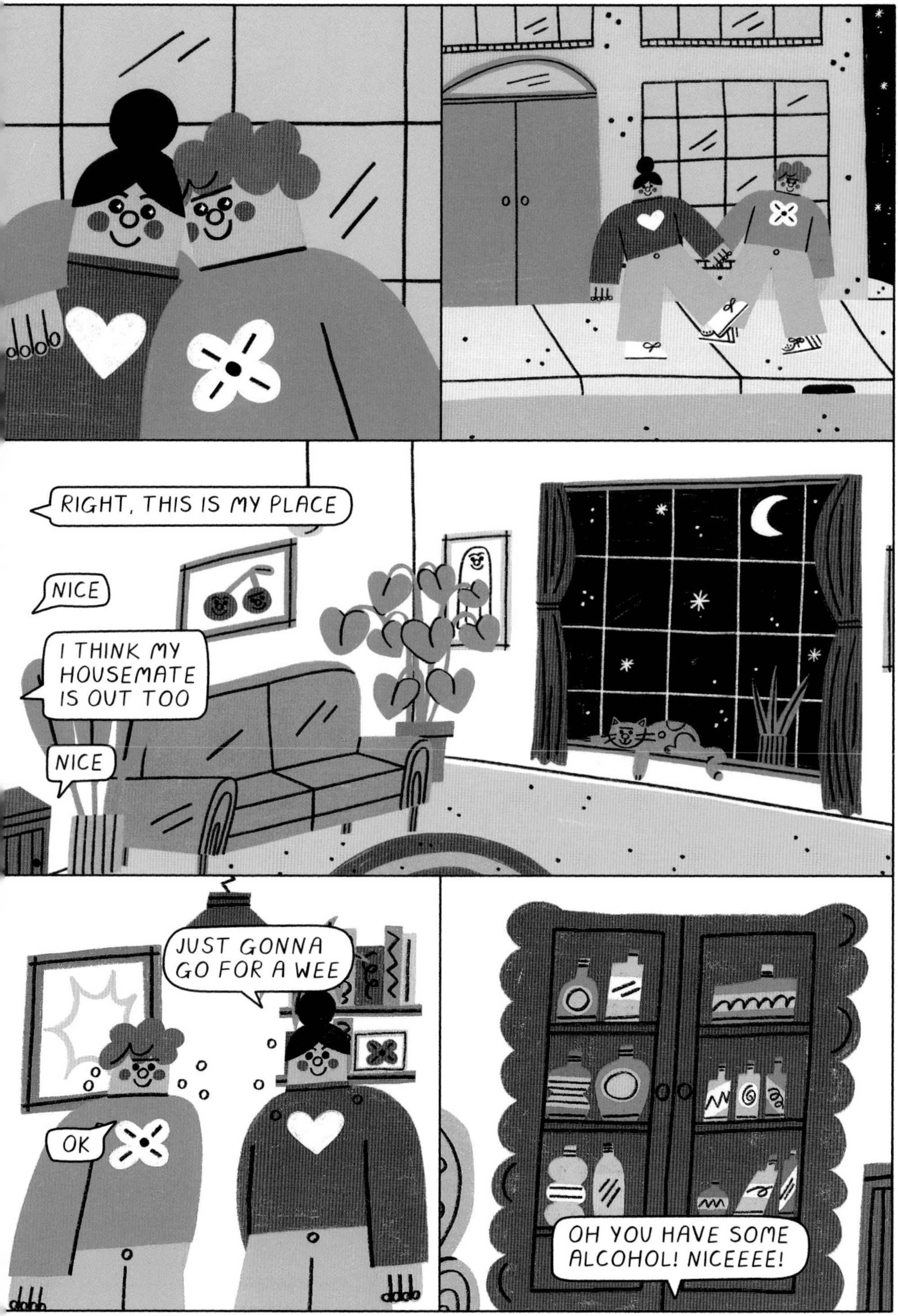
RIGHT, THIS IS MY PLACE
NICE
I THINK MY HOUSEMATE IS OUT TOO
NICE
JUST GONNA GO FOR A WEE
OK
OH YOU HAVE SOME ALCOHOL! NICEEEE!

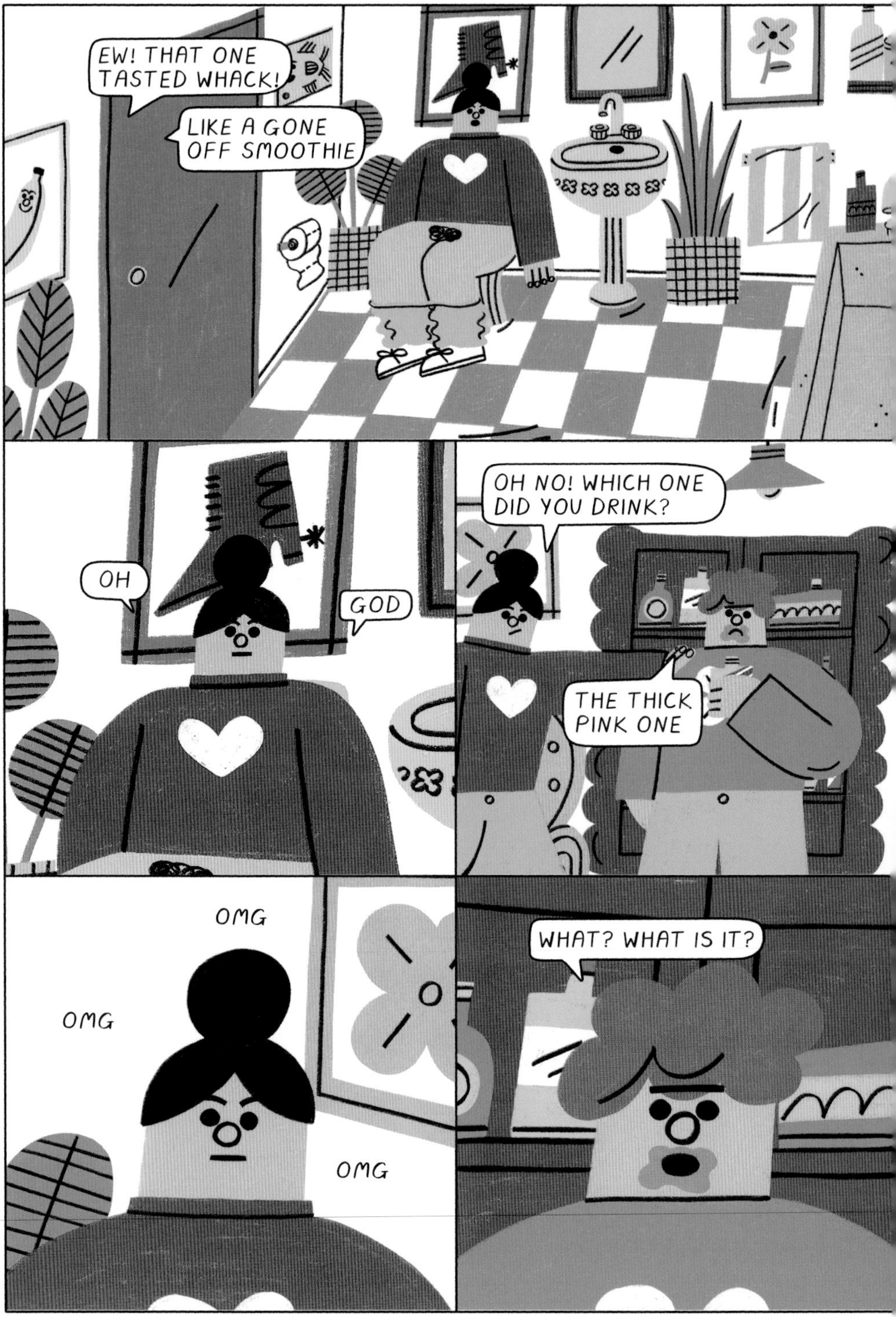
EW! THAT ONE TASTED WHACK!
LIKE A GONE OFF SMOOTHIE
OH
GOD
OH NO! WHICH ONE DID YOU DRINK?
THE THICK PINK ONE
OMG
OMG
OMG
WHAT? WHAT IS IT?

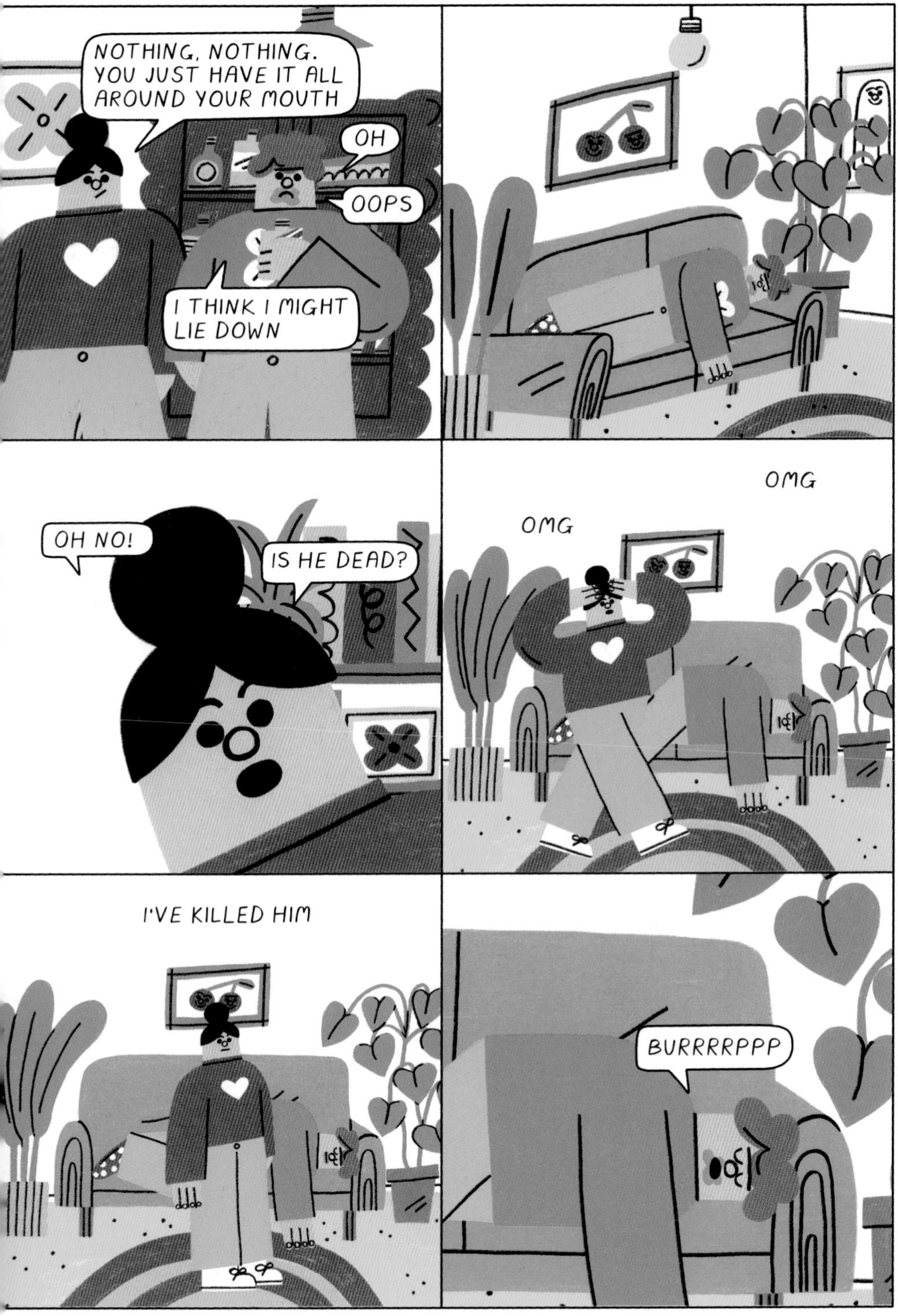
NOTHING, NOTHING. YOU JUST HAVE IT ALL AROUND YOUR MOUTH
OH
OOPS
I THINK I MIGHT LIE DOWN
OH NO!
IS HE DEAD?
OMG
OMG
I'VE KILLED HIM
BURRRRPPP

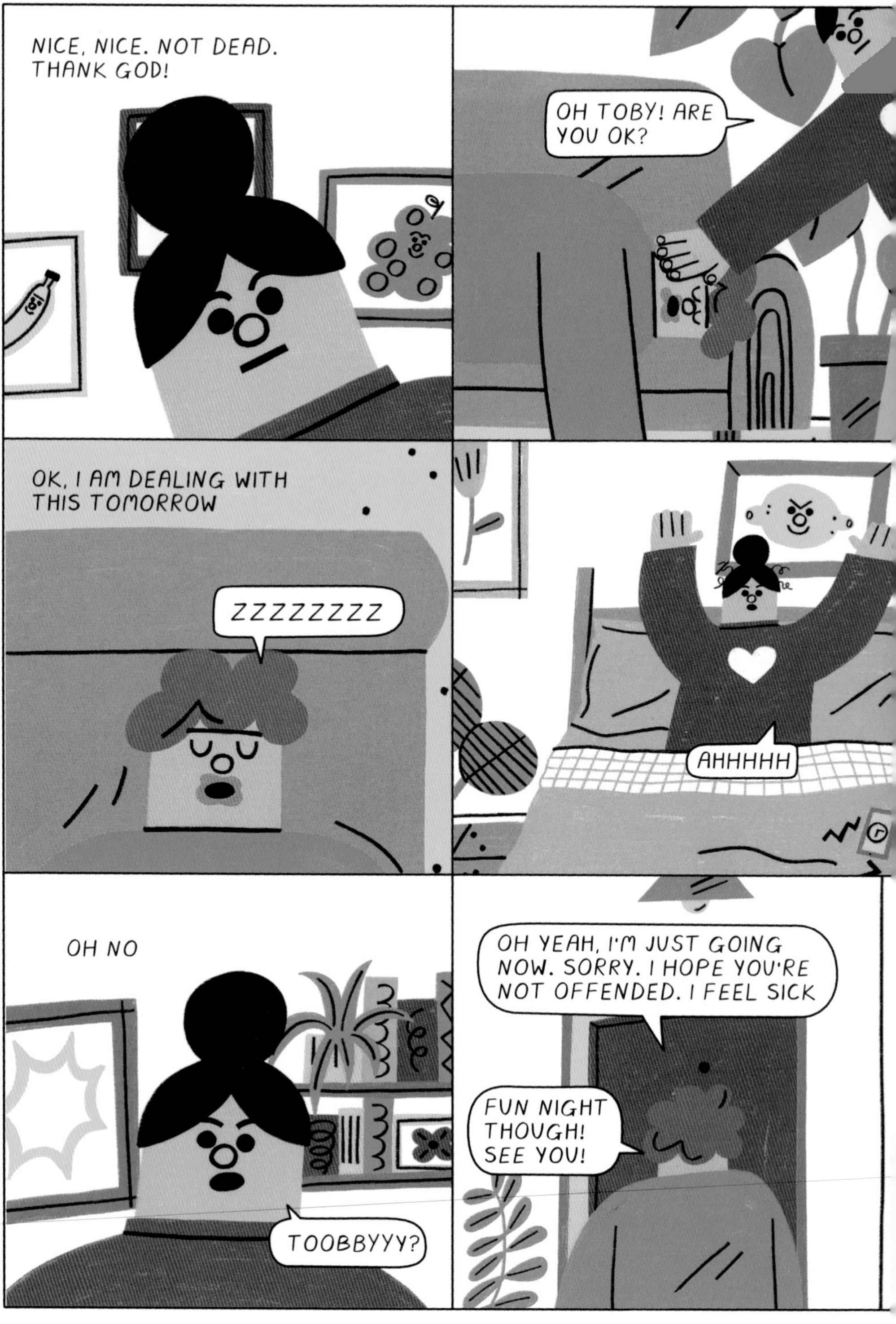
NICE, NICE. NOT DEAD. THANK GOD!
OH TOBY! ARE YOU OK?
OK, I AM DEALING WITH THIS TOMORROW
ZZZZZZZZ
AHHHHH
OH NO
TOOBBYYY?
OH YEAH, I'M JUST GOING NOW. SORRY. I HOPE YOU'RE NOT OFFENDED. I FEEL SICK
FUN NIGHT THOUGH! SEE YOU!

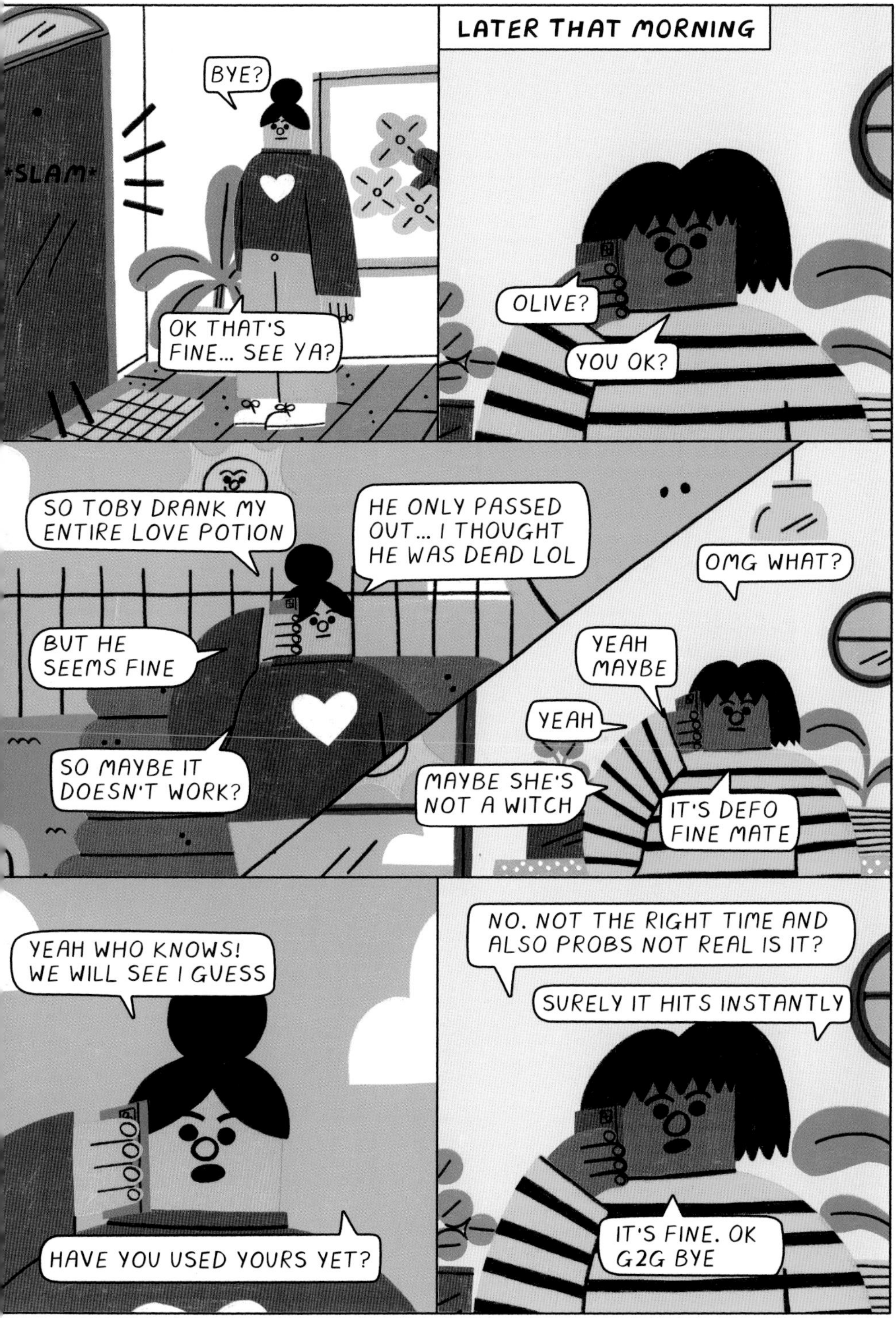

SLAM
BYE?
OK THAT'S FINE... SEE YA?
LATER THAT MORNING
OLIVE?
YOU OK?
SO TOBY DRANK MY ENTIRE LOVE POTION
HE ONLY PASSED OUT... I THOUGHT HE WAS DEAD LOL
OMG WHAT?
BUT HE SEEMS FINE
YEAH MAYBE
YEAH
SO MAYBE IT DOESN'T WORK?
MAYBE SHE'S NOT A WITCH
IT'S DEFO FINE MATE
YEAH WHO KNOWS! WE WILL SEE I GUESS
HAVE YOU USED YOURS YET?
NO. NOT THE RIGHT TIME AND ALSO PROBS NOT REAL IS IT?
SURELY IT HITS INSTANTLY
IT'S FINE. OK G2G BYE

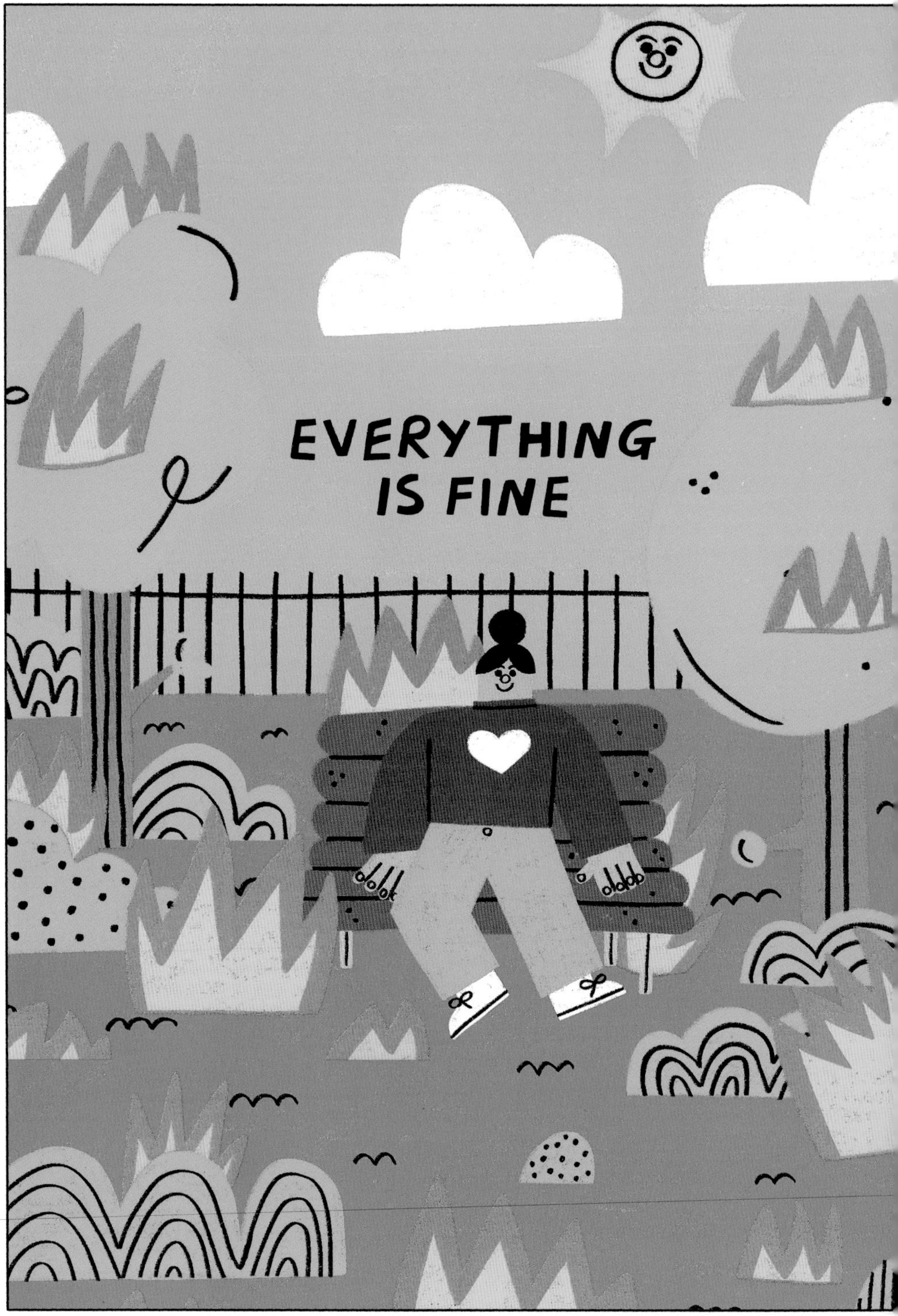
EVERYTHING
IS FINE

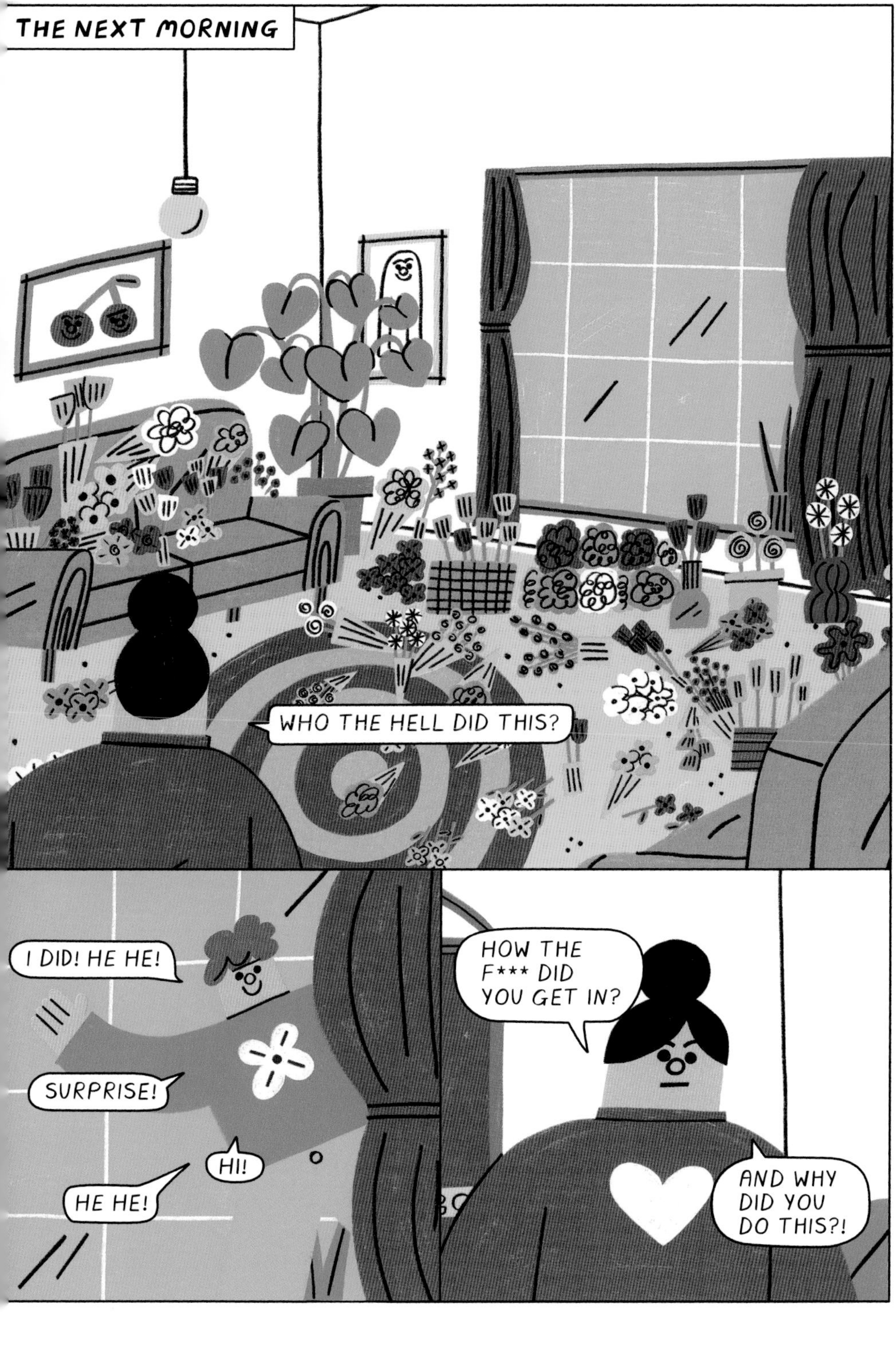
THE NEXT MORNING
WHO THE HELL DID THIS?
I DID! HE HE!
SURPRISE!
HI!
HE HE!
HOW THE F*** DID YOU GET IN?
AND WHY DID YOU DO THIS?!

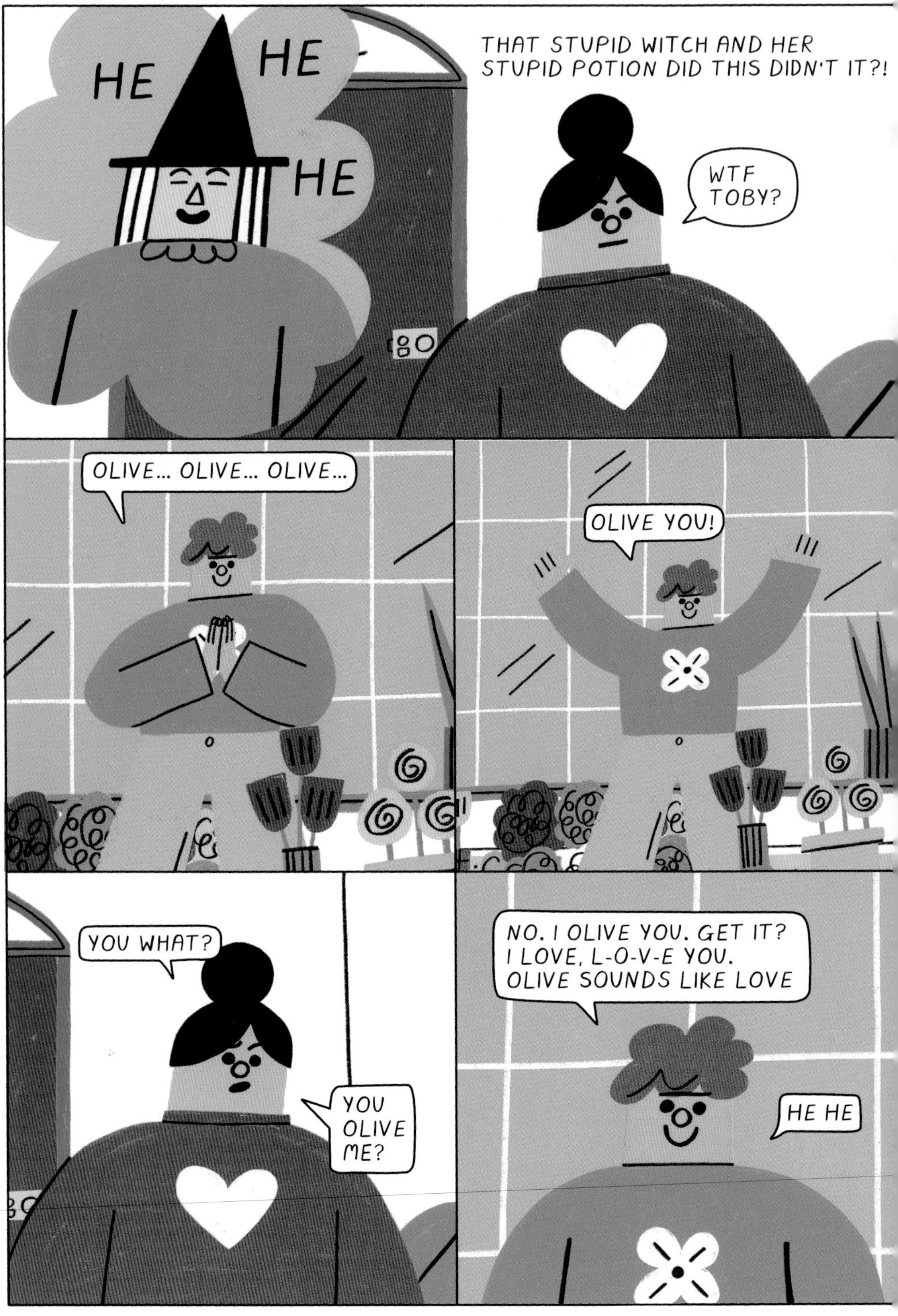

HE
HE
HE
THAT STUPID WITCH AND HER STUPID POTION DID THIS DIDN'T IT?!
WTF TOBY?
OLIVE... OLIVE... OLIVE...
OLIVE YOU!
YOU WHAT?
YOU OLIVE ME?
NO. I OLIVE YOU. GET IT? I LOVE, L-O-V-E YOU. OLIVE SOUNDS LIKE LOVE
HE HE

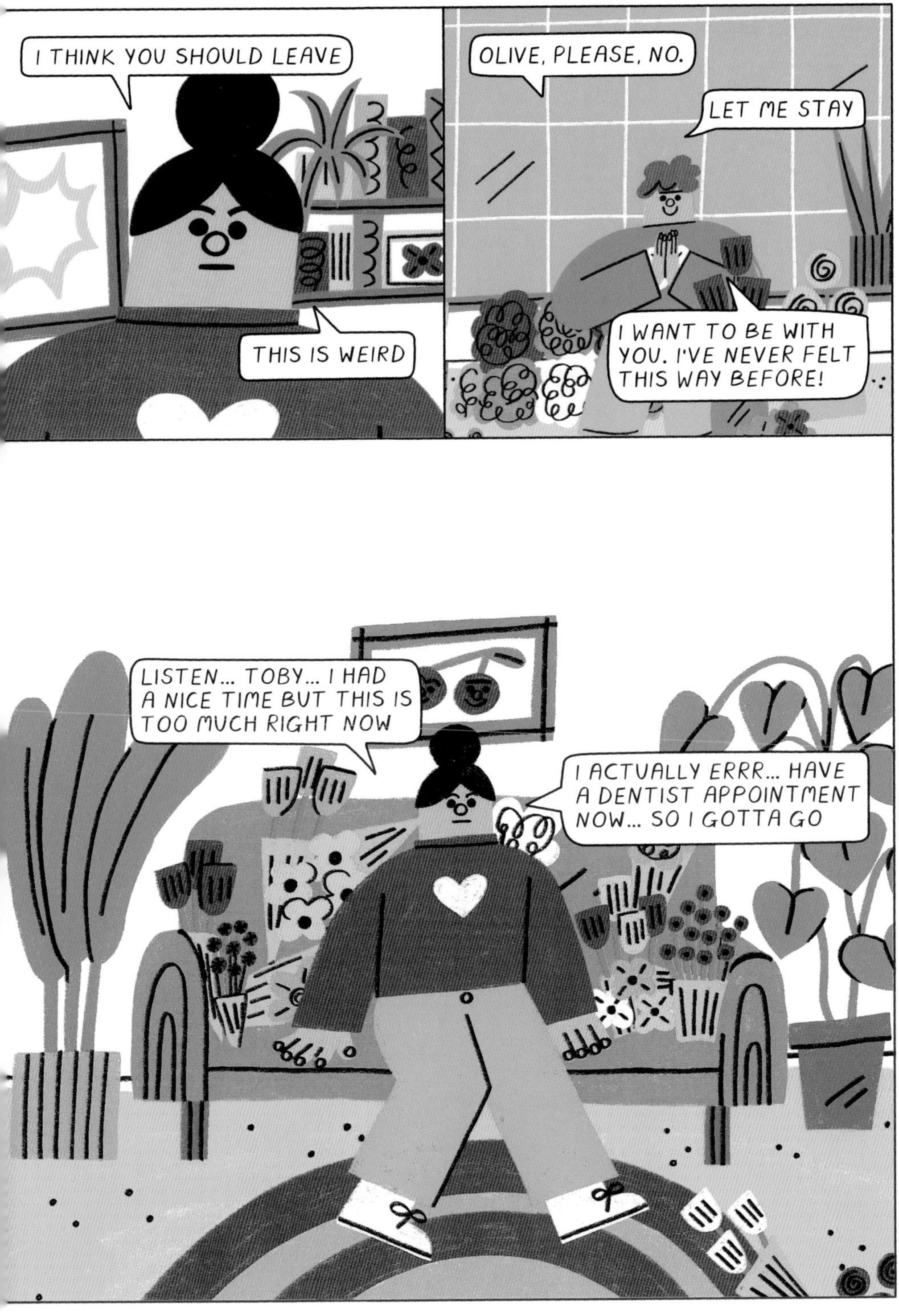
I THINK YOU SHOULD LEAVE
THIS IS WEIRD
OLIVE, PLEASE, NO.
LET ME STAY
I WANT TO BE WITH YOU. I'VE NEVER FELT THIS WAY BEFORE!
LISTEN... TOBY... I HAD A NICE TIME BUT THIS IS TOO MUCH RIGHT NOW
I ACTUALLY ERRR... HAVE A DENTIST APPOINTMENT NOW... SO I GOTTA GO

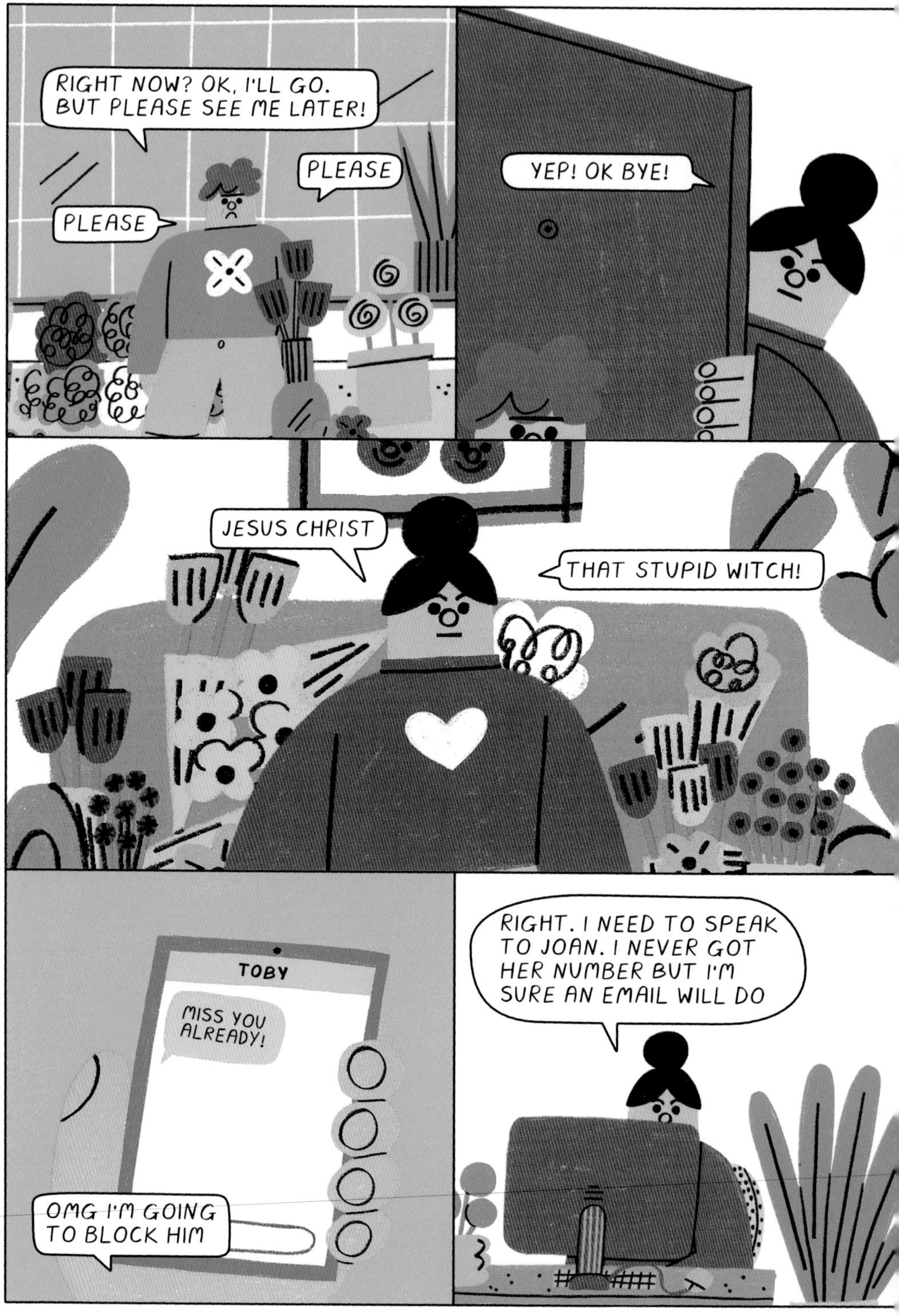
RIGHT NOW? OK, I'LL GO. BUT PLEASE SEE ME LATER!
PLEASE
PLEASE
YEP! OK BYE!
JESUS CHRIST
THAT STUPID WITCH!
TOBY
MISS YOU ALREADY!
OMG I'M GOING TO BLOCK HIM
RIGHT. I NEED TO SPEAK TO JOAN. I NEVER GOT HER NUMBER BUT I'M SURE AN EMAIL WILL DO

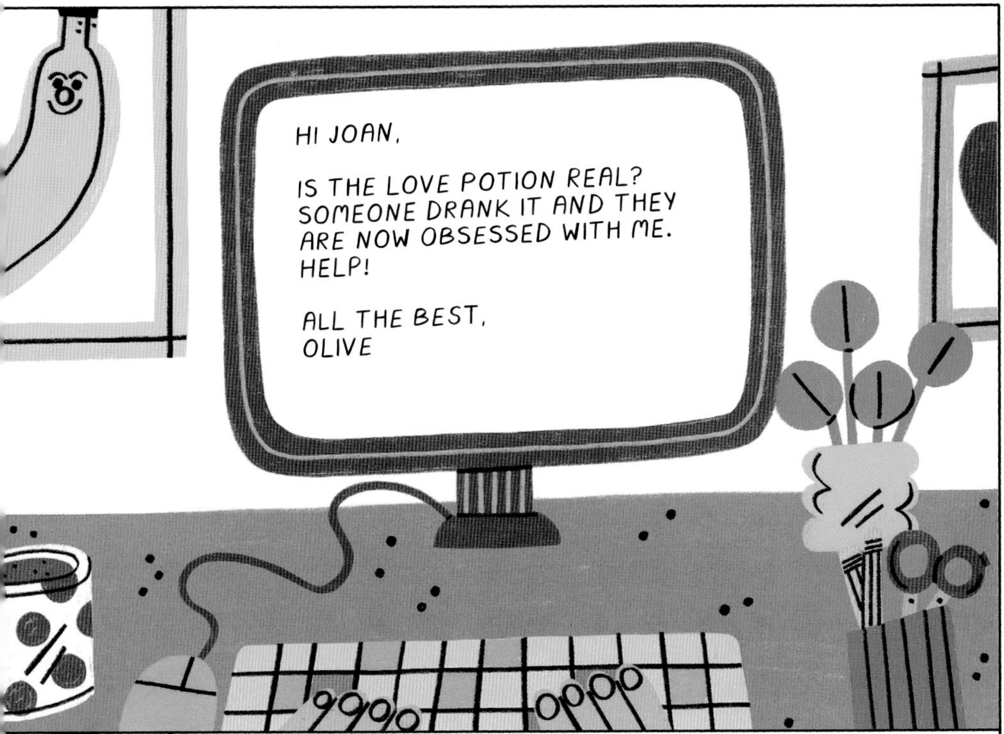
HI JOAN,
IS THE LOVE POTION REAL? SOMEONE DRANK IT AND THEY ARE NOW OBSESSED WITH ME. HELP!
ALL THE BEST,
OLIVE

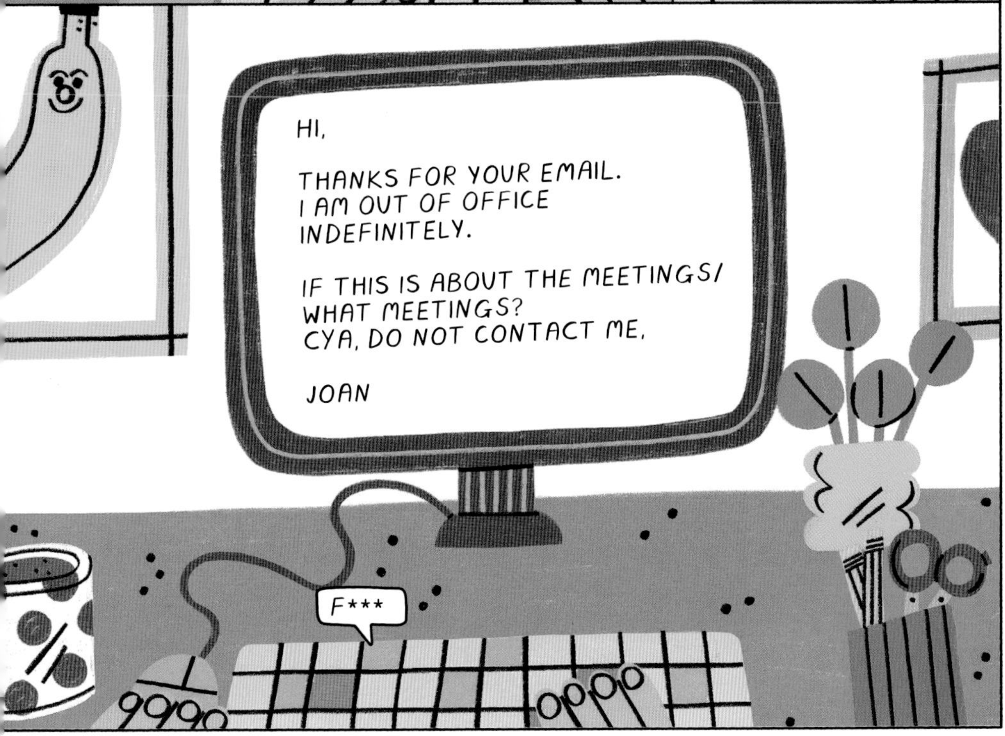
HI,
THANKS FOR YOUR EMAIL. I AM OUT OF OFFICE INDEFINITELY.
IF THIS IS ABOUT THE MEETINGS/ WHAT MEETINGS?
CYA, DO NOT CONTACT ME,
JOAN
F***

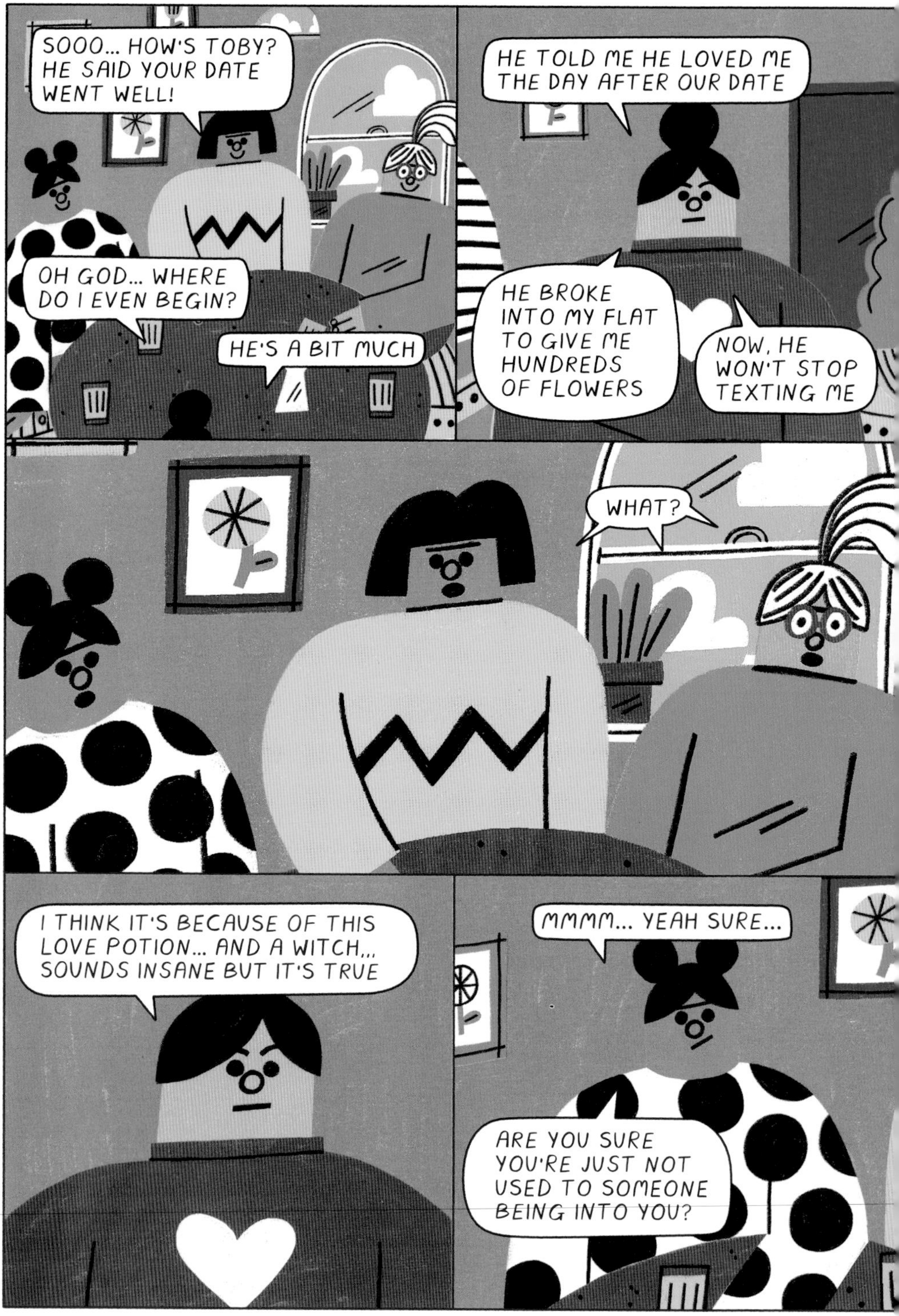
SOOO... HOW'S TOBY? HE SAID YOUR DATE WENT WELL!
OH GOD... WHERE DO I EVEN BEGIN?
HE'S A BIT MUCH
HE TOLD ME HE LOVED ME THE DAY AFTER OUR DATE
HE BROKE INTO MY FLAT TO GIVE ME HUNDREDS OF FLOWERS
NOW, HE WON'T STOP TEXTING ME
WHAT?
I THINK IT'S BECAUSE OF THIS LOVE POTION... AND A WITCH,,, SOUNDS INSANE BUT IT'S TRUE
MMMM... YEAH SURE...
ARE YOU SURE YOU'RE JUST NOT USED TO SOMEONE BEING INTO YOU?

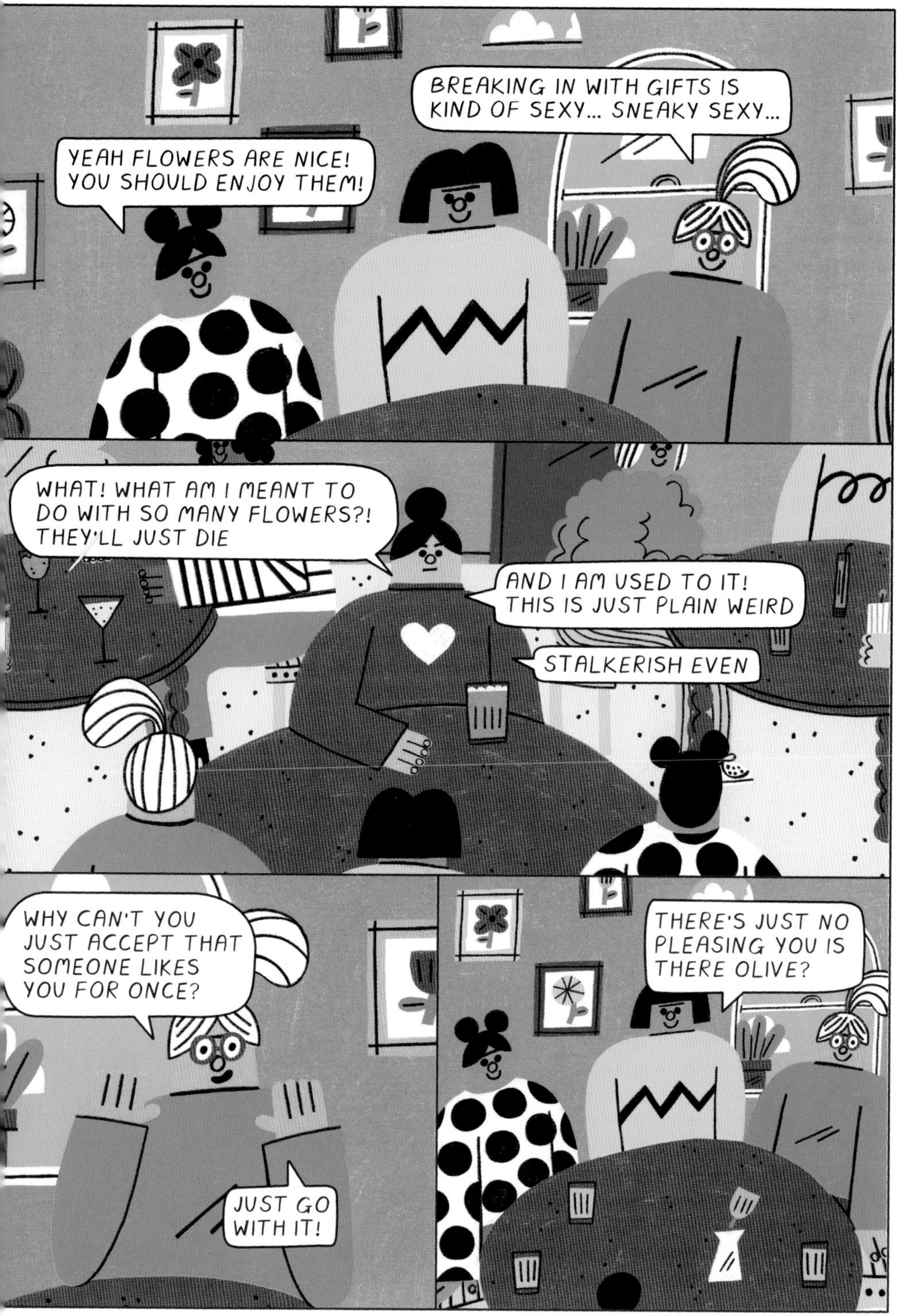
YEAH FLOWERS ARE NICE! YOU SHOULD ENJOY THEM!
BREAKING IN WITH GIFTS IS KIND OF SEXY... SNEAKY SEXY...
WHAT! WHAT AM I MEANT TO DO WITH SO MANY FLOWERS?! THEY'LL JUST DIE
AND I AM USED TO IT! THIS IS JUST PLAIN WEIRD
STALKERISH EVEN
WHY CAN'T YOU JUST ACCEPT THAT SOMEONE LIKES YOU FOR ONCE?
JUST GO WITH IT!
THERE'S JUST NO PLEASING YOU IS THERE OLIVE?

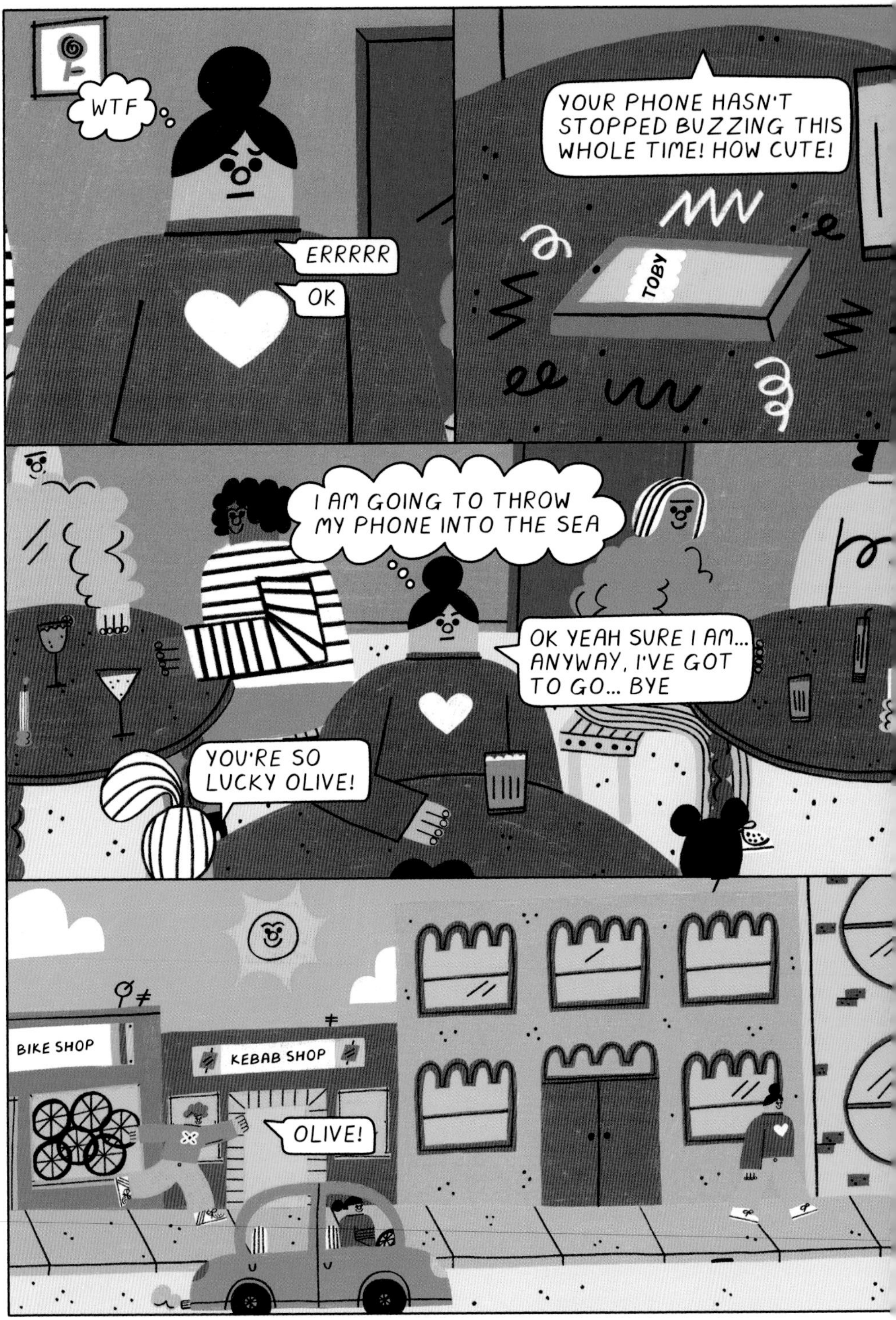
WTF
ERRRRR
OK
YOUR PHONE HASN'T STOPPED BUZZING THIS WHOLE TIME! HOW CUTE!
TOBY
I AM GOING TO THROW MY PHONE INTO THE SEA
OK YEAH SURE I AM... ANYWAY, I'VE GOT TO GO... BYE
YOU'RE SO LUCKY OLIVE!
BIKE SHOP
KEBAB SHOP
OLIVE!

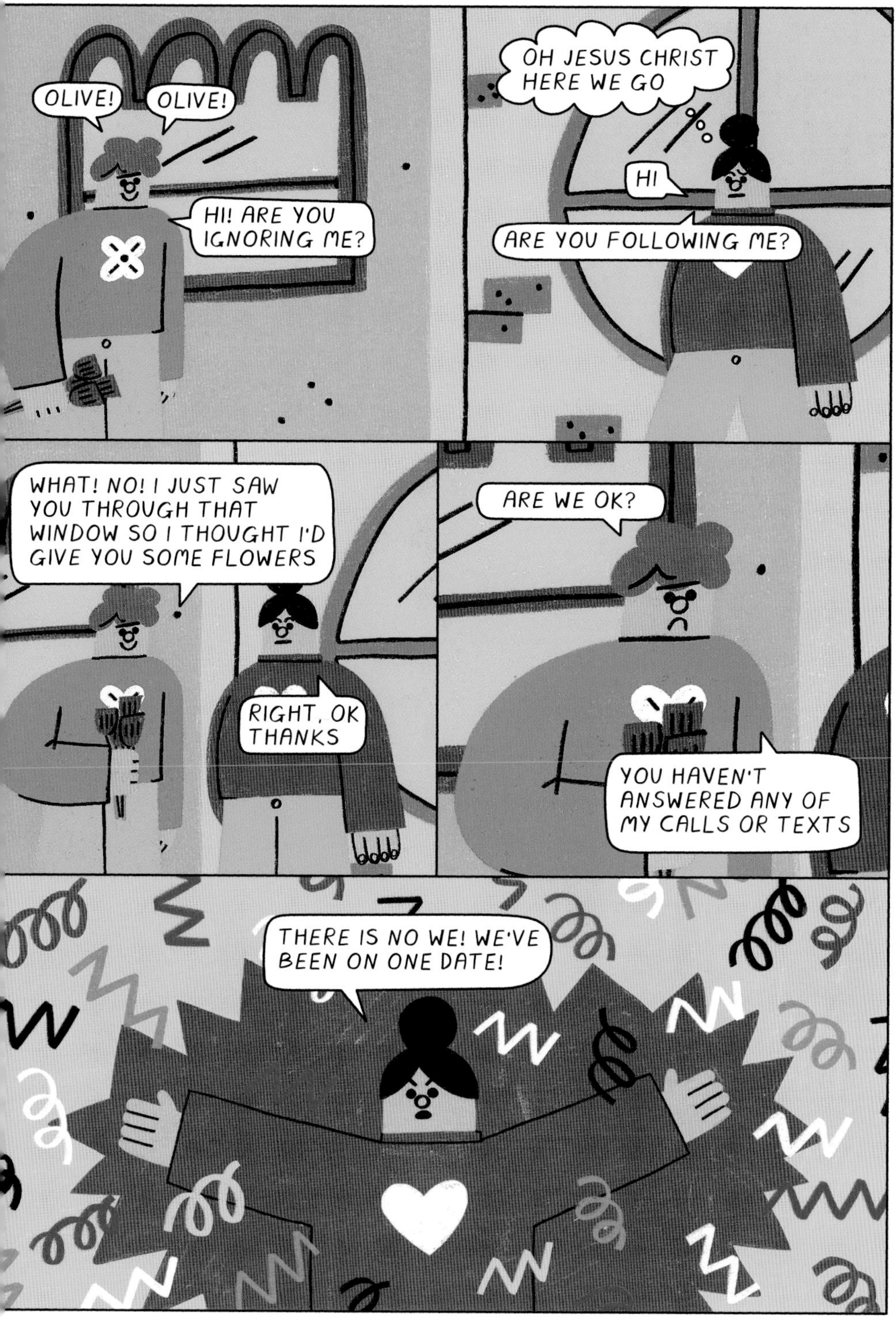
OLIVE!
OLIVE!
HI! ARE YOU IGNORING ME?
OH JESUS CHRIST HERE WE GO
HI
ARE YOU FOLLOWING ME?
WHAT! NO! I JUST SAW YOU THROUGH THAT WINDOW SO I THOUGHT I'D GIVE YOU SOME FLOWERS
RIGHT, OK THANKS
ARE WE OK?
YOU HAVEN'T ANSWERED ANY OF MY CALLS OR TEXTS
THERE IS NO WE! WE'VE BEEN ON ONE DATE!

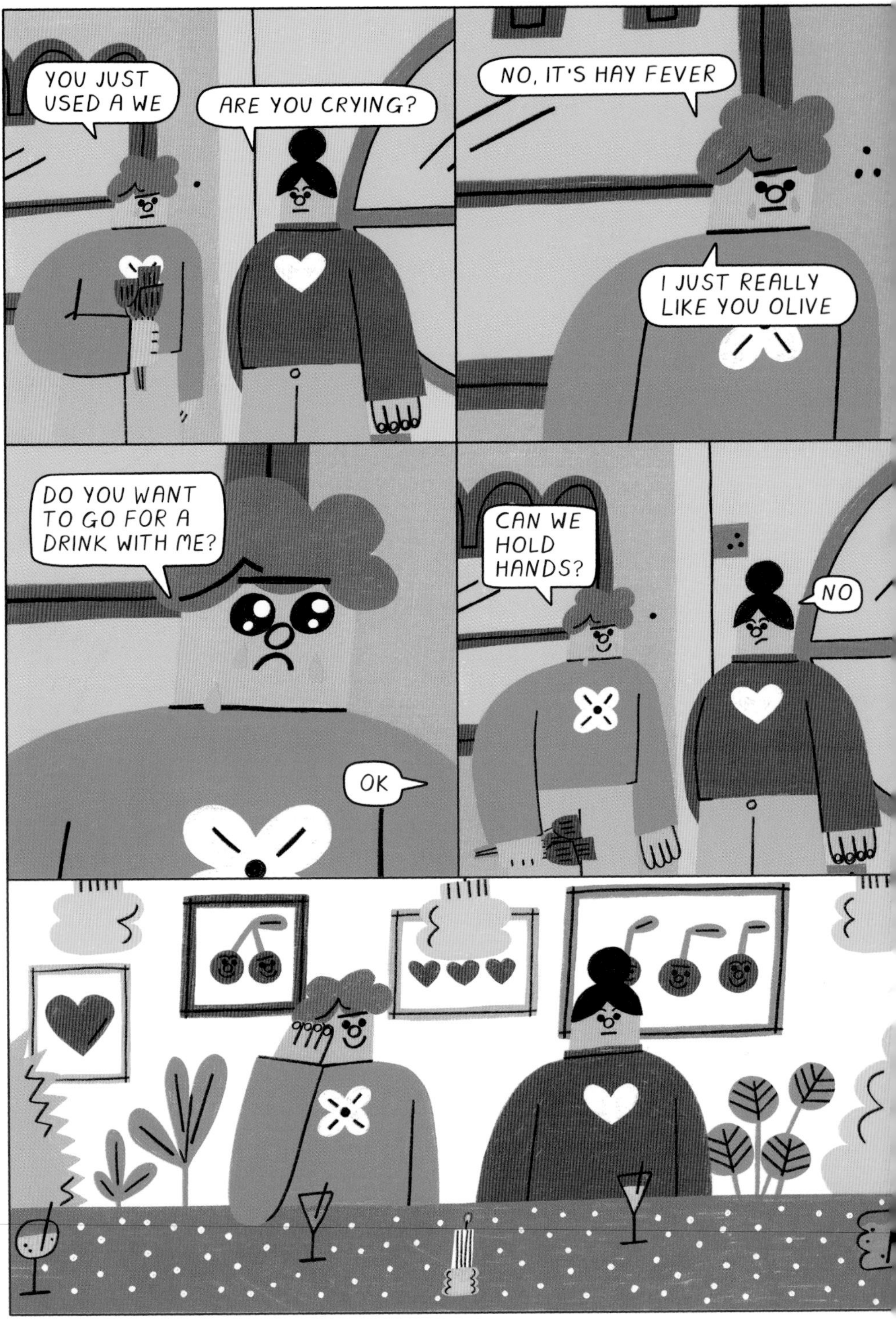
YOU JUST USED A WE
ARE YOU CRYING?
NO, IT'S HAY FEVER
I JUST REALLY LIKE YOU OLIVE
DO YOU WANT TO GO FOR A DRINK WITH ME?
OK
CAN WE HOLD HANDS?
NO

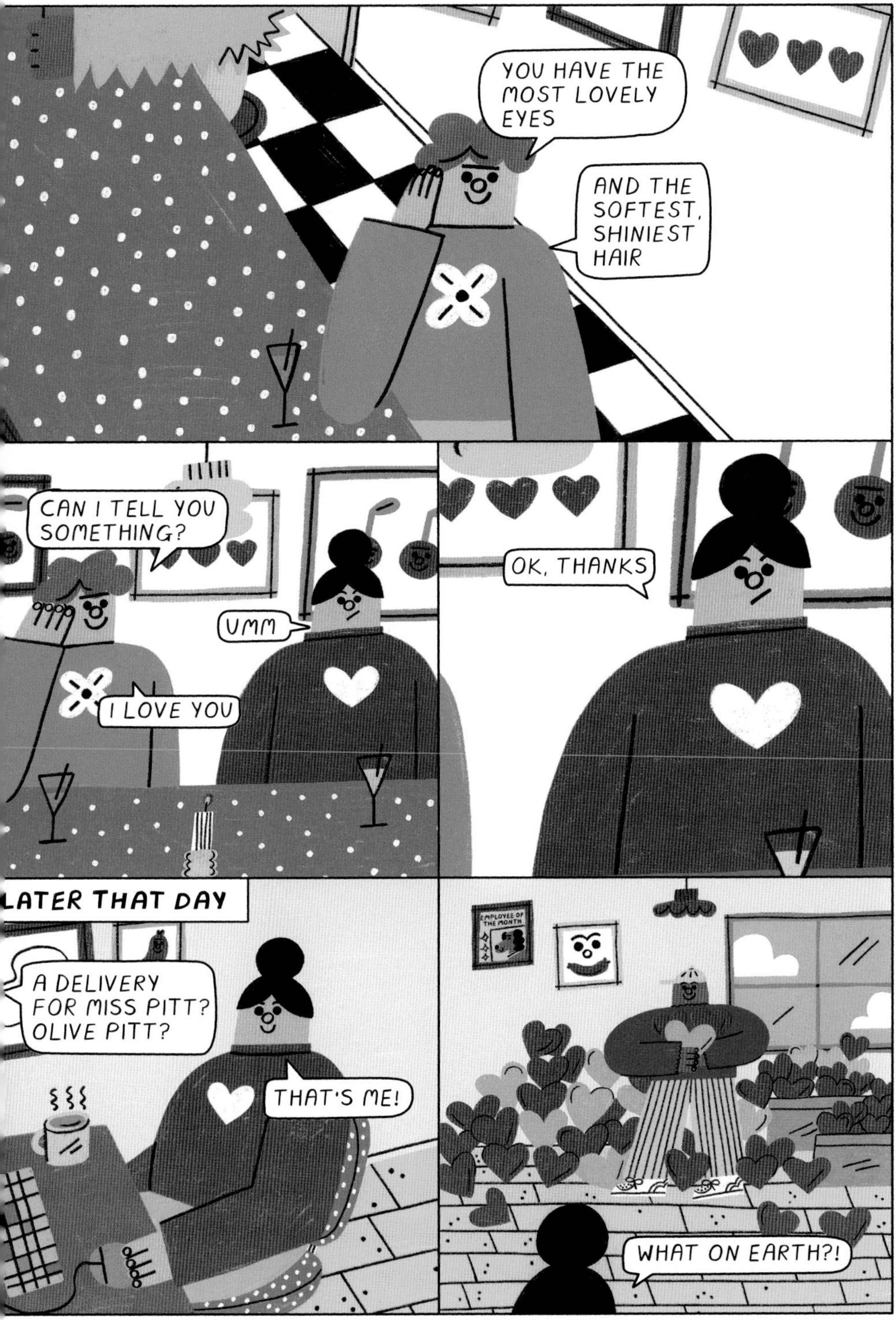
YOU HAVE THE MOST LOVELY EYES
AND THE SOFTEST, SHINIEST HAIR
CAN I TELL YOU SOMETHING?
UMM
I LOVE YOU
OK, THANKS
LATER THAT DAY
A DELIVERY FOR MISS PITT? OLIVE PITT?
THAT'S ME!
EMPLOYEE OF THE MONTH
WHAT ON EARTH?!

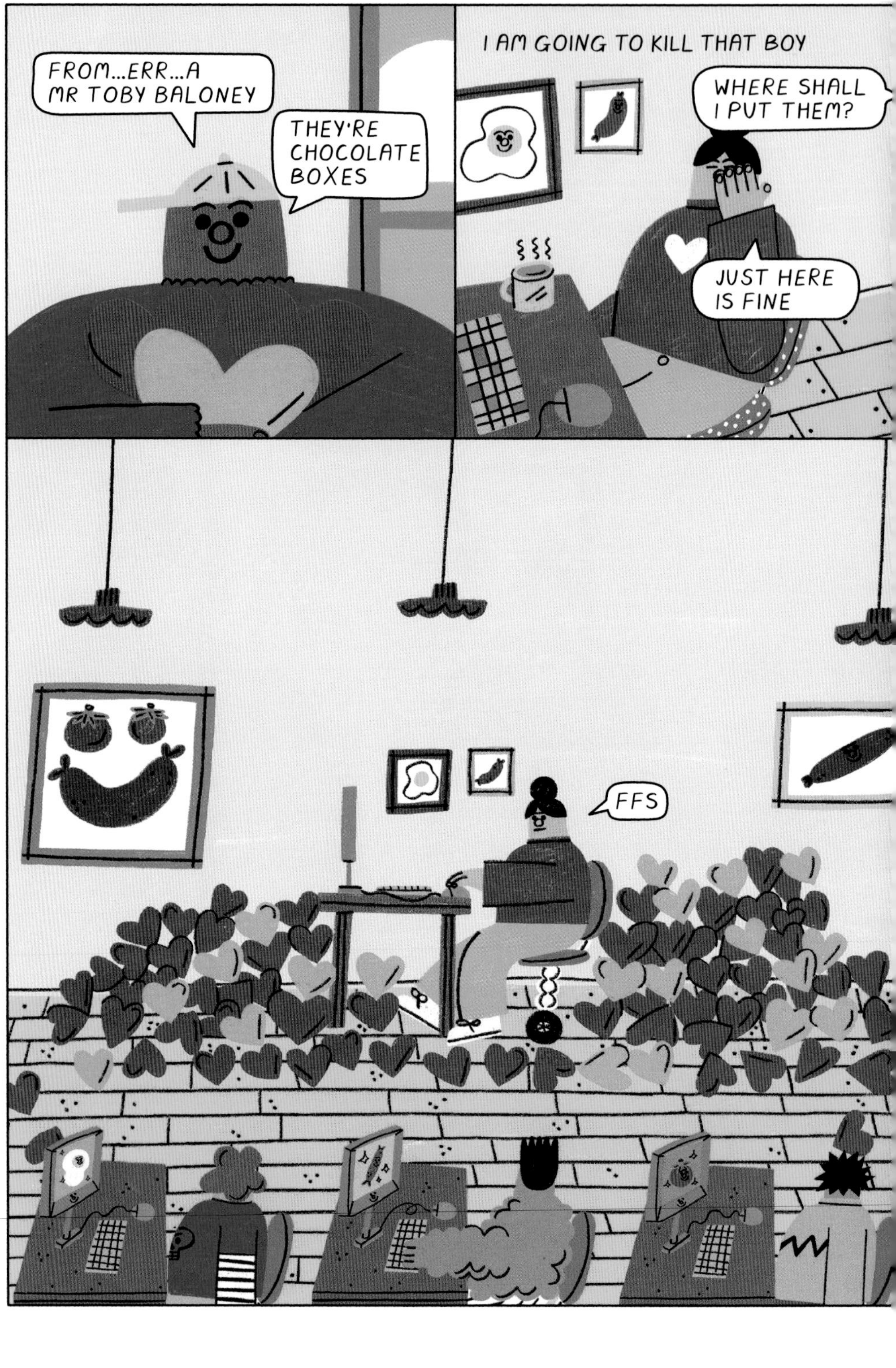
FROM...ERR...A MR TOBY BALONEY
THEY'RE CHOCOLATE BOXES
I AM GOING TO KILL THAT BOY
WHERE SHALL I PUT THEM?
JUST HERE IS FINE
FFS

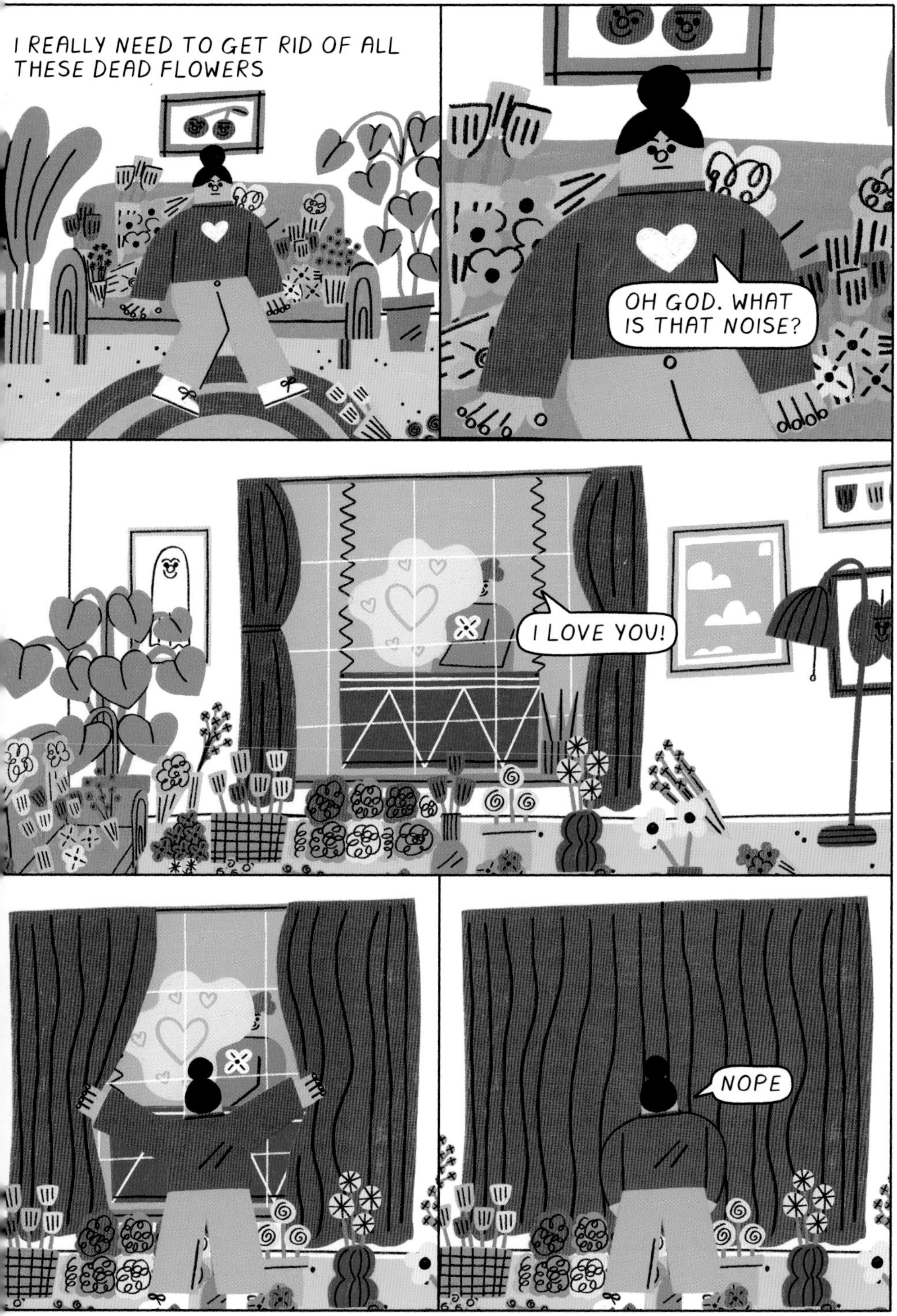
I REALLY NEED TO GET RID OF ALL THESE DEAD FLOWERS
OH GOD. WHAT IS THAT NOISE?
I LOVE YOU!
NOPE

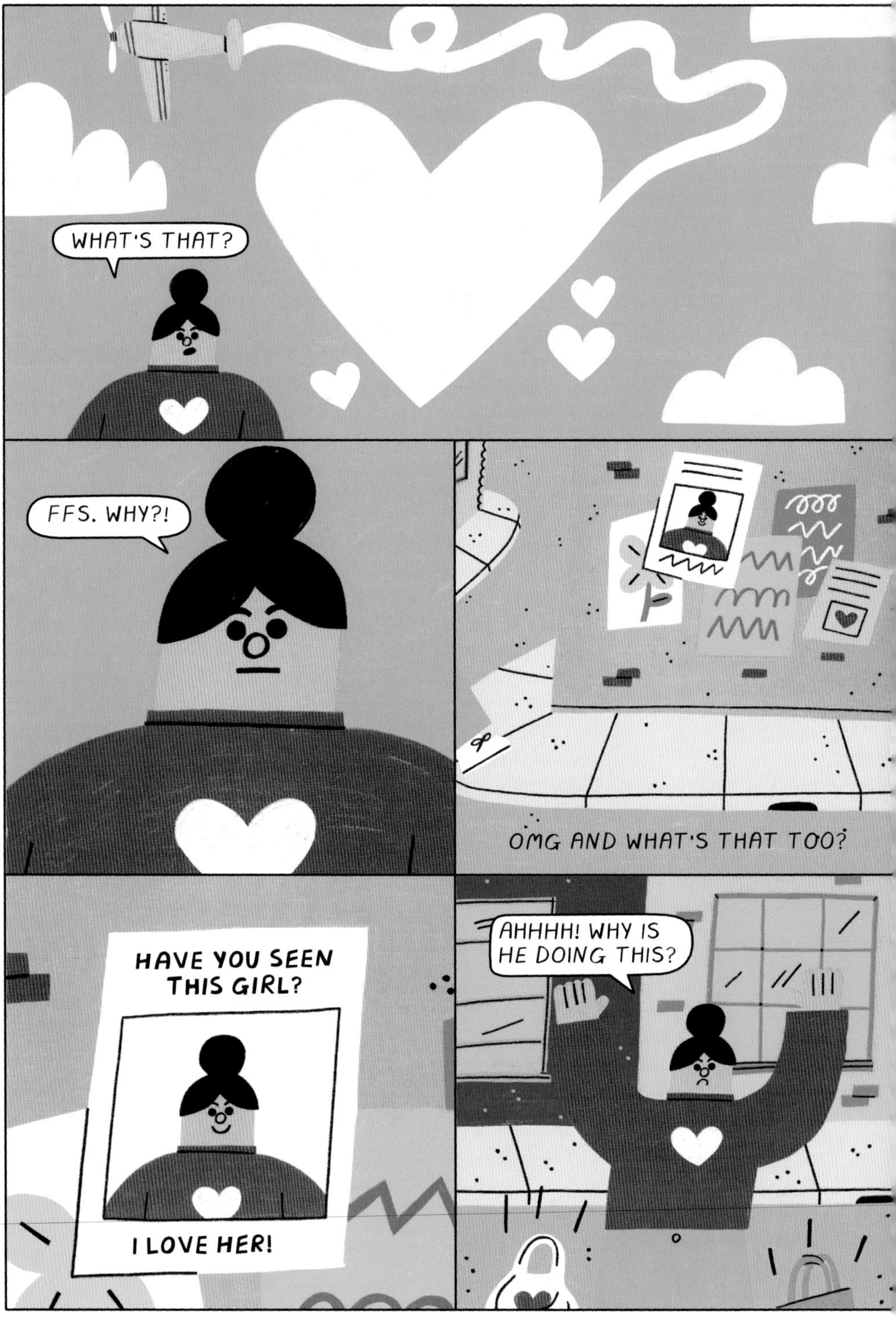
WHAT'S THAT?
FFS. WHY?!
OMG AND WHAT'S THAT TOO?
HAVE YOU SEEN THIS GIRL?
I LOVE HER!
AHHHH! WHY IS HE DOING THIS?

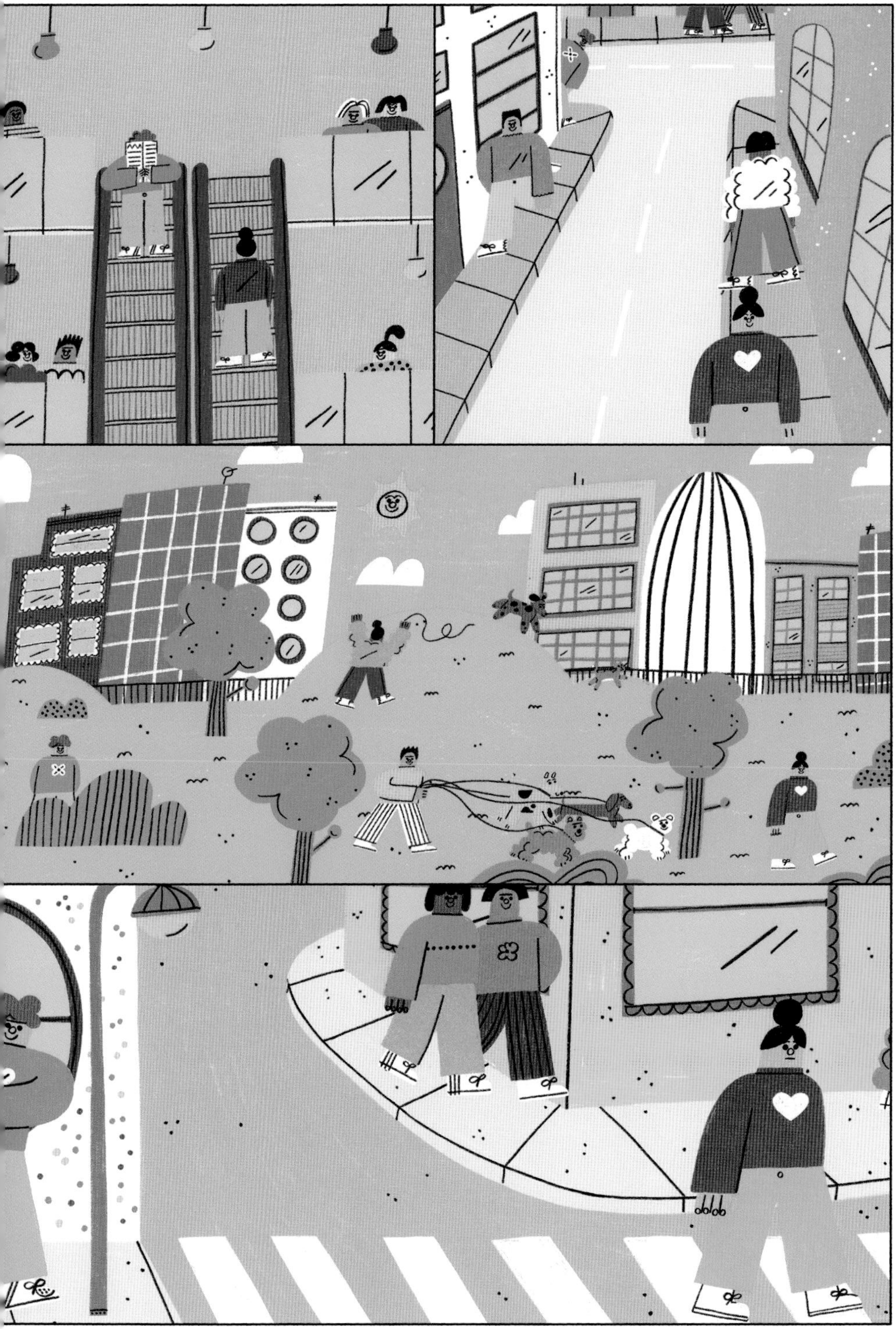

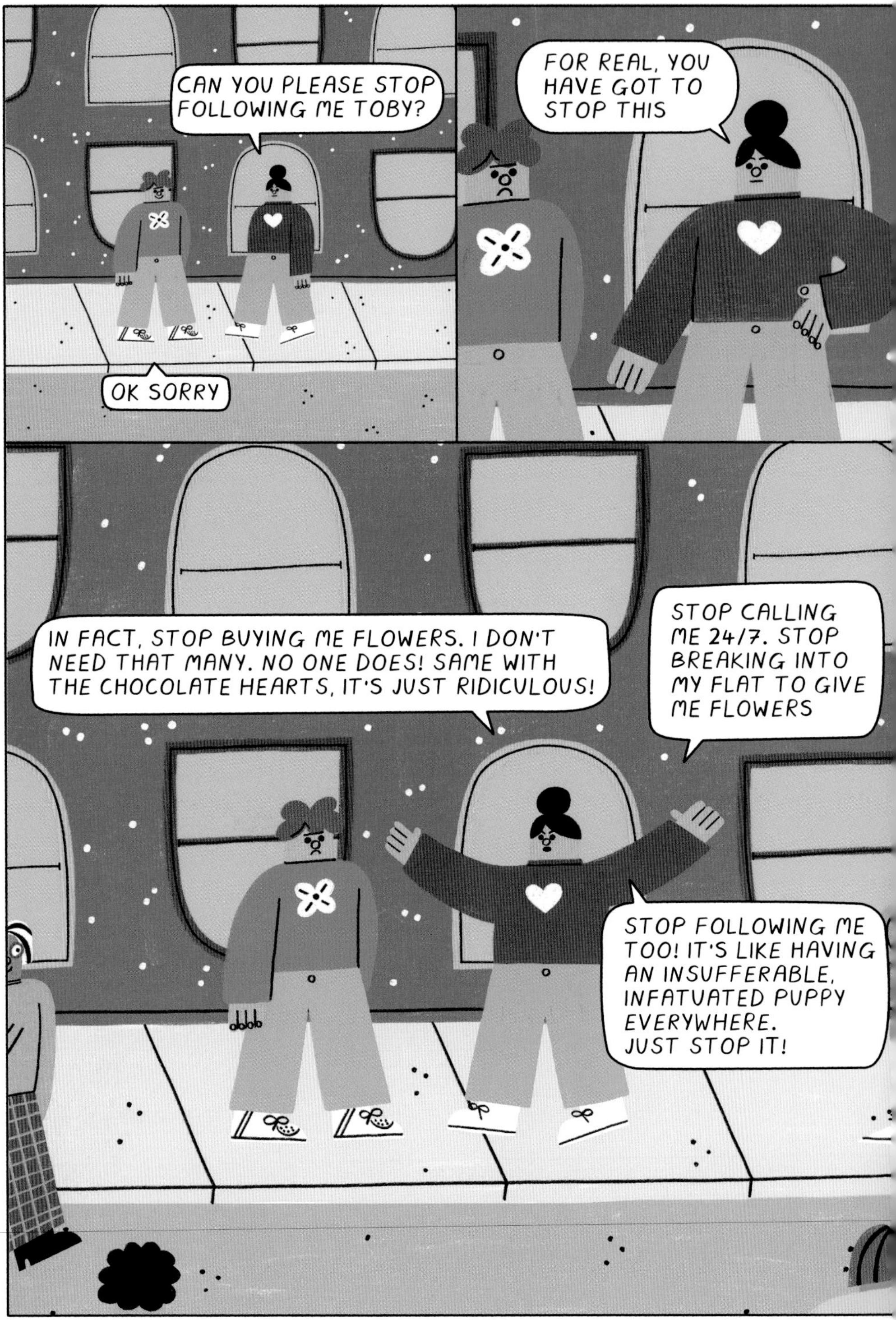
CAN YOU PLEASE STOP FOLLOWING ME TOBY?
OK SORRY
FOR REAL, YOU HAVE GOT TO STOP THIS
IN FACT, STOP BUYING ME FLOWERS. I DON'T NEED THAT MANY. NO ONE DOES! SAME WITH THE CHOCOLATE HEARTS, IT'S JUST RIDICULOUS!
STOP CALLING ME 24/7. STOP BREAKING INTO MY FLAT TO GIVE ME FLOWERS
STOP FOLLOWING ME TOO! IT'S LIKE HAVING AN INSUFFERABLE, INFATUATED PUPPY EVERYWHERE. JUST STOP IT!

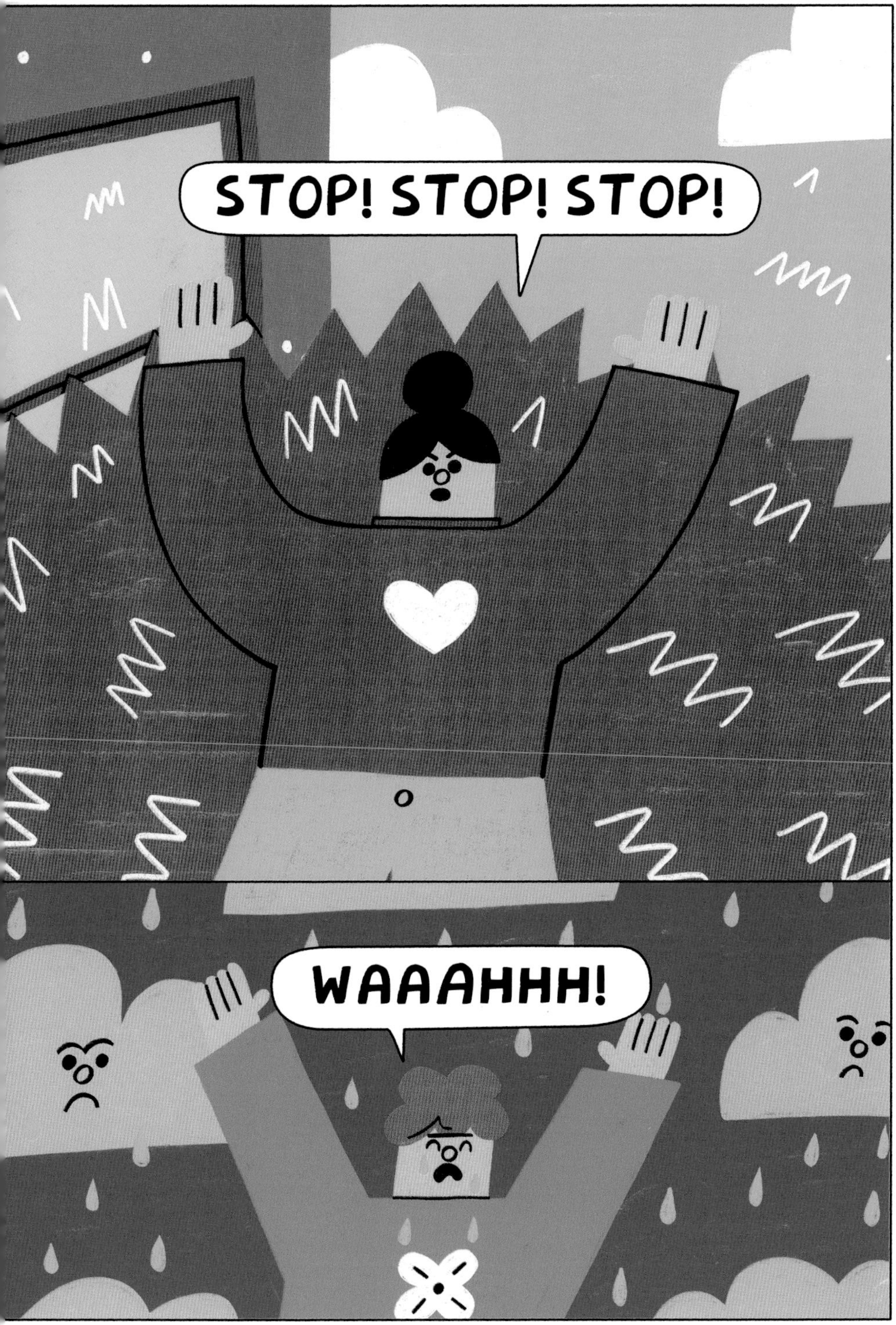
STOP! STOP! STOP!
WAAAHHH!

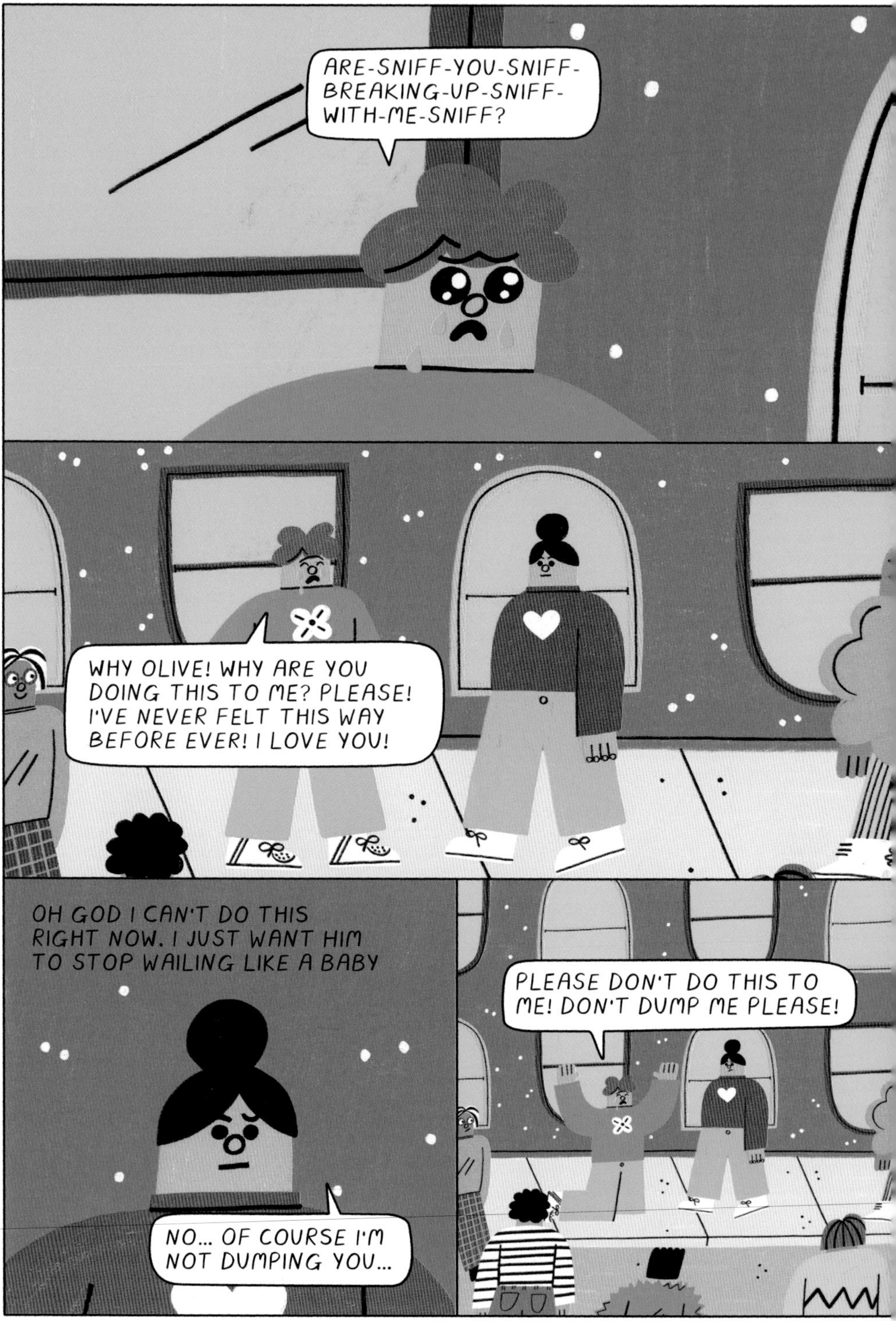
ARE-SNIFF-YOU-SNIFF-BREAKING-UP-SNIFF-WITH-ME-SNIFF?
WHY OLIVE! WHY ARE YOU DOING THIS TO ME? PLEASE! I'VE NEVER FELT THIS WAY BEFORE EVER! I LOVE YOU!
OH GOD I CAN'T DO THIS RIGHT NOW. I JUST WANT HIM TO STOP WAILING LIKE A BABY
NO... OF COURSE I'M NOT DUMPING YOU...
PLEASE DON'T DO THIS TO ME! DON'T DUMP ME PLEASE!

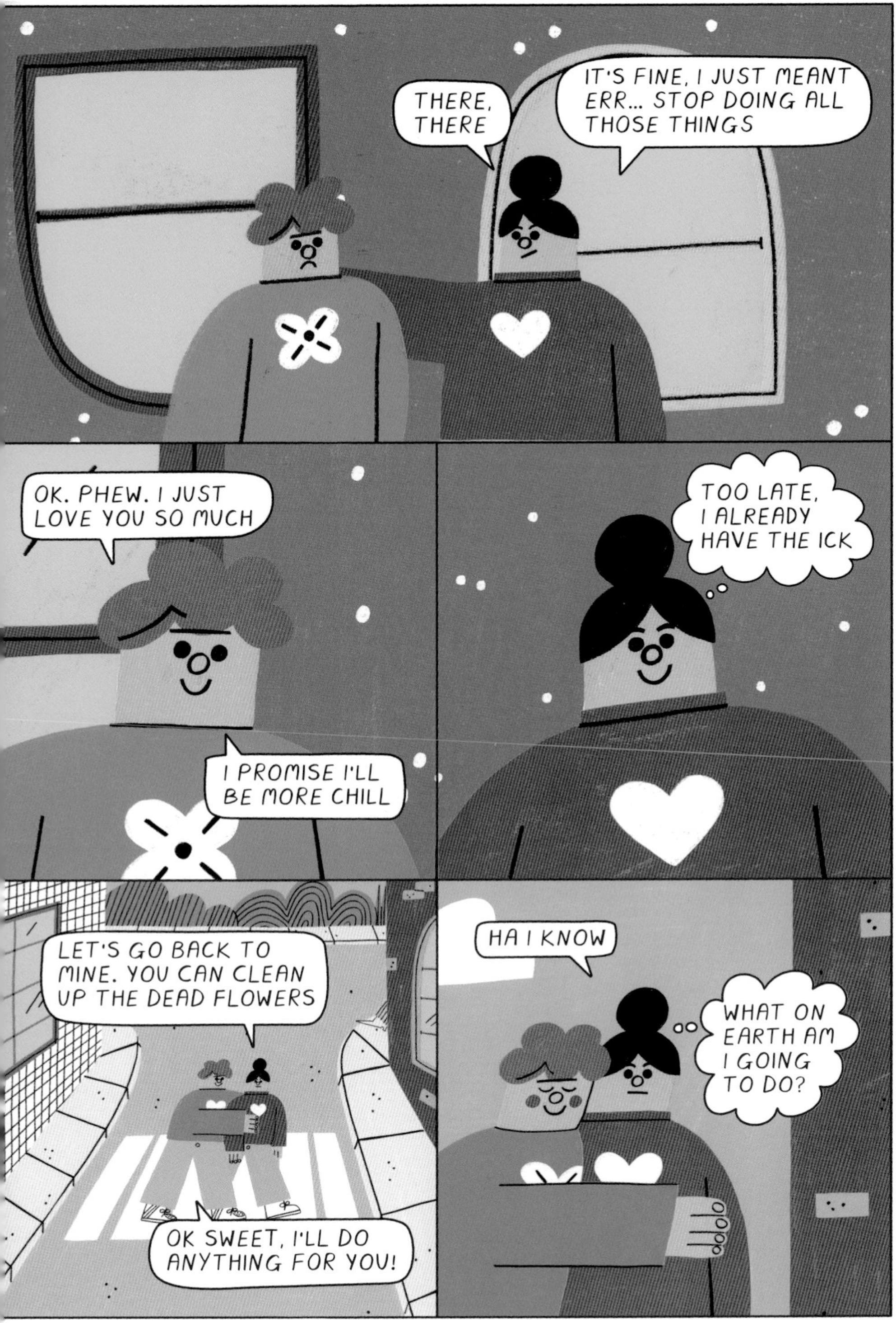

THERE, THERE
IT'S FINE, I JUST MEANT ERR... STOP DOING ALL THOSE THINGS
OK. PHEW. I JUST LOVE YOU SO MUCH
I PROMISE I'LL BE MORE CHILL
TOO LATE, I ALREADY HAVE THE ICK
LET'S GO BACK TO MINE. YOU CAN CLEAN UP THE DEAD FLOWERS
OK SWEET, I'LL DO ANYTHING FOR YOU!
HA I KNOW
WHAT ON EARTH AM I GOING TO DO?

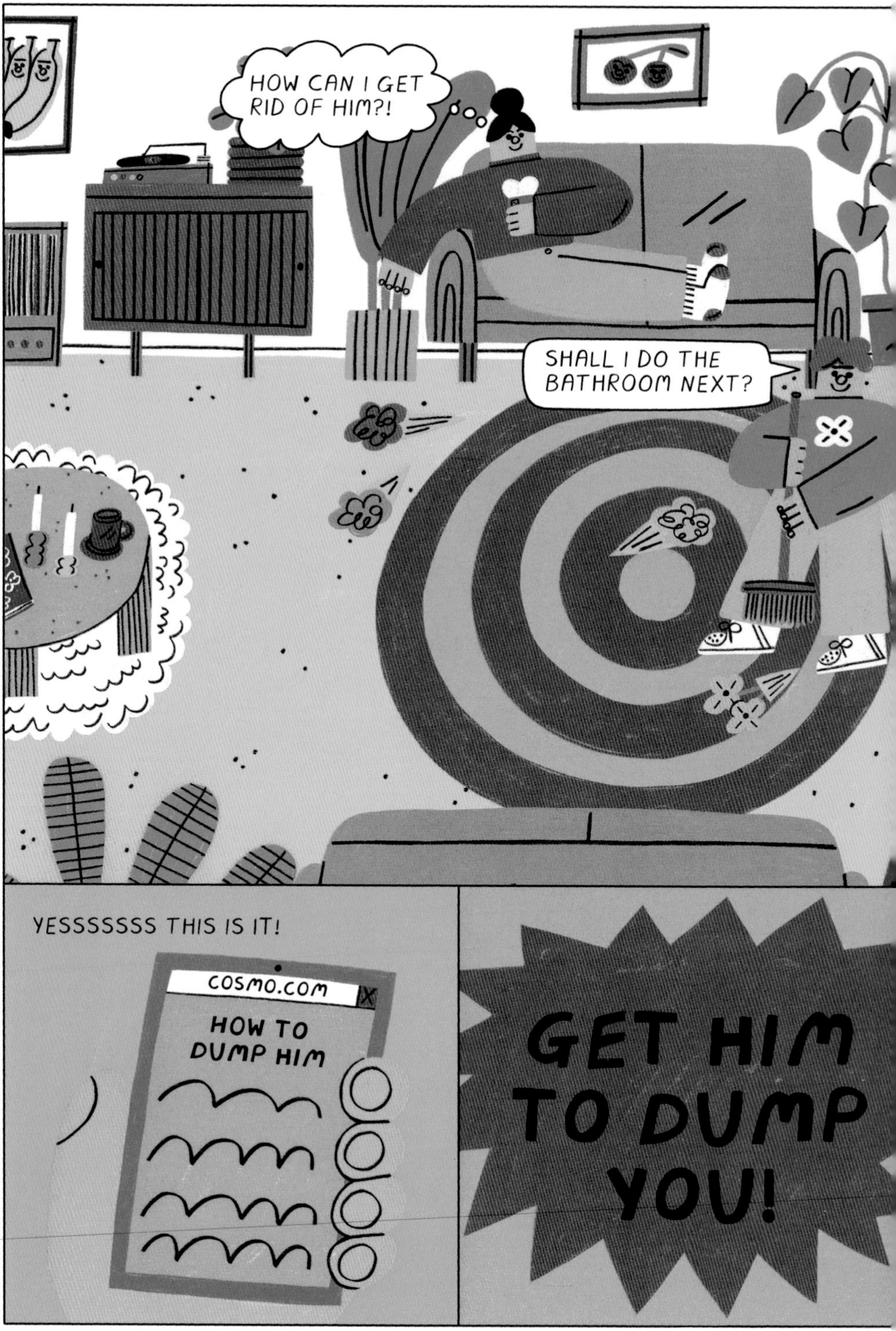
HOW CAN I GET RID OF HIM?!
SHALL I DO THE BATHROOM NEXT?
YESSSSSSS THIS IS IT!
COSMO.COM
HOW TO DUMP HIM
GET HIM TO DUMP YOU!

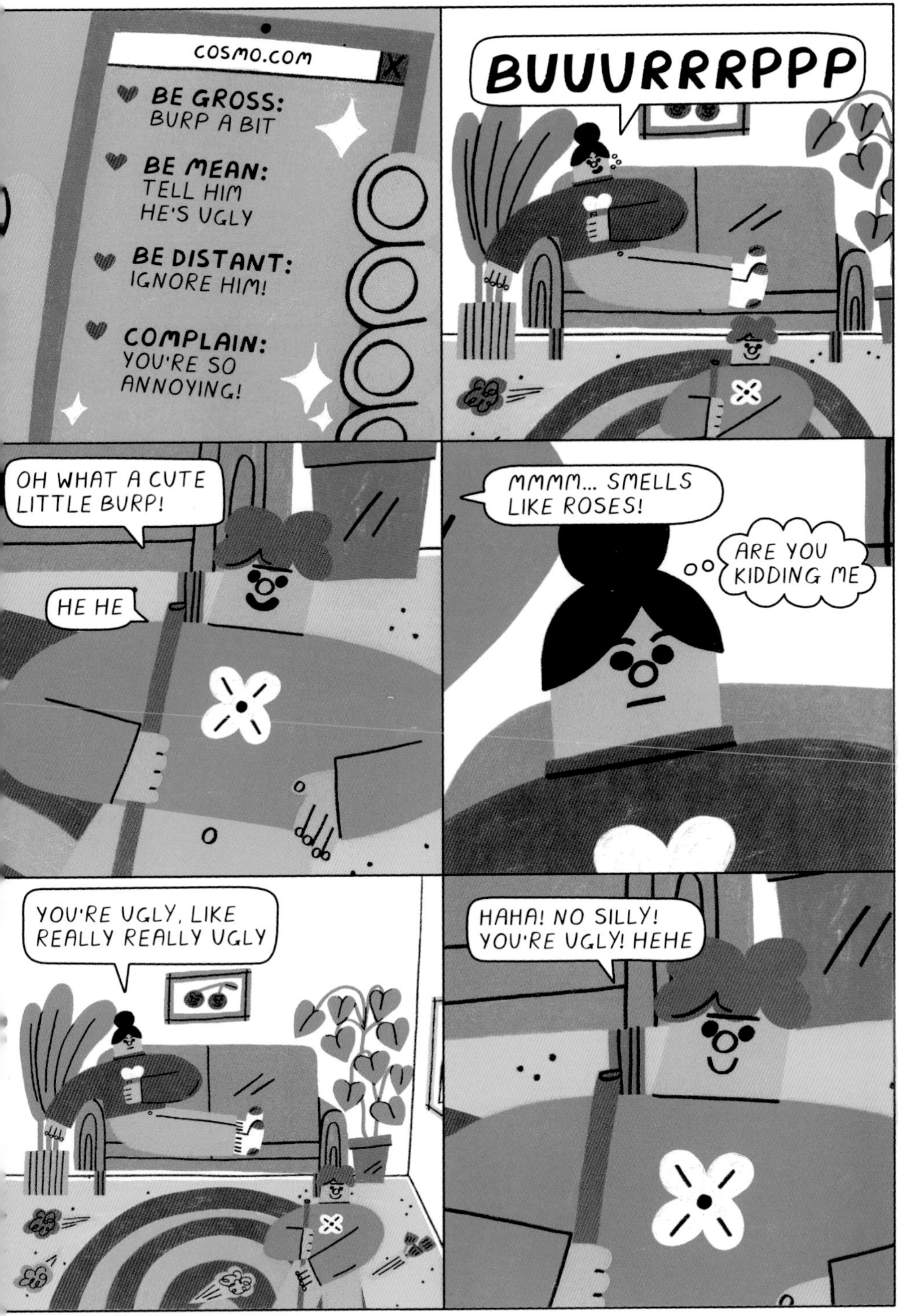
COSMO.COM
X
BE GROSS: BURP A BIT
BE MEAN: TELL HIM HE'S UGLY
BE DISTANT: IGNORE HIM!
COMPLAIN: YOU'RE SO ANNOYING!
BUUURRRRPPP
OH WHAT A CUTE LITTLE BURP!
HE HE
MMMM... SMELLS LIKE ROSES!
ARE YOU KIDDING ME
YOU'RE UGLY, LIKE REALLY REALLY UGLY
HAHA! NO SILLY! YOU'RE UGLY! HEHE

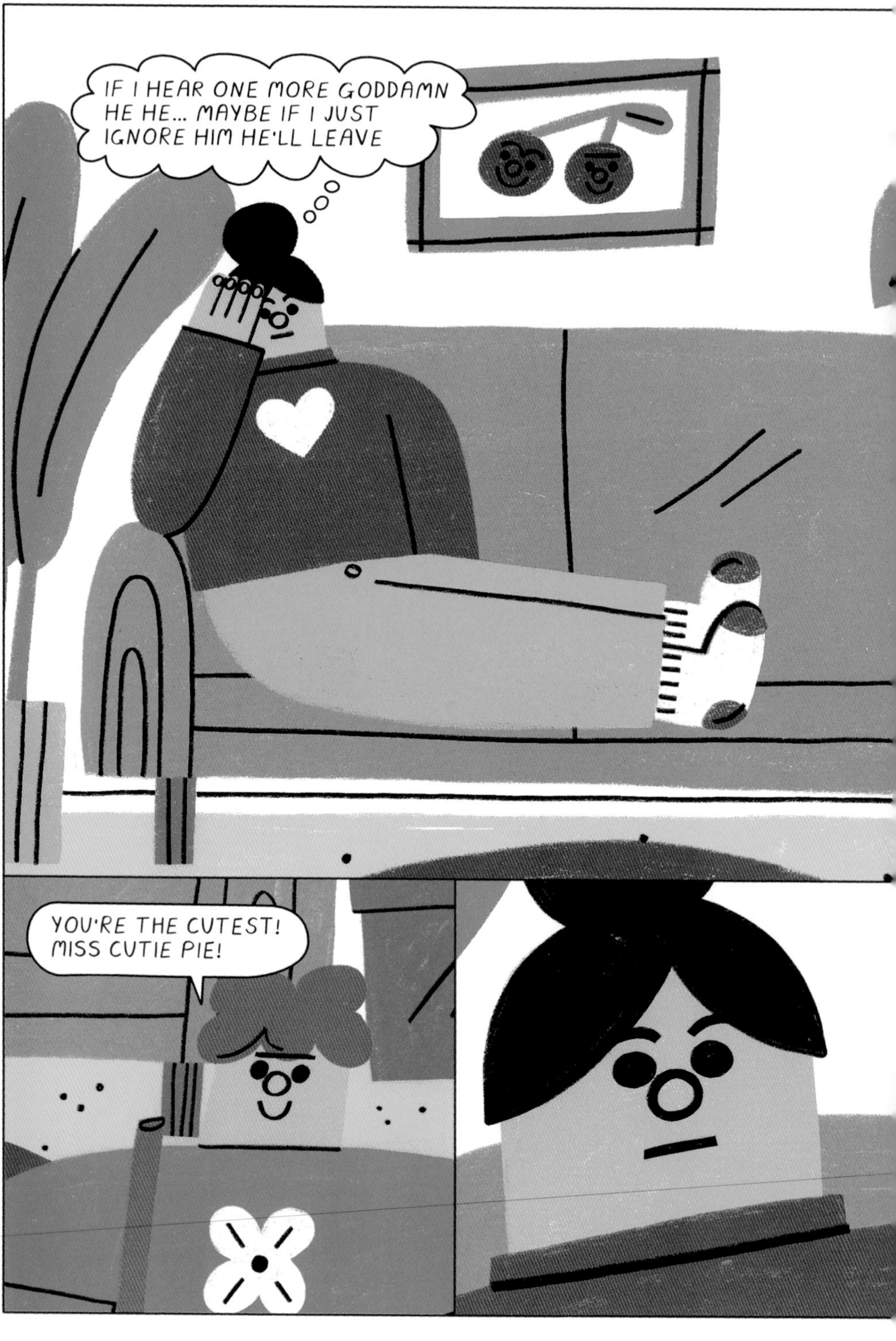
IF I HEAR ONE MORE GODDAMN HE HE... MAYBE IF I JUST IGNORE HIM HE'LL LEAVE
YOU'RE THE CUTEST! MISS CUTIE PIE!

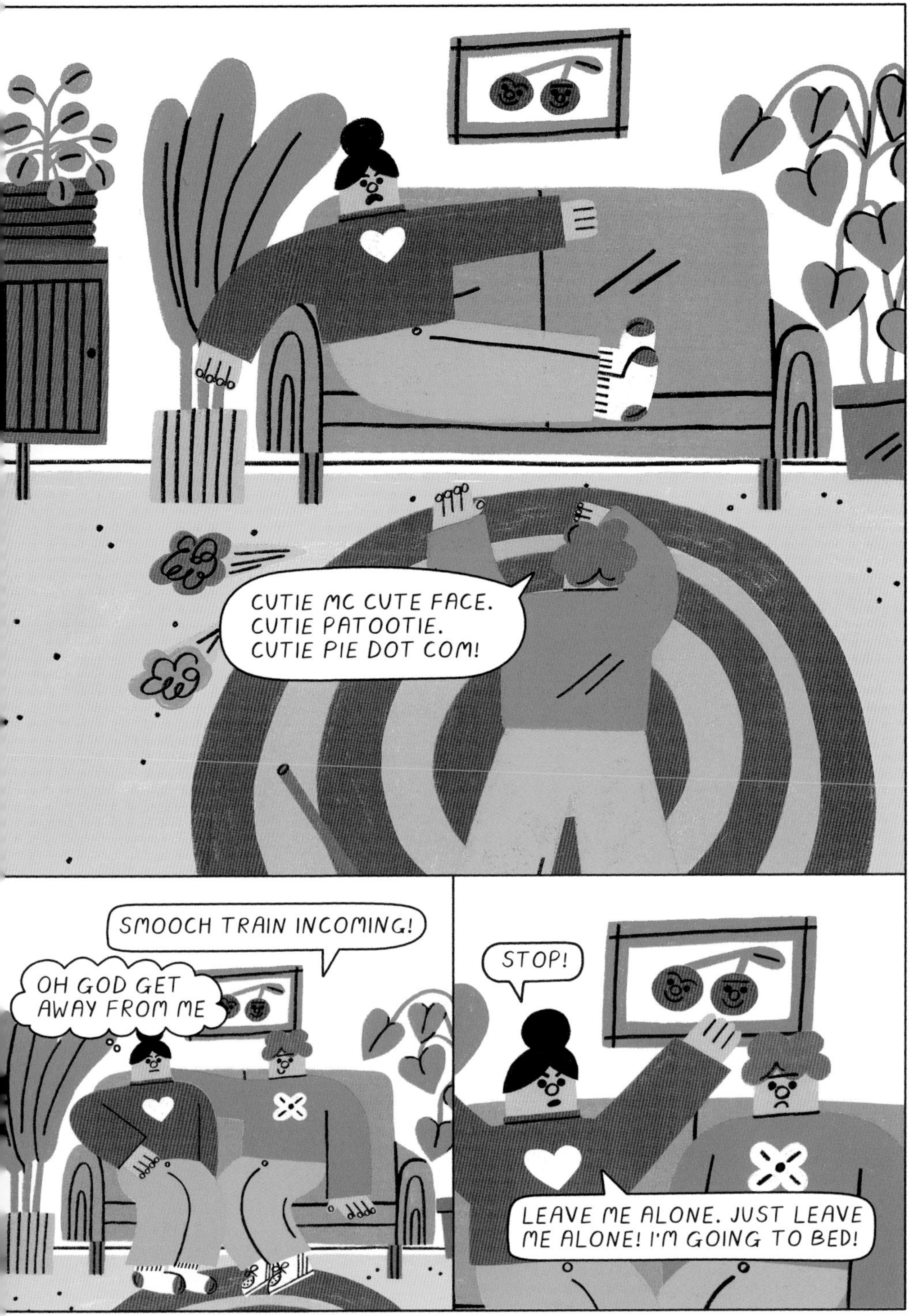
CUTIE MC CUTE FACE. CUTIE PATOOTIE. CUTIE PIE DOT COM!
SMOOCH TRAIN INCOMING!
OH GOD GET AWAY FROM ME
STOP!
LEAVE ME ALONE. JUST LEAVE ME ALONE! I'M GOING TO BED!

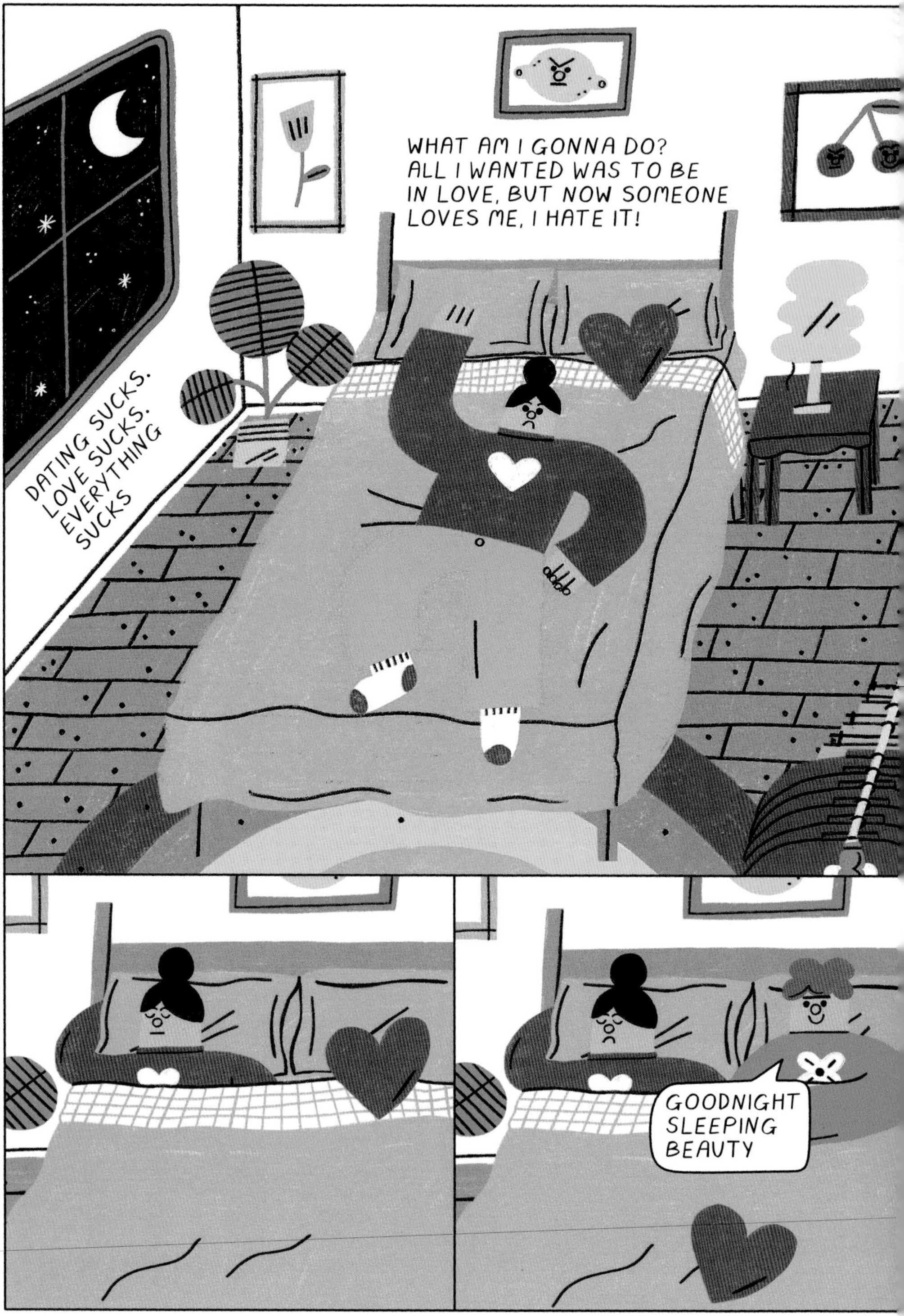
DATING SUCKS. LOVE SUCKS. EVERYTHING SUCKS
WHAT AM I GONNA DO? ALL I WANTED WAS TO BE IN LOVE, BUT NOW SOMEONE LOVES ME, I HATE IT!
GOODNIGHT SLEEPING BEAUTY

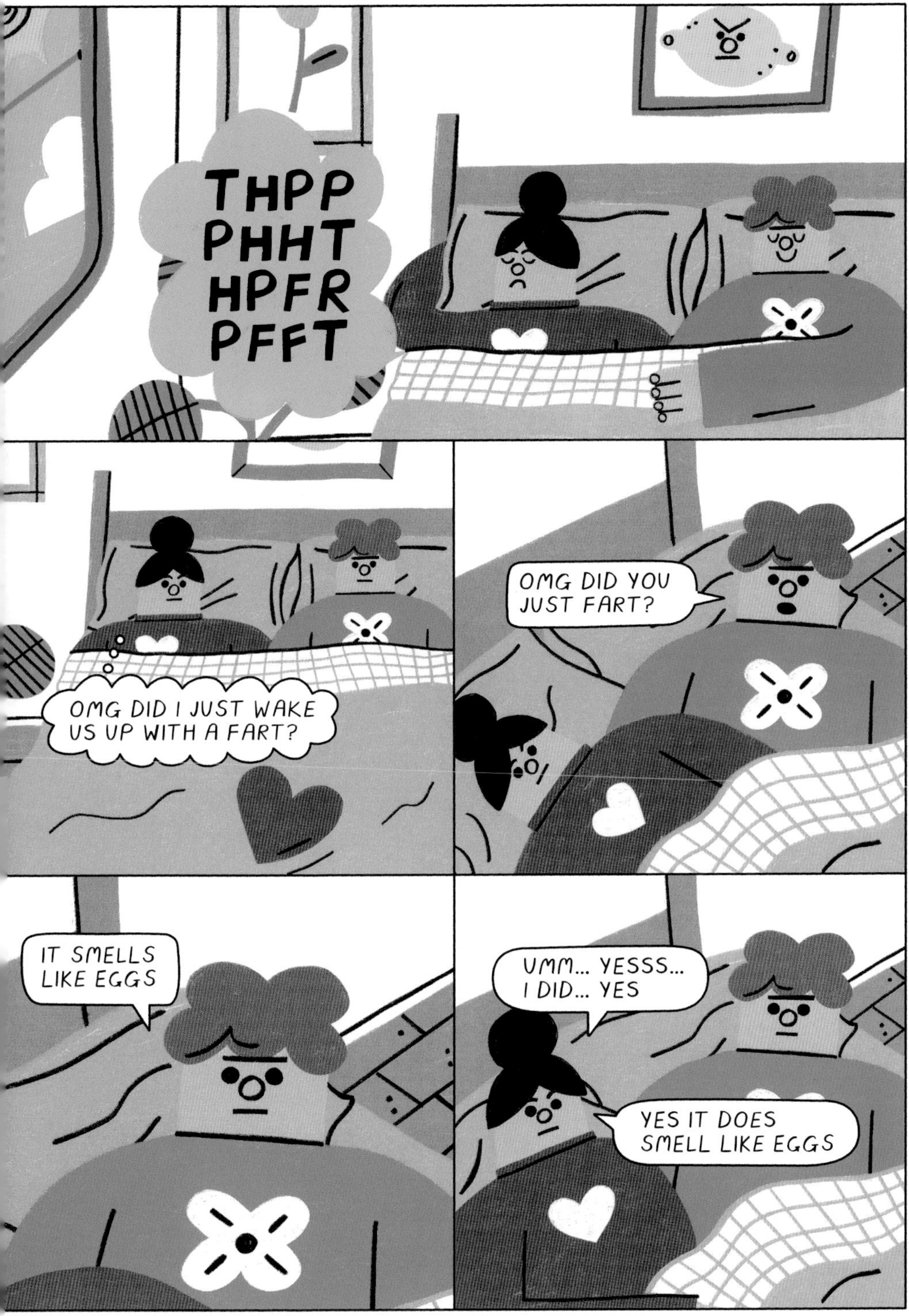
THPP PHHT HPFR PFFT
OMG DID I JUST WAKE US UP WITH A FART?
OMG DID YOU JUST FART?
IT SMELLS LIKE EGGS
UMM... YESSS... I DID... YES
YES IT DOES SMELL LIKE EGGS

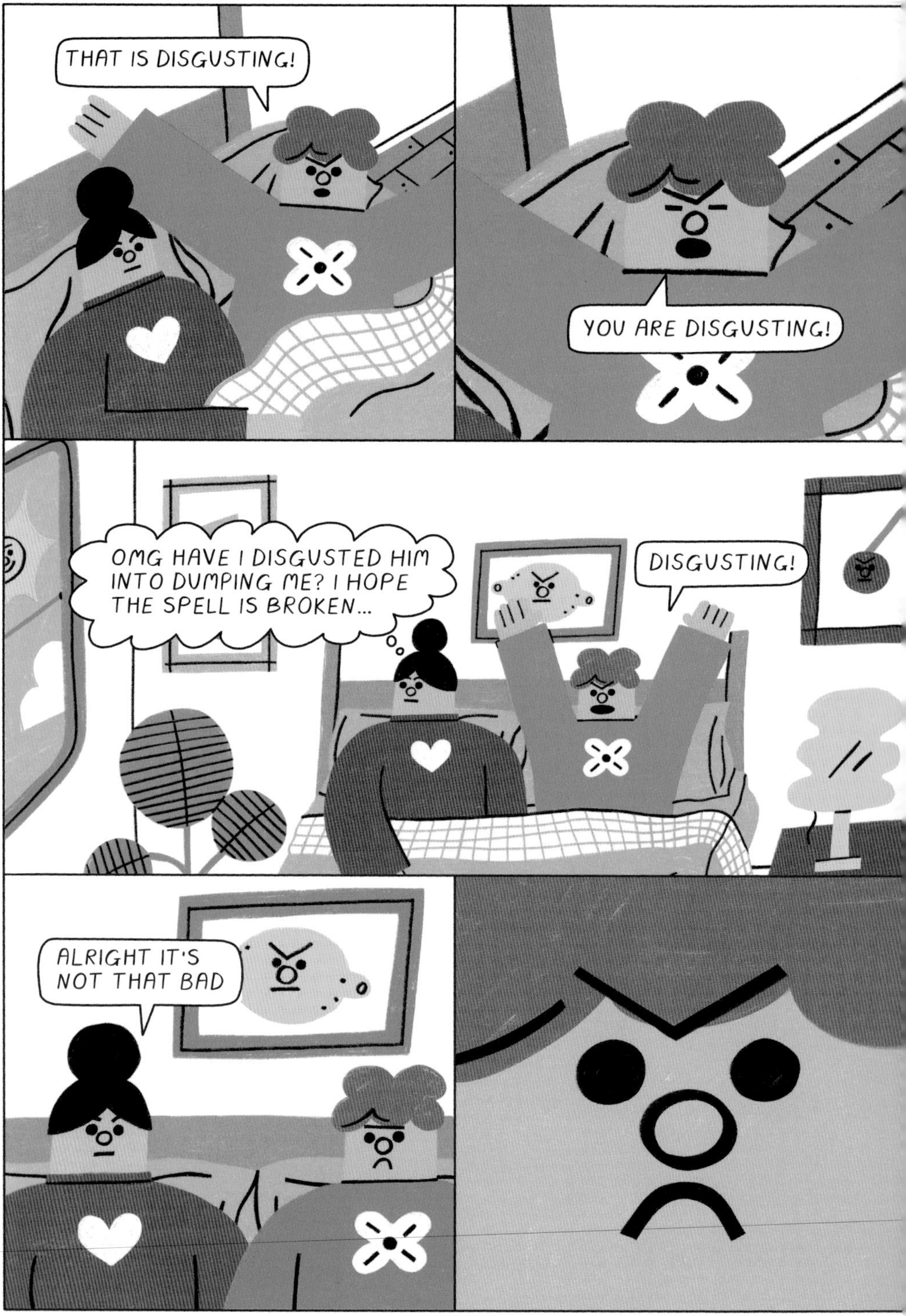
THAT IS DISGUSTING!
YOU ARE DISGUSTING!
OMG HAVE I DISGUSTED HIM INTO DUMPING ME? I HOPE THE SPELL IS BROKEN...
DISGUSTING!
ALRIGHT IT'S NOT THAT BAD

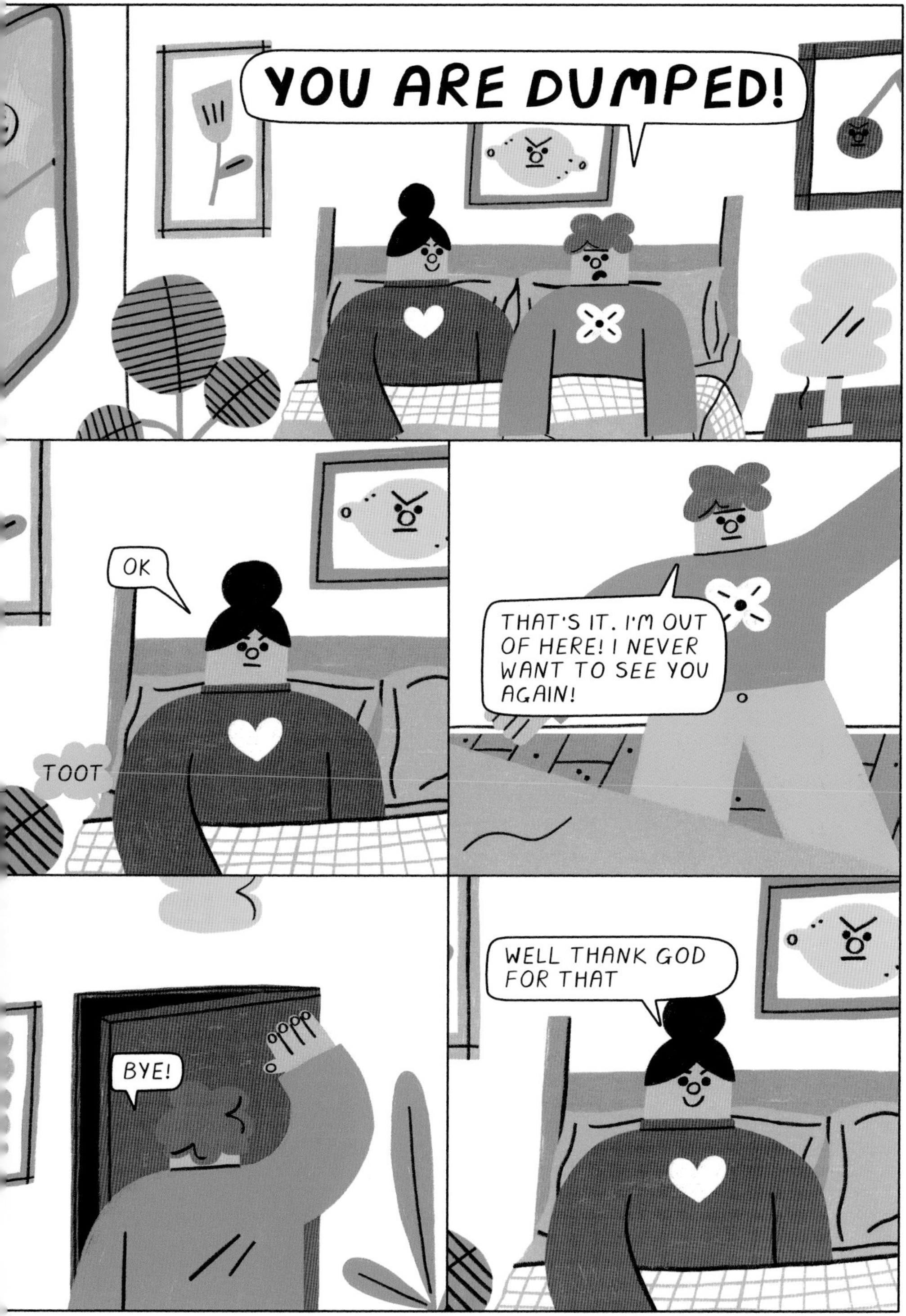
YOU ARE DUMPED!
OK
TOOT
THAT'S IT. I'M OUT OF HERE! I NEVER WANT TO SEE YOU AGAIN!
BYE!
WELL THANK GOD FOR THAT

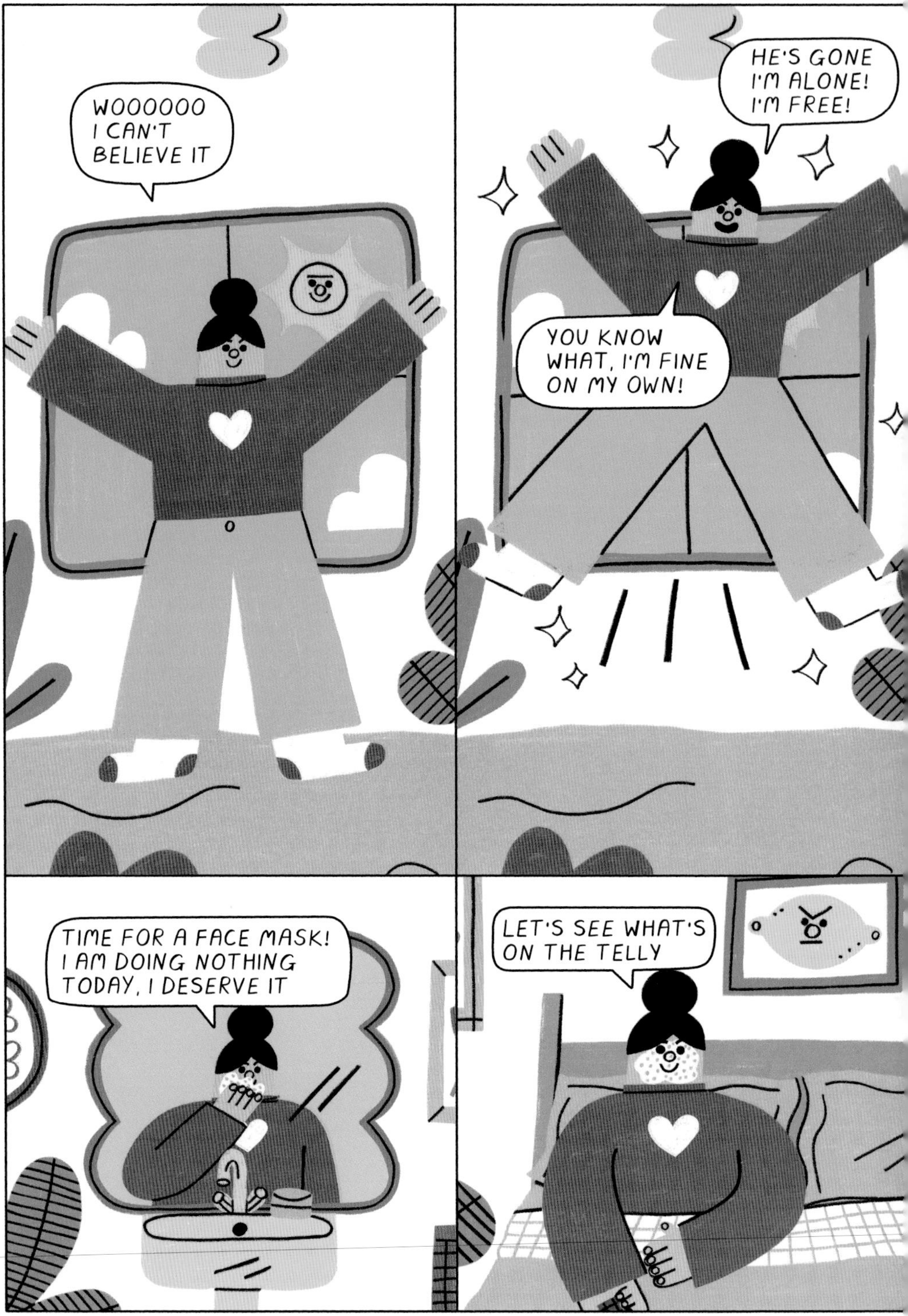
WOOOOOO I CAN'T BELIEVE IT
HE'S GONE I'M ALONE! I'M FREE!
YOU KNOW WHAT, I'M FINE ON MY OWN!
TIME FOR A FACE MASK! I AM DOING NOTHING TODAY, I DESERVE IT
LET'S SEE WHAT'S ON THE TELLY

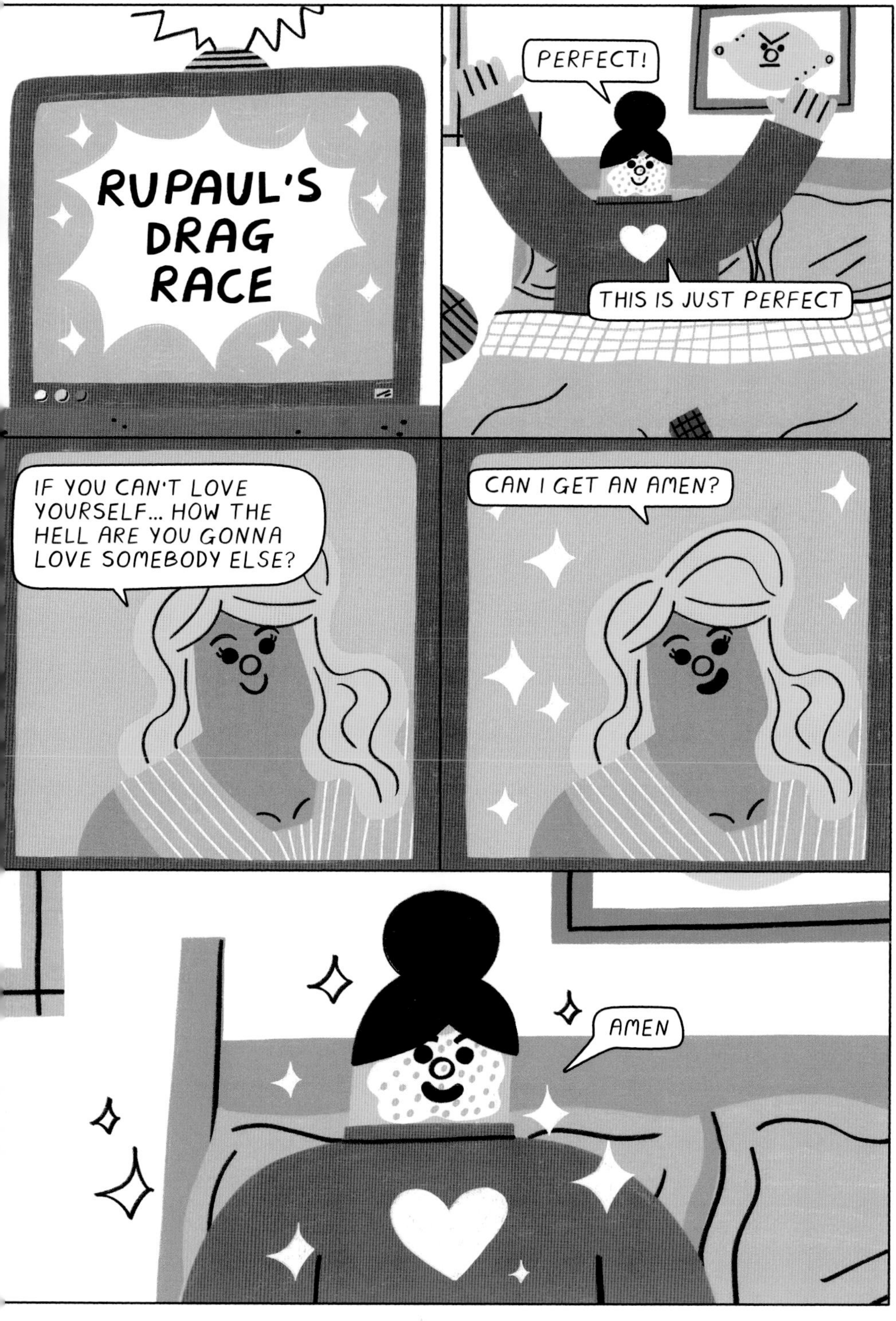
RUPAUL'S DRAG RACE
PERFECT!
THIS IS JUST PERFECT
IF YOU CAN'T LOVE YOURSELF... HOW THE HELL ARE YOU GONNA LOVE SOMEBODY ELSE?
CAN I GET AN AMEN?
AMEN

ACKNOWLEDGEMENTS

THANK YOU TO ALL THE STUPID GUYS* I DATED THAT
GAVE ME THE STARTING POINT FOR THESE COMICS,
AND THEN EVENTUALLY, A BOOK.

THANK YOU TO MY FRIENDS FOR LISTENING TO, AND
LAUGHING AT MY OWN BAD DATE STORIES, THE SUGGESTION
TO TURN THEM INTO A BOOK, AND FOR THE SOLID DATING
ADVICE. THANK YOU TO MY INSTAGRAM FOLLOWERS FOR
SENDING ME FUNNY, CRAZY, AND RIDICULOUS DATES TO
DRAW. WITHOUT YOU, THIS BOOK WOULDN'T HAVE HAPPENED.

THANK YOU TO MY FAMILY, MY SISTER SOPHIE AND MY MUM,
FOR ALWAYS BEING THERE FOR ME AND FOR YOUR ADVICE.
AND THANK YOU FOR YOUR FUNNY DATING STORIES
TOO, SOPHIE.

THANK YOU TO SAMHITA AND THE TEAM AT KYLE BOOKS
FOR BELIEVING THAT I COULD DO THIS! FOR GIVING ME THE
OPPORTUNITY TO MAKE THIS STORY POSSIBLE AND COME
TO LIFE, AND FOR WORKING SO HARD ON IT WITH ME. THANK
YOU TO THE DESIGNER, LYDIA, WHO HAD TO GO THROUGH
HUNDREDS AND HUNDRED OF MY DRAWINGS TO PUT THIS
BOOK TOGETHER SO WELL. THANK YOU TO MY LOVELY
AGENT, JOLENE, FOR BEING THERE EVERY STEP OF THE
WAY AND SUPPORTING ME SO MUCH. I COULDN'T HAVE
DONE IT WITHOUT YOU ALL!

THANK YOU TO EVERYONE WHO HAS EVER SUPPORTED
MY WORK. AND FINALLY, THANK YOU TO OLI FOR MATCHING
WITH ME ON HINGE, AND LIKING ME BACK.

*NOT ALL OF YOU WERE STUPID! SOME OF YOU WERE KIND...
BUT SOME OF YOU WERE ACTUALLY KIND OF AWFUL...